For Not To Be Taken
From the Room
reference

D1591399

The Gallup Poll

Public Opinion 1985

Other Gallup Poll Publications Available from Scholarly Resources

The Gallup Poll: Public Opinion, 1984
ISBN 0-8420-2234-1 (1985)

The Gallup Poll: Public Opinion, 1983
ISBN 0-8420-2220-1 (1984)

The Gallup Poll: Public Opinion, 1982
ISBN 0-8420-2214-7 (1983)

The Gallup Poll: Public Opinion, 1981
ISBN 0-8420-2200-7 (1982)

The Gallup Poll: Public Opinion, 1980
ISBN 0-8420-2181-7 (1981)

The Gallup Poll: Public Opinion, 1979
ISBN 0-8420-2170-1 (1980)

The Gallup Poll: Public Opinion, 1978
ISBN 0-8420-2159-0 (1979)

The Gallup Poll: Public Opinion, 1972–1977
2 volumes ISBN 0-8420-2129-9 (1978)

The International Gallup Polls: Public Opinion, 1979
ISBN 0-8420-2180-9 (1981)

The International Gallup Polls: Public Opinion, 1978
ISBN 0-8420-2162-0 (1980)

The Gallup International Public Opinion Polls:
France, 1939, 1944–1975
2 volumes ISBN 0-394-40998-1 (1976)

The Gallup International Public Opinion Polls:
Great Britain, 1937–1975
2 volumes ISBN 0-394-40992-2 (1976)

The Gallup Poll

Public Opinion 1985

George Gallup, Jr.

SR *Scholarly Resources Inc.*
Wilmington, Delaware

ACKNOWLEDGMENTS

The preparation of this volume has involved the entire staff of the Gallup Poll and their contributions are gratefully acknowledged. I particularly wish to thank James Shriver III, editor of the Gallup Poll, and Professor Fred L. Israel of the City College of New York, who was the principal coordinator.

G.G., Jr.

The paper used in this publication meets the minimum requirements of the American National Standard for permanence of paper for printed library materials, Z39.48, 1984.

Scholarly Resources Inc.
104 Greenhill Avenue
Wilmington, DE 19805-1897

Library of Congress Catalog Card Number: 79-56557
International Standard Serial Number: 0195-962X
International Standard Book Number: 0-8420-2249-X

CONTENTS

PREFACE*

Dramatic changes in the attitudes and behavior of Americans have occurred since the Gallup Poll published its first report to sponsoring newspapers on October 20, 1935. Some of the most profound changes during Gallup's fifty years of scientific polling include the following:

1) The proportion who say they would vote for a black, a Jew, or a Catholic for president has grown dramatically since the 1930s. So, too, has the expressed willingness to vote for a woman. In 1937 only 31% said they would vote for a woman for president, compared to 78% today. Surveys also show a marked increase in the acceptance of interracial and interfaith marriages.

2) In 1969, 68% of U.S. adults said premarital sex is wrong, while only 39% now hold this view.

3) In 1937 the public believed that a family of four needed $30 per week to make ends meet; the current figure is $302. Public estimates of food expenditures have soared from $11 per week in 1937 to $75 today.

4) In 1936, 34% of Americans thought the ideal family should include four children. This percentage increased to 47% in 1947 but subsequently has dropped to 11%. This question has proved to be an accurate barometer of actual population trends.

5) The percentage of Americans who exercise daily has soared from 24% in 1961 to 59% in late 1984. Active participation in sports also has grown substantially. This encouraging trend, however, is offset by other Gallup findings: the proportion who admit to occasional overindulgence in alcohol has almost doubled, from 18% in 1974 to 32% in 1985. And, despite warnings about the relationship between smoking and lung cancer and heart disease, little decline is noted in cigarette smoking. Although the use of marijuana is down, cocaine use is increasing.

---

*For an explanation of how the Gallup Poll determines its representative sample and develops its survey questions, see *The Gallup Poll: Public Opinion, 1984*, pp. xi–xlv.

6) Thirty years ago crime did not figure among the top community problems named by Americans, but now it is foremost in communities of all sizes. In 1965, one-third (34%) were fearful of venturing out of their homes after dark, while currently 45% say they are afraid to do so.

7) Although the decline has leveled out in 1985, the 58% who currently approve of trade unionism is far lower than in 1936 (72%) and even less than in 1957 (76%). Key factors in labor's declining support are negative feelings about certain union leaders and strikes against the public welfare.

8) At present there is a continuing conviction that the United States should work closely with other nations at many levels, but a strong reluctance, stemming from the Vietnam experience, to commit U.S. troops to involvement in the affairs of other nations.

9) Confidence in key U.S. institutions—Congress, the Supreme Court, public schools, and the media, for example—is only marginally higher than it was in the immediate post-Watergate days.

10) A survey in 1939 showed that a majority of adults thought it was indecent for women to wear shorts for street wear. In the 1940s the Gallup Poll asked the public: "Do you object to women drinking in public places?" or "Should school teachers be allowed to smoke outside the classroom?" Reflecting the changes in manners and morals, in 1950 the Gallup Poll asked: "Do you object to a woman saying 'hell or damn' in public?"

Despite certain dramatic changes in public opinion over the last fifty years, in other respects the nation has remained much the same since the mid-1930s, as discovered by the Gallup Poll:

1) The problems named today as the most important facing the nation closely parallel those named in the 1930s: unemployment, international tensions, the high cost of living, and government spending. Almost invariably, except during wartime or periods of threat of war, worry over the twin economic issues of unemployment and inflation has dominated the concerns of the American people.

2) The standard of living of Americans has increased dramatically over the last fifty years, yet the nation remains plagued by poverty. A recent Gallup survey showed one-fourth of the total sample (and nearly one-half of nonwhites) saying that there were times during the previous twelve months when they did not have enough money to buy the food, clothing, or medical supplies they needed.

3) Although the nation has shifted to a somewhat more liberal position on a number of key issues over the last half century, the populace continues to include about equal numbers of persons who describe themselves as either liberals or conservatives.

4) Americans continue to place a high premium on such traditional values as hard work, the family, and religion. The ideal life-style, as viewed by the vast majority of U.S. women, continues to be marriage with children. Of

late, that ideal also has come to include a full or part-time job outside the home.

5) Basic religious beliefs in God and an afterlife have remained intact, although a decline is noted in the proportion who say religion is very important in their lives.

6) Finally, despite the multitude of problems confronting society, Americans continue to be optimistic about the future of the nation. They believe that the country has survived difficult periods in the past, that we have the capability to change, and that there is much that the individual can do to bring about change in his community and in society as a whole. In fact, voluntarism, an American trait, remains at a high level.

An examination of the views of the millions of Americans who have been interviewed by the Gallup Poll over the last half century leads to the conclusions that the collective judgment of the American people has proved to be sound, that the public is willing to make great sacrifices for the national good in times of crisis, and that the will of the people sooner or later becomes law.

In the case of many legislative issues and proposals, the late George H. Gallup believed that the people are often years ahead of their legislative leaders: "Through nearly five decades of polling, we have found the collective judgment of the people to be extraordinarily sound, especially on issues which come within the scope of the typical person's experience. Often the people are actually ahead of their elected leaders in accepting innovations and radical changes."

Founded in 1935 the Gallup Poll was the first organization to provide newspaper readers with public opinion polling reports, based on scientific survey procedures. The Gallup Organization (1958) and its corporate predecessors—Public Opinion Surveys (1938) and Audience Research Institutes (1937)—were established to serve the needs of business, government, and others who wished to apply survey research to problem solving. The Gallup Organization is a member of Gallup International Research Institutes, founded in 1947, and is affiliated with survey organizations in thirty-nine nations around the globe.

Election surveys both here and abroad are a good indicator of a survey organization's technical proficiency. Evidence that progress has been made is seen in the fact that from 1936 through 1950 the average deviation of U.S. Gallup survey results from the actual election results was 3.6 percentage points; from 1952 through 1960, 1.7 percentage points; from 1962 through 1970, 1.6 percentage points; and from 1972 through 1984, 1.2 percentage points. The vote for the candidates in the 1984 presidential election exactly matched the final Gallup preelection survey results, making this forecast the most accurate one in the long history of the Gallup Poll.

George Gallup, Jr.

RECORD OF
GALLUP POLL ACCURACY

Year	Gallup Final Survey*		Election Result*	
1984	59.0%	Reagan	59.2%	Reagan
1982	55.0	Democratic	55.8	Democratic
1980	47.0	Reagan	50.8	Reagan
1978	55.0	Democratic	54.0	Democratic
1976	48.0	Carter	50.0	Carter
1974	60.0	Democratic	58.9	Democratic
1972	62.0	Nixon	61.8	Nixon
1970	53.0	Democratic	54.3	Democratic
1968	43.0	Nixon	43.5	Nixon
1966	52.5	Democratic	51.9	Democratic
1964	64.0	Johnson	61.3	Johnson
1962	55.5	Democratic	52.7	Democratic
1960	51.0	Kennedy	50.1	Kennedy
1958	57.0	Democratic	56.5	Democratic
1956	59.5	Eisenhower	57.8	Eisenhower
1954	51.5	Democratic	52.7	Democratic
1952	51.0	Eisenhower	55.4	Eisenhower
1950	51.0	Democratic	50.3	Democratic
1948	44.5	Truman	49.9	Truman
1946	58.0	Republican	54.3	Republican
1944	51.5	Roosevelt	53.3**	Roosevelt
1942	52.0	Democratic	48.0	Democratic
1940	52.0	Roosevelt	55.0	Roosevelt
1938	54.0	Democratic	50.8	Democratic
1936	55.7	Roosevelt	62.5	Roosevelt

*The figure shown is the winner's percentage of the Democratic-Republican vote except in the elections of 1948, 1968, and 1976. Because the Thurmond and Wallace voters in 1948 were largely split-offs from the normally Democratic vote, they were made a part of the final Gallup Poll preelection.

**Civilian vote 53.3, Roosevelt soldier vote 0.5 = 53.8% Roosevelt. Gallup final survey based on civilian vote.

estimate of the division of the vote. In 1968 Wallace's candidacy was supported by such a large minority that he was clearly a major candidate, and the 1968 percents are based on the total Nixon-Humphrey-Wallace vote. In 1976, because of interest in McCarthy's candidacy and its potential effect on the Carter vote, the final Gallup Poll estimate included Carter, Ford, McCarthy, and all other candidates as a group.

Average Deviation for 24
    National Elections . . . . 2.3 percentage points

Average Deviation for 17
    National Elections
    Since 1950, inclusive . . . . 1.5 percentage points

Trend in Deviation Reduction

Elections	Average Error
1936–48	4.0
1950–58	1.7
1960–68	1.5
1970–82	1.4
1966–82	1.2
1972–84	1.2

CHRONOLOGY

The chronology is provided to enable the reader to relate poll results to specific events, or series of events, that may have influenced public opinion.

1984

December 3	Toxic fumes from a chemical plant leak kill more than 2,000 in Bhopal, India.
December 5	President Ronald Reagan proposes cuts of $34 billion from the 1986 budget, exclusive of defense.
December 7	The unemployment rate for November fell 0.3%, to an even 7%.
December 13	Industrial production advanced 0.4% in November.
December 17	U.S. balance of payments showed a record deficit of $32.9 billion during the third quarter of 1984.
December 19	The United States withdraws from the United Nations Educational, Scientific and Cultural Organization.
December 20	Prices at the consumer level rose two-tenths of 1% during November, the smallest increase since June.
December 22	Bernhard Goetz, a rider on a New York City subway train, shoots and wounds four teen-age boys after one of them asks him for $5. The shooting starts a national debate on what action a citizen should be permitted to take in life-threatening situations.

1985

January 4	Sales of automobiles in the United States rose 13.1% in 1984, with some 76% of cars produced in America.
January 7	The United States and the Soviet Union agree to resume negotiations in March on the reduction of nuclear arms.
January 9	Unemployment rose slightly during December to 7.1%.
January 10	The United States notifies the World Court that it will not participate in proceedings related to Nicaragua's suit against the United States for alleged military aggressions.
January 14	Major banks again cut their prime interest rate, this time to 10.75%, the lowest since August 1983.
January 20	At the White House, President Reagan and Vice-President George Bush take their oaths of office for a second term.
January 21	President Reagan takes the oath again inside the Capitol and then delivers his inaugural address.
January 22	The nation's real gross national product increased 6.8% in 1984, the highest gain since 1951.
January 24	The U.S. space shuttle *Discovery* begins its first secret military mission.
January 29	The Dow Jones Industrial Average closes at an all-time high of 1,292.62.
January 30	The Organization of Petroleum Exporting Countries cuts prices on crude oil.
February 1	Unemployment rose slightly in January to 7.3%.
February 4	New Zealand denies a request that a U.S. Navy destroyer be allowed to pay a port call in that country because the United States refuses to say whether the ship carries nuclear weapons.
February 5	Farmers facing economic ruin because of high interest rates and lower market prices call for immediate financial assistance from the federal government.

February 6	President Reagan, celebrating his seventy-fourth birthday, delivers his State of the Union address to a joint session of Congress.
February 14	Annual reports by the "Big 3" American automakers—General Motors, Ford, and Chrysler—showed their total profits in 1984 stood at $9.81 billion, far above the previous high.
February 18	Killings and arrests in South Africa bring an abrupt halt to a trend toward a lessening of racial tensions. Dozens of demonstrations across America call for an end to apartheid.
February 21	The economy grew at an annual rate of 4.9% during the final three months of 1984. President Reagan acknowledges that he wants to remove the leftist Sandinista government of Nicaragua.
March 1	President Reagan steps up his support for the guerrillas or *contras* fighting to overthrow the Sandinista regime.
	The index of leading economic indicators shows that the economy is on the move after a period of economic uncertainty. The index rose 1.7% in January, the sharpest jump in nineteen months.
March 4	Thousands of Ohio citizens face the possible loss of their money when several savings and loan institutions closed their doors. The banking problem continued throughout the month.
March 8	Unemployment edged downward in February to 7.2%.
March 10	Konstantin Chernenko, president of the Soviet Union and general secretary of the Soviet Communist party, dies. The Central Committee, acting on a recommendation of the ruling Politburo, appoints Mikhail Gorbachev as the new party secretary.
	Disarmament talks between the United States and the Soviet Union begin on schedule in Geneva.
March 13	President Reagan complains that cuts in domestic programs proposed by the Senate for the 1986 budget will not go far enough. He again rules out any tax increase.
March 15	Raymond Donovan, the first sitting member of a president's cabinet ever to be indicted, resigns as secretary of labor.

March 21	The Senate approves the construction of twenty-one additional MX missiles. The House gives its approval on March 28.
April 4	Congress turns down President Reagan's appeal for military support for the *contras*.
April 5	The unemployment rate stood at 7.2% in March; it has remained between 7.0% and 7.4% since May 1984.
April 18	The economy grew at an annual rate of only 1.3% during the first three months of 1985.
April 30	The nation marks the tenth anniversary of the fall of Saigon and the end of the Vietnam War.
May 2–9	President Reagan completes an eventful and dramatic trip to Europe. His visits to a concentration camp site and a German military cemetery monopolize public attention and overshadow the economic summit conference of the seven major industrial democracies.
May 2	E. F. Hutton, one of the nation's largest brokerage companies, pleads guilty to some 2,000 federal charges related to the illegal manipulation of its checking accounts. Hutton agrees to pay $2 million in fines and to pay back up to $8 million to banks it had defrauded.
May 3	Unemployment held at 7.2% in April.
May 13	A violent confrontation in Philadelphia between police and a radical group called MOVE ended with eleven deaths and the destruction of sixty-one houses, following an air attack by the police.
May 17	The Federal Reserve Board cut its basic interest rate for loans to member institutions to 7.5%. The action, aimed at stimulating economic growth, put the discount rate at its lowest level since 1978.
May 20	The Dow Jones Industrial Average finishes above 1,300 for the first time in history.
May 28	President Reagan calls for a sweeping revision of the nation's tax laws.

June 7	Unemployment held at 7.2% in May.
June 10	President Reagan announces that the United States will stay with restrictions established by the second Strategic Arms Limitation Treaty, although the Senate never ratified it.
June 14–30	An airplane hostage drama, played out mostly in Beirut, rivets the attention of the world. The seizure by Shiite Muslim extremists of a TWA jet with 153 persons aboard, including 104 Americans, is a grim reminder of the 1979–81 hostage crisis in Iran. This time, however, the last of the hostages are freed after seventeen days; one American is killed.
June 18	Major banks cut their prime interest rate to 9.5%, the lowest level since 1978.
June 23	In history's third worst aviation disaster, an Air India Boeing 747 crashes into the Atlantic Ocean near Ireland, killing 329.
July 1	The United States and the Soviet Union announce that a summit conference between President Reagan and Soviet leader Gorbachev will be held in Geneva on November 19–20.
July 2	The Supreme Soviet elects Andrei Gromyko, who had been foreign minister of the Soviet Union since 1957, as president of the USSR. Eduard Shevardnadze is named as his successor.
July 5	Unemployment for June remained at 7.2% for the fifth straight month.
July 10	In one of the most abrupt reversals in the history of marketing, the Coca-Cola Company announces that it will once again sell a soft drink using the same recipe that it has used for ninety-nine years.
July 11	The Senate votes to impose economic sanctions on South Africa as a protest against that country's racial policies.
July 13	President Reagan undergoes major intestinal surgery, and a growth removed from his colon proves to be cancerous.
July 16	The June rate for fixed-rate home mortgages falls to the lowest average level since 1979.

July 18	The gross national product increased at an annual rate of 1.7% during the second quarter of 1985.
July 20	The announcement that actor Rock Hudson has Acquired Immune Deficiency Syndrome (AIDS) increases public awareness of this health crisis. During 1985 the number of AIDS victims grew to more than 13,000 in the United States.
	The government of South Africa declares an indefinite state of emergency in certain districts, as racial unrest escalates.
July 30	The U.S. trade deficit for June was $13.42 billion, the second highest ever.
August 1	The long congressional struggle to come up with a federal budget for 1986 ends, with both houses agreeing to a compromise calling for outlays of $967.6 billion and revenues of only $793.7 billion.
August 2	Unemployment remained at 7.2% in July, for the sixth consecutive month.
August 5	President Reagan announces that a patch of skin removed from his nose on July 30 is cancerous.
August 27	The Census Bureau issues a report showing that poverty edged downward in 1984, after advancing for five consecutive years. The overall poverty rate was 14.4%, but among blacks it was 33.8%. A family of four is considered to be at the poverty level if its cash income is less than $10,609; median family income in 1984 stood at $26,430.
August 28	President Reagan advances his reputation as a champion of free trade when he says he will not impose quotas on the importation of shoes.
August 30	The index of leading economic indicators rose 0.4% in July.
August 31	By the end of August, 1985 had become the most tragic year in the history of commercial aviation, with more than 1,400 persons killed in airplane crashes.
September 6	The unemployment rate dropped to 6.9% in August, the lowest since 1980.

September 9	President Reagan announces additional restrained sanctions against South Africa. In an executive order, he bans most computer sales and bank loans, as well as gold Krugerrands. He also forbids most exports of nuclear technology.
September 16	For the first time since 1914, the United States becomes a debtor nation; that is, foreigners owned more assets in the United States than vice versa.
September 19	A powerful earthquake in central Mexico kills more than 5,000.
September 30	The automobile industry has its biggest sales year in history, according to figures released after the end of the 1985 model year.
October 2	Rock Hudson dies of AIDS.
October 7–12	On October 7, four Palestinians seize the Italian cruise ship *Achille Lauro* as it carries some 400 passengers to Port Said, Egypt. The hijackers demand the release of fifty Palestinians held by Israel. After surrendering to Egyptian authorities, it is determined that Leon Klinghoffer, an elderly American, has been killed. When the hijackers seek to leave Egypt, bound for Tunis, American Navy F-14 planes bring down the aircraft, forcing it to land in Sicily, where Italian authorities take the hijackers into custody.
November 7	The Dow Jones Industrial Average closes above 1,400 for the first time in history.
November 14	In northern Colombia a snow-capped volcano, which had not erupted in nearly 400 years, explodes in full fury, killing at least 20,000 people.
	President Reagan proposes the most extensive people-to-people exchanges in the history of U.S.-Soviet relations.
November 19–21	The Geneva summit meeting takes place between President Reagan and Soviet leader Gorbachev.
December 5	The Dow Jones Industrial Average climbs past 1,500 for the first time in history.

Skiing 7
Waterskiing 7
Racquetball 6
Sailing 6
Touch football/flag 6

Frequency of Participation

(During Last Twelve Months)

	1–4 times	5–20 times	Over 20 times	Average times
Jogging/running	11%	33%	56%	67
Swimming	19	43	38	40
Tennis	33	39	28	28
Golf	34	38	28	28
Fishing	36	41	23	27
Bowling	44	31	25	24
Motorboating	40	40	20	23
Hunting	43	40	17	23
Sailing	57	33	10	17
Skiing	44	43	13	14
Camping	56	33	11	11
Horseback riding	56	39	5	10

JANUARY 3
SPORTS PARTICIPATION

Interviewing Date: 11/9–12/84
Survey #245–G

Asked of those who participate in sports: Which of these sports and activities have you, yourself, participated in within the last twelve months? [Respondents were handed a card listing fifty sports and activities.]

	National
Swimming	41%
Bicycling	33
Fishing	30
Camping	23
Jogging	22
Bowling	21
Aerobics, dancercize	20
Weight training	19
Billiards, pool	18
Softball	18
Calisthenics	15
Motorboating	14
Volleyball	14
Basketball	13
Hunting	13
Golf	12
Ping-Pong/table tennis	12
Baseball	11
Tennis	11
Canoeing/rowing	10
Roller skating	9
Horseback riding	8
Target shooting	8

Selected National Trend

	1984	1980	1966	1959
Swimming	41%	37%	33%	33%
Bicycling	33	27	17	*
Fishing	30	24	*	32
Bowling	21	24	27	18
Softball	18	16	15	*
Volleyball	14	13	12	4
Motorboating	14	12	16	*
Hunting	13	13	*	16
Basketball	13	18	15	*
Golf	12	8	11	8
Tennis	11	14	9	4
Roller skating	9	12	5	4
Horseback riding	8	7	8	5
Skiing	7	6	5	*
Waterskiing	7	7	6	*
Sailing	6	4	2	*

*These activities were not included.

Note: Americans continued to participate in sports and recreational activities at a record level, with swimming, bicycling, and fishing the most popular activities. For the 1984 Gallup Leisure Activities Index, a carefully selected cross section of U.S. adults were asked which of fifty activities they had participated in within the last twelve months. The current findings, with few exceptions, parallel those recorded in the 1983 audit, which showed participation to be the highest ever recorded in Gallup surveys.

As in surveys conducted at regular intervals since 1959, swimming is the most popular activity in 1984 with 41% participation, down from its all-time high of 50% in 1983. In second place is bicycling at 33%, as has been the case in three surveys since 1980, with the percentage of adults participating having doubled since 1966. Bowling has dropped from third place in 1983 to sixth place in the 1984 survey, to be replaced by fishing at 30%.

Gaining in popularity are aerobic dancing and weight training, in seventh and eighth places in the current survey, with about one adult in five having taken part in each activity within the twelve-month period tested. In fact, the percentage of persons engaged in aerobic dancing, dancercize, or Jazzercise has almost doubled since last year from 12% to 20%, while weight training has increased from 15% to 19%. Rounding out the ten most popular activities are camping, 23%; jogging/running, 22%; billiards or pool and softball, each 18%.

The following have been engaged in by 5% or less of American adults within the last twelve months: badminton and ice skating, each 5%; archery and marathon or distance running, each 4%; snorkeling and handball, each 3%; martial arts, paddle or platform tennis, scuba diving, skateboarding, soccer, and yoga, each 2%; squash, surfing, and windsurfing, 1%; and less than 1% for hang gliding, lacrosse, skeet/trap shooting, and sky diving.

Not surprisingly, age is the single most important factor in determining the percentages of adults engaged in these activities: about twice as many adults under 30 take part in sports as among the adult population as a whole. Men are more likely than women to participate in hunting, shooting, fishing, racquetball, billiards or pool, martial arts,

weight training, and golf, in order of degree. On the other hand, the following are more popular with women than with men: bicycling, aerobic dancing, and roller skating.

Sports and recreational activities in which one's income and educational level play an important part are sailing, skiing, tennis, golf, waterskiing, and racquetball. For example, among such up-market population segments as persons with over $40,000 annual household income and/or a college degree, the percentages engaged in these activities are twice those for the nation as a whole.

JANUARY 6
WAR AND PEACE

Interviewing Date: 11/26–12/9/84 (U.S. only)*
Special Telephone Survey

Asked by Gallup affiliated organizations in twenty-seven nations: I'd like your opinion of the chances of a world war breaking out in the next ten years. If 10 means it is absolutely certain that a world war will break out and 0 means that there is no chance of a world war breaking out, where on this scale of 10 to 0 would you rate the chances of world war breaking out in the next ten years?

	50–50 or greater	Less than 50%	No opinion
Colombia	58%	38%	4%
United States	47	45	8
Costa Rica	45	53	2
Australia	43	53	4
Philippines	40	53	7
Uruguay	40	53	7
Canada	39	53	8
Brazil	37	54	9
Argentina	36	52	12
France	32	67	1
Spain	32	58	10
Luxembourg	31	67	2
Ireland	29	63	8
Switzerland	29	69	2

*Interviews in other nations were conducted during the last weeks of 1984.

Belgium	26	67	7
United Kingdom	26	69	5
Japan	25	66	9
Denmark	25	66	9
Norway	25	71	4
West Germany	23	68	9
Italy	23	76	1
Netherlands	23	72	5
Austria	22	72	6
Finland	22	72	6
South Korea	22	54	24
Sweden	20	76	4
Greece	19	74	7

Italy	23	28	46	3
West Germany	18	26	49	7

Interviewing Date: 11/30–12/3/84
Survey #246-G

Asked in the United States: Do you think the United States is or is not doing all it can to keep peace in the world?

Yes, is 54%
No, is not 40
No opinion 6

Will 1985 be a peaceful year, more or less free of international disputes; a troubled year, with much international discord; or remain the same?

	Peaceful	Troubled	Remain the same	No opinion
Sweden	12%	57%	25%	6%
Australia	7	49	37	7
Colombia	17	46	32	5
Luxembourg	10	46	38	6
Belgium	8	44	43	5
Uruguay	30	42	21	7
Ireland	13	41	40	6
Netherlands	7	40	46	7
Denmark	5	39	48	8
Brazil	31	39	23	7
Philippines	19	39	38	4
Costa Rica	16	39	35	10
South Korea	14	39	35	12
Canada	8	38	48	6
Norway	17	36	55	2
Switzerland	14	35	42	9
United States	15	34	43	8
France	6	34	52	8
United Kingdom	9	34	51	6
Finland	11	32	44	13
Greece	14	32	36	18
Argentina	26	31	32	11
Austria	12	30	45	13
Japan	5	30	36	29
Spain	15	30	39	16

By Sex
Male

Yes, is 55%
No, is not 41
No opinion 4

Female

Yes, is 54%
No, is not 39
No opinion 7

By Ethnic Background
White

Yes, is 58%
No, is not 37
No opinion 5

Nonwhite

Yes, is 34%
No, is not 57
No opinion 9

Black

Yes, is 31%
No, is not 59
No opinion 10

By Education
College Graduate

Yes, is 48%
No, is not 50
No opinion 2

College Incomplete

Yes, is 50%
No, is not 46
No opinion 4

High-School Graduate

Yes, is 60%
No, is not 34
No opinion 6

Less Than High-School Graduate

Yes, is 56%
No, is not 34
No opinion 10

By Region
East

Yes, is 55%
No, is not 40
No opinion 5

Midwest

Yes, is 56%
No, is not 39
No opinion 5

South

Yes, is 57%
No, is not 35
No opinion 8

West

Yes, is 48%
No, is not 48
No opinion 4

By Age
18–29 Years

Yes, is 47%
No, is not 47
No opinion 6

30–49 Years

Yes, is 49%
No, is not 44
No opinion 7

50 Years and Over

Yes, is 65%
No, is not 31
No opinion 4

By Politics
Republicans

Yes, is 72%
No, is not 25
No opinion 3

Democrats

Yes, is 42%
No, is not 51
No opinion 7

Independents

Yes, is 51%
No, is not 44
No opinion 5

Asked in the United States: Do you think the USSR is or is not doing all it can to keep peace in the world?

Yes, is 10%
No, is not 81
No opinion 9

By Sex
Male

Yes, is 10%
No, is not 83
No opinion 7

Female

Yes, is 10%
No, is not 79
No opinion 11

By Ethnic Background
White

Yes, is 10%
No, is not 82
No opinion 8

Nonwhite

Yes, is 8%
No, is not 78
No opinion 14

Black

Yes, is 8%
No, is not 77
No opinion 15

By Education
College Graduate

Yes, is 6%
No, is not 89
No opinion 5

College Incomplete

Yes, is 8%
No, is not 88
No opinion 4

High-School Graduate

Yes, is 11%
No, is not 81
No opinion 8

Less Than High-School Graduate

Yes, is 14%
No, is not 69
No opinion 17

By Region
East

Yes, is 13%
No, is not 77
No opinion 10

Midwest

Yes, is 10%
No, is not 83
No opinion 7

South

Yes, is 11%
No, is not 78
No opinion 11

West

Yes, is 5%
No, is not 89
No opinion 6

By Age
18–29 Years

Yes, is 11%
No, is not 82
No opinion 7

30–49 Years

Yes, is 9%
No, is not 82
No opinion 9

50 Years and Over

Yes, is 10%
No, is not 80
No opinion 10

By Politics
Republicans

Yes, is 9%
No, is not 86
No opinion 5

Democrats

Yes, is 11%
No, is not 78
No opinion 11

Independents

Yes, is 10%
No, is not 81
No opinion 9

Note: The much awaited talks between Secretary of State George Shultz and Foreign Minister Andrei Gromyko, to begin in Geneva on January 7, come at a time when many Americans and other people around the globe predict international discord during 1985 and see the possibility of a world war during the next decade. One-third of Americans (34%) interviewed in this twenty-seven-nation survey, conducted by Gallup International Research Institutes* in the final weeks of 1984, predict that 1985 will be a troubled year with much international discord, while 43% say the situation will remain the same as in 1984; only 15% think the next twelve months will be peaceful.

Although Americans are among the more optimistic regarding international discord during 1985, their long-range view on the prospects of war are more pessimistic than those in any other nation except Colombia. Nearly half of U.S. citizens today (47%) think the chances of a world war breaking out in the next ten years are 50–50 or greater. The comparable percentage among Colombians is 58%, but in all other nations the figure is 45% or lower. Most optimistic are the Greeks, with only 19% saying the chances of an all-out war in the next decade are 50% or higher.

*Gallup International Research Institutes, a survey network providing research capabilities and facilities through its thirty-six affiliates, serves a wide range of clients on five continents. These clients include corporations, governments, universities, and foundations in eighty-six countries. GIRI derives from the Gallup Research Institutes, operating before World War II, and Gallup International, founded in 1947 with eleven member organizations.

A majority of Americans (54%) believes the United States is doing all it can to keep peace in the world, but 40% hold the opposite view. By contrast, a total of 10% of U.S. survey respondents say the USSR is doing all it can to keep peace, while 81% say it is not.

JANUARY 10
PREDICTIONS FOR 1985

Interviewing Date: 11/26–12/9/84
Special Telephone Survey

So far as you are concerned, do you think that 1985 will be better or worse than 1984?

Better 61%
Worse 20
Same (volunteered) 12
Don't know 7

Selected National Trend

	Better	Worse	Same	Don't know
1984	70%	15%	7%	8%
1983	50	32	10	8
1982	41	44	11	4
1981	49	26	19	6
1980	31	56	*	13
1979	33	55	*	12
1978	45	30	18	7
1972	57	22	*	21
1960	56	7	28	9

*"Same" responses recorded with "don't know."

The following figures are the current survey results for member organizations of the Gallup International Research Institutes, grouped by developing and industrial nations and ranked from most to least optimistic:*

	Better	Worse	Same	Don't know
Developing Nations				
South Korea ...	56%	10%	31%	3%
Brazil	52	25	16	7
Argentina	50	15	28	7

				Don't
Uruguay	36	13	46	5
Philippines ...	26	46	25	3
Colombia	24	58	13	5
Costa Rica	18	32	40	10
Average	38	28	28	6

Industrial Nations	Better	Worse	Same	Don't know
United States ..	61%	20%	12%	7%
Australia	57	18	16	9
Greece	53	21	14	12
Italy	45	31	22	2
Canada	44	21	22	2
Sweden	43	42	11	5
Great Britain ..	34	34	23	9
Switzerland ...	32	51	11	6
Denmark	30	17	47	6
Norway	29	11	59	1
Spain	29	28	34	9
Netherlands ...	26	28	41	5
Luxembourg ..	26	23	48	3
West Germany	25	12	58	5
Ireland	25	45	24	6
Finland	23	59	16	2
Japan	21	6	43	30
Austria	16	20	57	6
France	15	41	36	8
Belgium	12	51	34	3
Average	32	29	32	7

*Interviews were conducted in these nations during the last weeks of 1984.

Note: Despite concern over international tensions, optimism among Americans continues to run high, with a higher proportion here than in twenty-six other nations predicting that 1985 will be better than 1984. The level of optimism among Americans is lower now than it was at the start of 1984, but still is higher than at any other time over the last quarter century. As many as six in ten Americans (61%) anticipate that 1985 will be still better than 1984 in terms of their personal lives, while 20% say worse, and another 12% foresee little change.

JANUARY 13
ECONOMIC SITUATION

Interviewing Date: 11/30–12/3/84
Survey #246-G

As you know, the economy has recovered from recession, with increased production, employment, and profits. Of course, no one knows for sure, but what is your best guess as to how long this recovery will last before the economy turns down again? Will the recovery end this year, early next year, later next year, or later than that?

This year, early next year	19%
Later next year	22
Later than that	38
Never end (volunteered)	4
Has already ended (volunteered)	4
No opinion	13

By Income

$40,000 and Over

This year, early next year	20%
Later next year	26
Later than that	43
Never end (volunteered)	2
Has already ended (volunteered)	4
No opinion	5

$30,000–$39,999

This year, early next year	18%
Later next year	23
Later than that	44
Never end (volunteered)	4
Has already ended (volunteered)	2
No opinion	9

$20,000–$29,999

This year, early next year	19%
Later next year	25
Later than that	39
Never end (volunteered)	1
Has already ended (volunteered)	4
No opinion	12

$10,000–$19,999

This year, early next year 18%
Later next year 22
Later than that 36
Never end (volunteered) 6
Has already ended (volunteered) 5
No opinion 13

Under $10,000

This year, early next year 18%
Later next year 15
Later than that 30
Never end (volunteered) 4
Has already ended (volunteered) 7
No opinion 26

Selected National Trend

	This year, early next year	Later next year	Later than that	Never end	No opinion
May 1984	26%	21%	34%	3%	16%
Sept. 1983	18	20	38	5	19

During the next twelve months, do you think the interest rates people pay for borrowing money will go up, stay the same, or go down?

Go up 41%
Stay the same 29
Go down 25
No opinion 5

By Income

$40,000 and Over

Go up 41%
Stay the same 23
Go down 34
No opinion 2

$30,000–$39,999

Go up 29%
Stay the same 39
Go down 28
No opinion 4

$20,000–$29,999

Go up 40%
Stay the same 31
Go down 25
No opinion 4

$10,000–$19,999

Go up 40%
Stay the same 31
Go down 23
No opinion 6

Under $10,000

Go up 50%
Stay the same 23
Go down 16
No opinion 11

Selected National Trend

	Go up	Stay the same	Go down	No opinion
April 1984	74%	16%	6%	4%
Nov. 1983	42	31	20	7

About the big things people buy for their homes—like major appliances, furniture, or a TV set—generally speaking, do you think that now is a good time or a bad time to buy big things for the house?

Good time 48%
Bad time 32
Good and bad (volunteered) 11
No opinion 9

By Income

$40,000 and Over

Good time 67%
Bad time 19
Good and bad (volunteered) 7
No opinion 7

$30,000–$39,999

Good time	.61%
Bad time	.24
Good and bad (volunteered)	.11
No opinion	. 4

$20,000–$29,999

Good time	.54%
Bad time	.29
Good and bad (volunteered)	.11
No opinion	. 6

$10,000–$19,999

Good time	.41%
Bad time	.37
Good and bad (volunteered)	.12
No opinion	.10

Under $10,000

Good time	.28%
Bad time	.43
Good and bad (volunteered)	.14
No opinion	.15

Selected National Trend

	Good time	Bad time	Good and bad	No opinion
June 1983	41%	33%	15%	11%
Dec. 1982	29	50	13	8
Dec. 1981	27	51	11	11

Many homeowners have found that their house has increased in value a great deal in recent years. How about the next couple of years— do you think that house values will continue to go up a lot, or will they go up a little, or will they go down?

Go up a lot	.17%
Go up a little	.52
Go down	.12
Stay the same (volunteered)	.14
No opinion	. 5

By Income

$40,000 and Over

Go up a lot	.16%
Go up a little	.61
Go down	. 9
Stay the same (volunteered)	.13
No opinion	. 1

$30,000–$39,999

Go up a lot	.17%
Go up a little	.58
Go down	.12
Stay the same (volunteered)	.10
No opinion	. 3

$20,000–$29,999

Go up a lot	.20%
Go up a little	.52
Go down	.13
Stay the same (volunteered)	.13
No opinion	. 2

$10,000–$19,999

Go up a lot	.15%
Go up a little	.53
Go down	.12
Stay the same (volunteered)	.15
No opinion	. 5

Under $10,000

Go up a lot	.21%
Go up a little	.38
Go down	.14
Stay the same (volunteered)	.15
No opinion	.12

Selected National Trend

	Go up a lot	Go up a little	Go down	Stay the same	No opinion
June 1983	19%	54%	11%	11%	5%
June 1982	19	47	20	9	5
June 1981	34	46	10	5	5

During the next twelve months, do you expect your income to go up more than prices go up, about the same, or less than prices go up?

More than prices 17%
Same as prices 41
Less than prices 35
No opinion 7

By Income
$40,000 and Over

More than prices 33%
Same as prices 37
Less than prices 29
No opinion 1

$30,000–$39,999

More than prices 19%
Same as prices 50
Less than prices 24
No opinion 7

$20,000–$29,999

More than prices 17%
Same as prices 42
Less than prices 35
No opinion 6

$10,000–$19,999

More than prices 10%
Same as prices 45
Less than prices 38
No opinion 7

Under $10,000

More than prices 12%
Same as prices 32
Less than prices 45
No opinion 11

Selected National Trend

	More than prices	Same as prices	Less than prices	No opinion
November 1983	14%	46%	33%	7%
December 1982	12	37	44	7
December 1981	11	32	50	7

Note: American consumers continue to view the economic outlook for 1985 in mostly optimistic terms, with 64% in a recent Gallup Poll saying they expect the recovery to last at least until late this year, and only 23% predicting an earlier downturn. Not only does the survey offer evidence of overall consumer optimism, but also the outlook for lower inflation and interest rates is bullish. For example, in April, 74% thought personal interest rates during the next twelve months would go up; currently 41% hold this belief. On the other hand, in April only 6% said interest rates would drop; now, the comparable figure is 25%. The public's current expectations for interest rates are similar to those found in November 1983.

The latest survey also shows 48% saying now would be a good time to buy big-ticket items, such as major appliances, furniture, or a television set. This is the highest proportion expressing this opinion in regular surveys since mid-1981 and may reflect both overall consumer buoyancy about the economy as well as the hope that interest rates are on their way down.

In addition, in June 1981 one-third of consumers said they thought housing values would go up a lot during the next couple of years, while another 46% said they would go up a little, doubtless a reflection of inflationary pressures that then were pushing housing costs up rapidly. The latest figures are "a lot," 17%; and "a little," 52%. In the same period, the proportion who felt housing costs would stay the same or go down increased from 15% in 1981, to 26% at present.

Another indication of changing consumer expectations, including the prospects for inflation, is that marginally more people now than in earlier surveys think their incomes in the next twelve months will rise more than prices. However, despite a modest increase in this sentiment, a large majority continues to believe price increases will outstrip their income (35%), or that their income and prices will go up at about the same rate (41%).

	Local schools	Your own school
A rating	12%	21%
B rating	52	51
C rating	27	20
D rating	4	4
Fail	1	2
Don't know	4	2

JANUARY 15
TEACHERS' ATTITUDES TOWARD THE PUBLIC SCHOOLS*

Interviewing Date: 4/30–5/9/84
Special Mail Survey

Teachers Grade Public Schools

Asked of teachers: Students are often given the grades A, B, C, D, and Fail to denote the quality of their work. Suppose the public schools themselves, in this community, were graded in the same way. What grade would you give the public schools here? How about the public school in which you teach? What grade would you give your own school?

*This first Phi Delta Kappa/Gallup Poll of Teachers' Attitudes Toward the Public Schools was taken in May 1984, to establish benchmark measurements from which opinion trends can be tracked in subsequent surveys. Of particular importance are the public's and parents' opinions compared to those of the teachers. The poll originally appeared in two installments (October 1984 and January 1985) of the *Phi Delta Kappan*, which has published the annual Gallup Polls of the Public's Attitudes Toward the Public Schools since 1969. Phi Delta Kappa International has sponsored these polls since 1981.

Teachers Grade Teachers, Administrators, School Boards, and Parents

Asked of teachers: What grade would you give the teachers in the local public schools? The administrators in the local public schools? The local school board? What grade would you give the parents of students in the local public schools for bringing up their children?

	Teachers	Administrators	School board	Parents
A rating	18%	10%	4%	2%
B rating	60	34	25	19
C rating	17	34	36	45
D rating	2	15	19	24
Fail	**	5	13	7
Don't know	3	2	3	3

**Less than 1%

Teachers Grade Teacher Education

Asked of teachers: What grade would you give the teachers' education training you received?

	All teachers	Elementary teachers	High-school teachers
A rating	14%	14%	14%
B rating	35	37	34
C rating	10	34	31
D rating	10	8	11
Fail	6	4	8
Don't know	2	3	2

School Prayer

Asked of teachers: Do you favor or oppose a proposed amendment to the U.S. Constitution that would allow voluntary prayer in the public schools?

	All teachers	Elementary teachers	High-school teachers	U.S. public
Yes	52%	56%	47%	74%
No	33	30	37	19
Don't know	15	14	16	7

Why Teachers Leave the Profession

Asked of teachers: Many public school teachers are leaving the classroom. Here are some reasons that are sometimes given. Which three of these do you think are the main reasons why teachers are leaving their jobs?*

	All	Elementary	High-school	U.S. public (1982)
Low teachers' salaries	87%	85%	89%	52%
Discipline problems in schools	46	49	41	63
Low standing of teaching as profession	38	37	38	15
Students unmotivated, uninterested in school	37	31	41	37
Lack of public financial support for education	26	24	28	24
Parents don't support teachers	21	25	16	37
Outstanding teachers' performance goes unrewarded	20	16	25	13
Difficulty of advancement	19	19	19	14
Parents not interested in children's progress	11	11	11	25

*Multiple responses were given.

Attracting and Retaining Good Teachers

Asked of teachers: Does the school in which you teach have difficulty in getting good teachers?

	All teachers	Elementary teachers	High-school teachers
Yes	37%	31%	45%
No	57	65	48
No opinion	6	4	7

Asked of teachers: Does the school in which you teach have difficulty in keeping good teachers?

	All teachers	Elementary teachers	High-school teachers
Yes	48%	43%	55%
No	47	52	39
No opinion	5	5	6

Teachers' Compensation

Asked of teachers: Do you think salaries for teachers in this community are too high, too low, or just about right?

	All teachers	Elementary teachers	High-school teachers	U.S. public
Too high	*%	*%	*%	7%
Too low	90	89	89	37
Just about right	9	10	9	41
No opinion	1	1	2	15

*Less than 1%

Differential Pay in Subject Areas With Teacher Shortages

Asked of teachers: Today there is a shortage of teachers in science, math, technical subjects, and vocational subjects. If your local schools needed teachers in these subjects, would you favor or oppose paying them higher wages than teachers of other subjects?

	All teachers	Elementary teachers	High-school teachers	U.S. public
Favor	21%	18%	25%	48%
Oppose	75	80	70	43
No opinion	4	2	5	9

Merit Pay

Asked of teachers: How do you, yourself, feel about the idea of merit pay for teachers? In general, do you favor or oppose it?

	All teachers	Elementary teachers	High-school teachers	U.S. public
Favor	32%	29%	35%	76%
Oppose	64	67	62	19
No opinion	4	4	3	5

Asked of those who favor/oppose: Why do you favor/oppose merit pay for teachers?*

	All teachers	Elementary teachers	High-school teachers
Oppose			
Difficult to give fair evaluation	23%	22%	24%
Would create problems/morale problems	12	14	10
Administrators can't evaluate fairly	12	12	13
Political problems	8	9	7
Can't be objectively measured	12	12	12
Other	5	4	5

Favor			
Good teachers would be rewarded	25	23	27
Children would benefit	1	**	1
Other	7	6	8

*Multiple responses were given.
**Less than 1%

Asked of teachers: Suppose that your own school were to adopt the merit pay plan. Who, in your opinion, should determine which teachers should be given merit increases?*

	All teachers	Elementary teachers	High-school teachers
Committee of teachers	63%	62%	65%
School principal	57	60	53
Committee of outside educators	42	42	40
Students	22	18	26
Parents	19	21	17
Other	11	11	11
No one qualified	2	2	3
Don't know	3	3	4

*Multiple responses were given.

Asked of teachers: Aside from whether you favor or oppose merit pay, do you feel there are any teachers in the school where you teach who are sufficiently outstanding to warrant merit pay, or not?

	All teachers	Elementary teachers	High-school teachers
Yes	76%	72%	81%
No	16	19	11
No opinion	8	9	8

Asked of those who favor merit pay: What percentage of teachers do you feel warrants merit pay?

	All teachers	Elementary teachers	High-school teachers
Under 10%	13%	11%	16%
10% to 19%	23	22	25
20% to 29%	17	15	19
30% to 59%	23	25	20
60% to 99%	17	21	13
No answer	7	6	7
Average	33	36	30

Major Problems Confronting the Public Schools

*Asked of teachers: What do you think are the biggest problems with which the public schools in this community must deal?**

	All	Elementary	High-school	U.S. public
Parents' lack of interest/support	31%	35%	26%	5%
Lack of proper financial support	21	20	21	14
Pupils' lack of interest/truancy	20	17	23	4
Lack of discipline	16	20	18	27
Problems with administration	10	8	12	3
Poor curriculum/poor standards	7	7	7	15
Use of drugs	5	3	6	18
Low teachers' salaries	5	5	5	4
Difficulty getting good teachers	4	3	4	14
Large schools/overcrowding	4	5	2	4
Teachers' lack of interest	4	5	4	5
Lack of respect for teachers/other students	4	4	4	3
One-parent households	4	4	4	**
Lack of public support	3	3	4	**
Communication problems	3	4	3	1
Government interference/regulation	3	2	4	1
Integration/busing	2	2	2	6
Lack of proper facilities	2	2	3	2
School board policies	2	2	2	**
Parental involvement with school activities	2	3	2	1
Mismanagement of funds/programs	2	3	2	2
Moral standards	2	2	2	1
Drinking/alcoholism	2	2	3	4
Lack of needed teachers	2	2	1	1
Crime/vandalism	1	**	2	3

*Multiple responses were given.
**Less than 1%

The Discipline Problem

Asked of teachers: How serious a problem would you say discipline is in the public schools in your community—very serious, fairly serious, not too serious, or not at all serious?

	All	Elementary	High-school	U.S. public
Very serious	16%	17%	15%	34%
Fairly serious	33	29	36	34
Not too serious	35	38	32	22
Not at all serious	14	12	17	4
No opinion	2	4	*	6

*Less than 1%

*Asked of teachers: About how often do each of the problems listed occur at the school where you teach?**

	Most of the time/ fairly often	
	All teachers	U.S. public
Schoolwork and homework assignments not completed ..	76%	64%
Behavior that disrupts class ...	47	60
Truancy/being absent from school	47	53
Talking back to, disobeying teachers	43	56
Cheating on tests	40	46
Sloppy or inappropriate dress	37	47
Skipping classes	35	56
Stealing money or personal property belonging to other students, teachers, or staff ..	32	38
Vandalizing of school property	29	39
Theft of school property	23	34
Use of drugs at school	17	53
Selling of drugs at school	13	47
Drinking alcoholic beverages at school	10	35
Carrying of knives, firearms, or other weapons at school	8	29
Sexual activity at school	8	24
Racial fights between whites, blacks, Hispanics, or other minorities	4	22
Taking money or property by force, using weapons or threats	2	18
Physical attacks on teachers or staff	1	15

*Multiple responses were given.

Asked of teachers: Many people say that discipline is one of the major problems of the public schools today. Would you please look over this list and check the reasons you think are most important to explain why there is a discipline problem?*

	All teachers	U.S. public (1983)
Lack of discipline in home ...	94%	72%
Lack of respect for law and authority throughout society	74	54
Students who are constant troublemakers often can't be removed from school	66	42
Courts have made school administrators so cautious they don't deal severely with student misbehavior	65	41
Punishment is too lenient	50	39
Decline in teaching of good manners	48	37
One-parent families	42	26
Viewing television programs that emphasize crime and violence	39	39
Teachers themselves do not command respect	23	36
Teachers who are not properly trained to deal with discipline problems	19	42
Failure on part of teachers to make classroom work more interesting	11	31

*Multiple responses were given.

Support for Public School Testing

Asked of teachers: In your opinion, should children be promoted from grade to grade only if they can pass examinations?

	All teachers	Elementary teachers	High-school teachers	U.S. public
Yes	43%	33%	54%	71%
No	52	63	40	25
No opinion	5	4	6	4

Asked of teachers: Should all high-school students in the United States be required to pass a standard nationwide examination in order to get a high-school diploma?

	All teachers	Elementary teachers	High-school teachers	U.S. public
Should be required	48%	52%	44%	65%
Should not be required	45	41	50	29
No opinion	7	7	6	6

	All teachers	U.S. public
Yes	63%	89%
No	30	7
No opinion	7	4

Remedial Classes or Repeating a Grade

Asked of teachers: Should students who fail be required to take special remedial classes in the subjects they fail, or should they be required to repeat the whole year's work?

	All teachers	U.S. public (1978)
Special remedial classes	78%	81%
Repeat whole year's work	13	14
No opinion	9	5

Raising College Entrance Requirements

Asked of teachers: Do you feel that four-year colleges and universities should raise their entrance requirements, or not?

	All teachers	U.S. public
Should	47%	27%
Should not	39	59
No opinion	14	14

State Board Examination for Teachers

Asked of teachers: In addition to meeting college requirements for a teacher's certificate, should those who want to become teachers also be required to pass a state board examination to prove their knowledge in the subjects they will teach, before they are hired?

Desirability of Teaching as a Profession

Asked of teachers: Would you like to have a daughter of yours take up teaching in the public schools as a career? Would you like to have a son of yours take up teaching in the public schools as a career?

	All Teachers		U.S. Public	
	Daughter	Son	Daughter	Son
Yes	43%	31%	50%	46%
No	46	59	39	42
No opinion	11	10	11	12

Unions, Strikes, and Arbitration

Asked of teachers: Most teachers in the nation now belong to unions or associations that bargain over salaries, working conditions, and the like. Has unionization, in your opinion, helped, hurt, or made no difference in the quality of public education in the United States?

	All teachers	Elementary teachers	High-school teachers	U.S. public
Helped	49%	48%	50%	18%
Hurt	18	20	15	37
No difference	26	25	28	33
No opinion	7	7	7	12

Asked of teachers: Should public school teachers be permitted to strike, or not?

	All teachers	Elementary teachers	High-school teachers	U.S. public
Yes	63%	58%	70%	37%
No	26	30	20	56
No opinion	11	12	10	7

Asked of teachers: In case an agreement cannot be reached between a teachers' union (or association) and the school board, would you favor or oppose a plan that would require the dispute to be settled by the decision of an arbitrator or panel acceptable to both the union and school board?

	All teachers	Elementary teachers	High-school teachers	U.S. public
Favor	90%	88%	92%	79%
Oppose	3	4	2	7
No opinion	7	8	6	14

How Teachers See Themselves

Asked of teachers: Now we would like your impression about different professions and occupations, based on your personal experience or on what you've heard or read. To indicate your impression, please use this scale that goes from the lowest rating of 0 to the highest rating of 10.

First rate the professions listed below for the amount each contributes to the general good of society. The more you feel it contributes to the good of society, the higher the number you would pick; the less you feel it contributes, the lower the number you would pick.

	Highest Rating	
	All teachers	U.S. public
Public school teachers	59%	29%
Physicians	46	41
Clergy	43	46
Public school principals	19	28
Judges	13	12
Lawyers	6	12
Funeral directors	5	20
Business executives	4	–
Local political officeholders ...	4	8
Bankers	3	14
Realtors	2	7
Advertising practitioners	2	4

Asked of teachers: Now rate these professions for the amount of prestige or status you feel people in each profession have in your community.

	Highest Rating	
	All teachers	U.S. public
Public school teachers	1%	19%
Physicians	68	59
Clergy	20	42
Public school principals	3	25
Judges	45	31
Lawyers	32	31
Funeral directors	4	17
Business executives	26	–
Local political officeholders ...	15	16
Bankers	22	35
Realtors	3	6
Advertising practitioners	4	8

Subject Requirements

Asked of teachers: If you were the one to decide, which of the following subjects would you require every public high-school student who plans to go on to college to take?

	All teachers	U.S. public
Mathematics	96%	96%
English	95	94
History/U.S. government	95	84
Science	95	84
Foreign language	77	57
Physical education	74	43
Health education	73	52
Business	63	68
Art	54	24
Music	49	32
Industrial arts/homemaking ...	46	37*

*U.S. public was asked about "vocational training."

Asked of teachers: For how many years would you require every public high-school student who plans to go on to college to take these subjects?

	Average years required
Mathematics	3.4
English	3.8
History/U.S. government	2.9

Science	2.8
Foreign language	2.1
Physical education	2.6
Health education	1.5
Business	1.5
Art	1.3
Music	1.3
Industrial arts/homemaking	1.4

Music	1.3
Industrial arts/homemaking	2.4

Asked of teachers: What about those public high-school students who do not plan to go on to college when they graduate? Which courses would you require them to take?

	All teachers	U.S. public
Mathematics	94%	92%
English	93	90
History/U.S. government	91	71
Science	90	61
Foreign language	28	19
Physical education	75	44
Health education	80	50
Business	45	76
Art	42	18
Music	40	18
Industrial arts/homemaking	78	83*

*U.S. public was asked about "vocational training."

Asked of teachers: For how many years would you require every public high-school student who does not plan to go on to college to take these subjects?

	Average years required
Mathematics	2.7
English	3.6
History/U.S. government	2.2
Science	2.4
Foreign language	1.4
Physical education	2.6
Health education	1.6
Business	2.1
Art	1.3

Sex Education

Asked of teachers: Do you feel the public high schools should or should not include sex education in their instructional program?

	All teachers	U.S. public
Should	86%	70%
Should not	8	22
No opinion	6	8

Asked of teachers: Do you feel the public elementary schools should or should not include sex education in grades 4 through 8?

	All teachers	U.S. public
Should	75%	45%
Should not	18	48
No opinion	7	7

Asked of teachers: Which of the following topics, if any, should be included for high-school students (elementary-school students):

Biology of reproduction?

	High school	Elementary school
Should	83%	70%
Should not	15	28
No opinion	2	2

Venereal disease?

	High school	Elementary school
Should	83%	40%
Should not	15	50
No opinion	2	10

Birth control?

Should	80%	29%
Should not	18	58
No opinion	2	13

Premarital sex?

Should	68%	21%
Should not	24	65
No opinion	8	14

Nature of sexual intercourse?

Should	62%	24%
Should not	28	63
No opinion	10	13

Abortion?

Should	64%	18%
Should not	27	65
No opinion	9	17

Homosexuality?

Should	55%	15%
Should not	31	68
No opinion	14	17

	U.S. Public	
	Should be included in high school	Should be included in elementary school
Biology of reproduction	54%	37%
Venereal disease	59	23
Birth control	55	20
Premarital sex	42	18
Nature of sexual intercourse	37	16
Abortion	38	12
Homosexuality	32	10

Goals of Education

Please rate the importance of each of the following possible goals of education on a scale of 0 to 10. A zero means a goal is not at all important and should not be part of the public school program. A 10 means a goal is the most important goal, before all others. A rating between 0 and 10 means you consider the goal to be somewhere in between in importance.

	Highest Rating	
	All teachers	U.S. public
To help develop good work habits, ability to organize one's thoughts, ability to concentrate	56%	48%
To develop ability to think creatively, objectively, analytically	56	51
To develop ability to speak and write correctly	55	68
To develop ability to use mathematics for everyday problems	53	54
To encourage desire to continue learning throughout one's life	51	41
To encourage respect for law and order, for obeying rules of society	46	52
To develop ability to live in complex and changing world	41	51
To prepare those who plan to attend college for college ...	36	46
To develop skills needed to get jobs for those not planning to attend college	34	54
To develop standards of what is "right and wrong"	33	64
To develop desire to excel	32	51
To develop understanding of democracy and to promote participation in political process	31	33
To develop ability to get along with different kinds of people	31	42
To develop respect for and understanding of other races, religions, nations, and cultures	30	39

To develop ability to deal with adult responsibilities and problems, i.e., sex, marriage, parenting, personal finances, alcohol and drug abuse 28 46

To help students make realistic plans for what they will do after high-school graduation 27 52

To develop understanding about different kinds of jobs and careers, including their requirements and rewards ... 20 56

To gain knowledge and understanding of science and scientific facts 17 45

To gain knowledge of important facts of history, geography, etc. 15 42

To develop appreciation for and participation in arts, music, literature, theater, etc. 14 35

To help students overcome personal problems 13 45

To develop ability to understand and use computers 12 43

To promote physical development through sports programs 8 20

To help students get good/high-paying jobs 6 46

To develop appreciation of "good" things in life 6 32

Extending the School Day or Year

Asked of teachers: How do you feel about extending the school day by one hour in the school in which you teach? Aside from the question of teacher/staff compensation, do you favor or oppose this idea?

	All teachers	U.S. public
Favor	24%	42%
Oppose	72	52
No opinion	4	6

Asked of teachers: In some nations, students attend school as many as 240 days a year,

as compared to about 180 days in the United States. Aside from the question of teacher/staff compensation, how do you feel about extending the public school year in this community by 30 days, making the school year about 210 days or 10 months long? Do you favor or oppose this idea?

	All teachers	U.S. public
Favor	28%	44%
Oppose	66	50
No opinion	6	6

Control of Instruction

Asked of teachers: In your opinion, who should have the greatest influence in deciding what is taught in the public schools of your community?

	All teachers	Elementary teachers	High-school teachers	U.S. public
Teachers	33%	31%	35%	11%
Local school board	19	17	20	27
State government	17	19	16	17
Federal government	3	2	3	9
Parents	2	2	2	24
No opinion	26	29	24	12

Asked of teachers: Who do you feel should have the most influence in the selection of books for use in public school classrooms and school libraries?

	All teachers	Elementary teachers	High-school teachers	U.S. public
Teachers	79%	76%	82%	42%
Principals, school administrators	4	5	2	15
School board	3	2	3	13

Parents	*	*	1	18
No opinion	14	17	12	12

*Less than 1%

Note: Attitudes of American teachers are markedly uniform. Very few differences are apparent among the nine subgroups in the teacher population by which the data were analyzed. Only in the case of elementary and high-school teachers do differences in views emerge, and then only rarely.

At the same time, the attitudes of teachers and the public are frequently at odds. Of the approximately thirty issues in the two installments of this teacher poll on which the opinion of the public is also available, teachers and the public agree on one-third of the issues and disagree on two-thirds.

Grading the schools. Teachers give high marks to U.S. public schools. Asked to grade the local schools, using the traditional grading system, two-thirds of the teachers award the schools either an A or a B. When asked to grade the school in which they themselves teach, an even higher percentage (72%) award an A or a B.

Grading teachers, administrators, school boards, and parents. The same favorable attitude also is apparent when teachers are asked to rate other members of their profession; however, teachers are less positive about the performance of administrators in the public schools and about local school boards. Almost eight teachers in ten (78%) would award their peers an A or a B, but substantially fewer would give administrators and school board members top grades. Teachers' grades for parents fall far below those they give to teachers, administrators, and school board members. Asked to grade the job that local parents are doing in bringing up their children, only one teacher in five gives parents an A or a B.

School prayer. Elementary teachers favor voluntary school prayer by a 2-to-1 ratio. High-school teachers are much more closely divided on this issue than are elementary-school teachers. The public approves of school prayer by a wider margin, 4 to 1.

Teachers' compensation. A major source of teacher dissatisfaction involves what teachers perceive as poor compensation. For example, nine teachers in ten state that their salaries are too low, and almost nine in ten say that low pay is the reason why teachers are leaving the profession. Similarly, when asked for ways to reduce school costs, only 5% react favorably to the idea of cutting teachers' salaries. The public tends to agree, by a significantly smaller percentage, that teachers are paid too little.

Merit pay. U.S. teachers, including all major subgroups in the teacher population, oppose the idea of merit pay by a 2-to-1 ratio. Their objections center on two main points: the difficulties in evaluation (i.e., determining who should receive merit pay), and the morale problems that might be created if merit pay plans were put into effect. At the same time, however, fully three-quarters of U.S. teachers admit that some teachers in their own schools are outstanding enough to warrant merit pay. Asked to estimate the percentage in their own schools who deserve it, teachers who favor merit pay say about 33%.

If merit pay were adopted by the local schools, teachers would want fellow teachers, administrators, or educators from outside the district, rather than noneducators, to decide who should receive it. Only about one-fifth of teachers believe that either students or parents should be involved in this decision. Similarly, teachers say that the criteria to be used in selecting candidates for merit pay should be both an evaluation by educators, either teachers or administrators, and an advanced degree or years of experience. Only a relatively small percentage of teachers believe that students' academic achievement or improvement, students' evaluations of teachers, or parents' opinions should influence the awarding of merit pay.

The views of the public provide a rather dramatic contrast to the attitudes of teachers. The public favors merit pay for teachers by a ratio of 4 to 1 (76% to 19%). The public also thinks that the most important criterion upon which to base merit pay should be the academic achievement or improvement of students as measured by standardized tests (68%), but only 39% of teachers agree.

Major problems and discipline. U.S. teachers have a much different perception of the problem of discipline in the public schools than does the public. Teachers believe that the most important problem facing local public schools (named by 31% of the respondents) is lack of parental support, not lack of discipline. Only about one teacher in six (16%) says that discipline is a very serious problem.

In addition, nonacademic disciplinary problems—incomplete assignments, cheating, talking back to teachers, and truancy—are mentioned frequently by teachers as occurring most of the time or fairly often. A relatively small percentage of teachers says that criminal activities—vandalizing or theft of property, use or selling of drugs or alcohol, carrying of weapons, physical attacks on students or staff—occur in their schools most of the time or fairly often.

The public's perceptions of discipline in the schools differ considerably from those of teachers, however. The public has named discipline as the most important problem facing the public schools since the Gallup surveys of attitudes toward the schools began in 1969. One-third of the public in 1984, compared to 16% of teachers, believe that disciplinary problems are very serious. Most significantly, however, the public perceives violence and criminal activities as much more prevalent in the schools than teachers do. Far larger percentages of the public than of teachers, for example, say that a variety of these kinds of problems occur most of the time or fairly often.

Teachers blame disciplinary problems on outside influences—specifically, the courts, lack of respect for authority, and especially lack of discipline in the home, which is mentioned by virtually all teachers (94%). Only about one-third of the teachers think that teachers themselves are at fault. The public agrees, although by a smaller percentage, that the principal source of disciplinary problems is lack of discipline in the home. On the other hand, the public is more prone to blame teachers for these problems.

Testing. Teachers are divided on the value of public-school testing programs. A slight majority opposes exams for grade promotion, and an even smaller majority favors exams for high-school graduation. Two thirds of those who approve of an exam for high-school graduation think that the

results should be released to the public and compared with results from other schools that serve the same racial and socioeconomic mix.

The public's view differs markedly from that of teachers on the issue of testing. Although the public approves of an exam for high-school graduation by a wide 7 to 3 ratio, only half of those who favor the exam also favor the release of results to the public and approve of comparing the results with those of other schools.

College entrance requirements and state board examinations. Teachers are mixed in their views on recommendations for improving the public schools that have been made by the recent wave of national commissions and task forces on education. By wide margins, teachers favor both higher salaries for teachers and state board examinations (63%) to prove their knowledge of subject matter. By a somewhat smaller margin, they also favor tougher college entrance requirements (47%). By contrast, the public opposes more difficult admissions standards for colleges and universities (59%).

Desirability of teaching as a profession. Teachers are somewhat negative about the desirability of teaching as a profession. They are evenly divided on whether they would like a daughter to enter teaching, but they are against a son going into it by a ratio of 2 to 1 (59% to 31%). By contrast, the public favors a daughter going into teaching by a ratio of about 5 to 4 (50% to 39%), but is divided as to whether a son should enter the profession.

Teachers' unions/teachers' strikes. Teachers' attitudes regarding the effects of unionization are in almost direct contrast to the attitudes of the general public. Whereas teachers by a margin of almost 3 to 1 (49% to 18%) say that unions have helped the quality of American education, the public by a 2-to-1 ratio believes that unionization has hurt education. Moreover, while teachers say that they should have the right to strike (63% favor this right), 56% of the public oppose such strikes. On the other hand, the public agrees with the views of teachers concerning compulsory arbitration in settling disputes: large majorities of teachers (90%) and of the public (79%) favor this arbitration.

How teachers see themselves. Teachers rate their contribution to society the highest of twelve professions, including physicians, clergy, business executives, and lawyers, but they also believe that their status is the lowest of all of these professions. The general public rates teachers' contribution to society somewhat lower than that of clergy or physicians, but rates teachers' status in the community somewhat higher than the teachers themselves do.

Subject requirements. The reform reports also made a number of recommendations for changing subject requirements. Virtually all teachers (95%) agree with the reports that English and math should be required of all students, not just the college bound. Specifically, teachers recommend an average for the college bound of 3.8 years of English, 3.2 years of math, and 3.0 years of science; for those not bound for college, 3.6 years of English, 2.7 years of math, and 2.7 years of science.

Furthermore, 59% of teachers would require all students to take computer science; 78%, vocational training for the noncollege bound; and 48%, vocational education even for the college bound. Seventy-seven percent of teachers would require about two years (2.1) of a foreign language for college-bound students. As for the public, its attitudes toward subject requirements are basically the same as those of teachers, with the exception that a smaller percentage of the public would require science of high-school students and a slightly larger percentage would require computer science.

Sex education. Teachers overwhelmingly support sex education in both the secondary schools and the elementary schools. Almost nine out of ten (86%) support sex education in high school, and three out of four (75%) support it in elementary school.

More specifically, for high-school students, large majorities of teachers approve the discussion of such topics as the biology of reproduction, venereal disease, and birth control. Smaller majorities approve of including in high-school sex education classes such topics as premarital sex, the nature of sexual intercourse, abortion, and homosexuality. For elementary-school students, the only topic that a majority of teachers (70%) thinks would be appropriate is the biology of reproduction.

The public supports sex education in the high schools by a smaller margin than teachers do (70% as opposed to 86%). However, the public is about evenly divided (45% for and 48% against) on the question of sex education in the elementary schools.

Goals of education. A majority (56%) of teachers rates developing good work habits, the ability to organize one's thoughts, and the ability to concentrate as a most important goal of education. The same percentage of teachers also rates the ability to think creatively, objectively, and analytically as a goal of the highest importance. A majority of teachers also cites developing the ability to speak and write, developing the ability to use mathematics for everyday problems, and encouraging the desire for lifelong learning as among the highest priorities of education.

Extending the school day/year. Another major recommendation of the national commissions and task forces was that either the school day or school year be lengthened to provide more time for instruction. Teachers oppose both of these recommendations by roughly the same margins: 72% oppose lengthening the school day, while 66% oppose lengthening the school year. Virtually every major subgroup in the teacher population opposes both of these recommendations.

Control of instruction. Teachers believe that they should have the most influence on what is taught in the public schools. They feel even more strongly that they should have the most influence in the selection of schoolbooks. By contrast, the public says that parents and school boards should have the most say about what is taught in the public schools, but the public agrees with teachers that the latter should have the most say about the selection of books and other instructional materials.

JANUARY 17
POLITICAL AFFILIATION

Interviewing Date: 11/30–12/3/84
Survey #246-G

In politics, as of today, do you consider yourself a Republican, a Democrat, or an independent?*

Republican 31%
Democrat 40
Independent 29

Selected National Trend

	Repub- lican	Demo- crat	Inde- pendent
1983	25%	44%	31%
1981	28	42	30
1979	22	45	33
1977	21	48	31
1975	22	45	33
1972	28	43	29
1968	27	46	27
1964	25	53	22
1960	30	47	23
1954	34	46	20
1950	33	45	22
1946	40	39	21
1944	39	41	20
1940	38	42	20
1937	34	50	16

*Those saying they have no party preference or who named other political parties (3%–4% in the latest surveys) are excluded.

As you feel today, which political party—the Republican or the Democratic—do you think serves the interests of the following groups best:

People like yourself?

Republican 43%
Democratic 38
Same; no opinion 19

By Sex
Male

Republican 48%
Democratic 33
Same; no opinion 19

Female

Republican 39%
Democratic 42
Same; no opinion 19

By Ethnic Background
White

Republican 47%
Democratic 34
Same; no opinion 19

Nonwhite

Republican 14%
Democratic 66
Same; no opinion 20

Black

Republican 9%
Democratic 75
Same; no opinion 16

By Education
College Graduate

Republican 55%
Democratic 34
Same; no opinion 11

College Incomplete

Republican 49%
Democratic 36
Same; no opinion 15

High-School Graduate

Republican 42%
Democratic 37
Same; no opinion 21

Less Than High-School Graduate

Republican 30%
Democratic 43
Same; no opinion 27

By Region

East

Republican 42%
Democratic 40
Same; no opinion 18

Midwest

Republican 44%
Democratic 35
Same; no opinion 21

South

Republican 44%
Democratic 37
Same; no opinion 19

West

Republican 41%
Democratic 40
Same; no opinion 19

By Age

18–29 Years

Republican 43%
Democratic 37
Same; no opinion 20

30–49 Years

Republican 45%
Democratic 36
Same; no opinion 19

50 Years and Over

Republican 41%
Democratic 40
Same; no opinion 19

By Income

$40,000 and Over

Republican 56%
Democratic 30
Same; no opinion 14

$30,000–$39,999

Republican 53%
Democratic 29
Same; no opinion 18

$20,000–$29,999

Republican 46%
Democratic 35
Same; no opinion 19

$10,000–$19,999

Republican 40%
Democratic 39
Same; no opinion 21

Under $10,000

Republican 27%
Democratic 51
Same; no opinion 22

By Occupation

Professional and Business

Republican 53%
Democratic 32
Same; no opinion 15

Clerical and Sales

Republican 36%
Democratic 47
Same; no opinion 17

Manual Workers

Republican 40%
Democratic 39
Same; no opinion 21

Nonlabor Force

Republican 38%
Democratic 41
Same; no opinion 21

By Labor Union Household
Labor Union Members
Republican 32%
Democratic 49
Same; no opinion 19

Nonlabor Union Members
Republican 45%
Democratic 36
Same; no opinion 19

Farmers?
Republican 31%
Democratic 45
Same; no opinion 24

Selected National Trend

	Republican	Democratic	Same; no opinion
1981	23%	44%	33%
1965	16	43	41
1960	19	45	36
1956	22	51	27
1947	17	56	27

Business and professional people?
Republican 69%
Democratic 16
Same; no opinion 15

Selected National Trend

	Republican	Democratic	Same; no opinion
1981	55%	22%	23%
1965	39	25	36
1960	47	21	32
1956	56	19	25
1947	50	21	29

Skilled workers?
Republican 41%
Democratic 39
Same; no opinion 20

Selected National Trend

	Republican	Democratic	Same; no opinion
1981	21%	51%	28%
1965	12	46	42
1960	18	45	37
1956	26	45	29
1947	16	52	32

Unskilled workers?
Republican 22%
Democratic 58
Same; no opinion 20

Selected National Trend

	Republican	Democratic	Same; no opinion
1981	14%	57%	29%
1965	9	53	38
1960	14	52	34
1956	23	52	25
1947	11	62	27

White collar workers?
Republican 59%
Democratic 23
Same; no opinion 18

Selected National Trend

	Republican	Democratic	Same; no opinion
1981	38%	32%	30%
1965	23	32	45
1960	31	29	40
1956	35	30	35
1947	29	30	41

Labor union members?
Republican 24%
Democratic 58
Same; no opinion 18

Blacks?

Republican 19%
Democratic 60
Same; no opinion 21

Small business people?

Republican 35%
Democratic 45
Same; no opinion 20

Women?

Republican 25%
Democratic 48
Same; no opinion 27

Unemployed?

Republican 26%
Democratic 52
Same; no opinion 22

Retired?

Republican 28%
Democratic 48
Same; no opinion 24

Note: Although the Republican party continues to trail the Democratic party as better serving the interests of many traditionally Democratic population groups, the GOP is perceived by voters as having broadened its appeal to many of these Democratic bastions during President Ronald Reagan's first term. The most striking example may be found in the public's perception of which party better serves the interest of skilled workers. Today, the Republican (41%) and Democratic (39%) parties share that perception about equally; in 1981, only 21% thought skilled workers' interests were better represented by the GOP, while 51% named the Democrats.

For serving "people like yourself," the Republican party has edged ahead of the Democratic party, 43% to 38%. In 1981 the Democrats had a wide 45% to 29% lead on serving the average American. The survey results suggest that the GOP may be starting to shed its image as the party of the rich, while the Democratic party is losing ground as the workingman's party. These images have been rooted deeply in the thinking of the electorate since New Deal days.

In addition to registering gains with the public as the party better able to serve the interests of hard-core Democratic groups, the GOP has improved upon the solid advantage it already enjoyed as better able to serve the interests of upscale groups such as business and professional people. While the Democratic party has lost ground in terms of many of the groups tested, it continues to hold a substantial advantage as the party better serving the interests of farmers, unskilled workers, labor union members, blacks, women, unemployed people, retirees, and small business people.

Today's findings parallel a substantial increase in the proportion of Americans claiming affiliation with the Republican party. Just prior to President Reagan's landslide reelection, GOP affiliation reached a level not seen since the Eisenhower era of the 1950s. Concurrently, the proportion of the electorate now expressing allegiance to the Democratic party is as low as it has been at any point since the end of World War II. For the year 1984 as a whole, 31% of Americans claimed Republican party affiliation, up from 25% in 1983. During the same period, Democratic affiliation declined from 44% to 40%.

JANUARY 20
PRESIDENT REAGAN

Special Report

President Ronald Reagan ends his first term with an average approval rating of 50% for his four years in office, similar to the ratings achieved by predecessors Jimmy Carter, Gerald Ford, Richard Nixon, Lyndon Johnson, and Harry Truman during comparable periods of their presidencies. Reagan's first-term average, however, is substantially lower than those accorded John Kennedy and Dwight Eisenhower.

The president begins his second term with the approval of about six in ten Americans. In the three Gallup surveys conducted since his landslide reelection last November, 61% of the public approved of his handling of his presidential duties, 31% disapproved, and 8% withheld judgment. Reagan's high point of 68% approval was recorded in May 1981, soon after he took office. His low point of 35% approval occurred in January 1983, as the nation began to recover from the 1981–82 recession.

Reagan's record to date is quite similar to all but those of Presidents Kennedy and Eisenhower. All received their highest ratings, or close to their highest, during their first year in office and averaged close to 50% approval during their presidencies. The table below compares the high, low, and average approval ratings of the postwar presidents during their entire tenure:

Presidential Performance Ratings

(Percent Approval)

	Tenure	High point	Low point	Average
Reagan	1981–84	68%	35%	50%
Carter	1977–80	75	21	47
Ford	1974–76	71	37	47
Nixon	1969–74	68	24	49
Johnson	1963–68	80	35	56
Kennedy	1961–63	83	56	71
Eisenhower	1953–60	79	49	65
Truman	1945–52	87	23	43

A common thread links the four postwar presidents who were reelected (Nixon, Eisenhower) or who were elected to full terms after assuming office under nonelective circumstances (Johnson, Truman): they received lower approval ratings during their second or elected terms than they had in their initial ones.

The following table summarizes the average performance ratings, by term, of all the postwar presidents:

Presidential Performance Ratings

(Career Averages)

	Term	Approve	Disapprove	No opinion
Reagan	1981–84	50%	39%	11%
Carter	1977–80	47	38	15

Ford	1974–76	47	37	16
Nixon	1973–74	35	54	11
	1969–72	56	28	16
Johnson	1965–68	52	35	13
	1963–64	75	11	14
Kennedy	1961–63	71	16	13
Eisenhower	1957–60	61	25	14
	1953–56	69	17	14
Truman	1949–52	37	47	16
	1945–48	54	32	14

To determine presidential performance ratings, the following question was asked:

Do you approve or disapprove of the way (incumbent) is handling his job as president?

Each performance rating was based on in-person interviews with approximately 1,500 adults, age 18 and older, conducted in more than 300 scientifically selected localities across the nation. For results based on samples of this size, one can say with 95% confidence that the error attributable to sampling and other random effects could be 3 percentage points in either direction.

JANUARY 24
FEDERAL BUDGET DEFICIT

Interviewing Date: 12/7–10/84
Survey #247-G

At present the federal budget deficit is running at a rate of nearly $200 billion per year. Basically, there are only a few ways this deficit can be reduced. Please tell me whether you approve of each of the following ways to reduce the deficit:

Raise income taxes?

	Percent approving
National	23%

By Sex

Male	25%
Female	21

By Ethnic Background

White	23%
Black	23

By Education

College graduate	37%
College incomplete	24
High-school graduate	20
Less than high-school graduate	15

By Region

East	24%
Midwest	26
South	17
West	27

By Age

18–29 years	18%
30–49 years	23
50–64 years	24
65 years and over	29

By Politics

Republicans	20%
Democrats	30
Independents	20

Make cuts in government spending for social programs?

	Percent approving
National	41%

By Sex

Male	46%
Female	37

By Ethnic Background

White	45%
Black	20

By Education

College graduate	46%
College incomplete	43
High-school graduate	42
Less than high-school graduate	35

By Region

East	38%
Midwest	41
South	48
West	37

By Age

18–29 years	38%
30–49 years	40
50–64 years	47
65 years and over	44

By Politics

Republicans	57%
Democrats	28
Independents	41

Make cuts in defense spending?

	Percent approving
National	61%

By Sex

Male	64%
Female	59

By Ethnic Background

White	60%
Black	72

By Education

College graduate	72%
College incomplete	65
High-school graduate	55
Less than high-school graduate	59

East	63%
Midwest	62
South	53
West	71

By Age

18–29 years	56%
30–49 years	62
50–64 years	64
65 years and over	63

By Politics

Republicans	53%
Democrats	71
Independents	60

Make cuts in "entitlement" programs such as Social Security, Medicaid, and the like?

	Percent approving
National	11%

By Sex

Male	14%
Female	8

By Ethnic Background

White	12%
Black	7

By Education

College graduate	18%
College incomplete	15
High-school graduate	8
Less than high-school graduate	6

By Region

East	11%
Midwest	9
South	13
West	11

By Age

18–29 years	10%
30–49 years	12
50–64 years	11
65 years and over	11

By Politics

Republicans	17%
Democrats	7
Independents	9

Note: If the American people had the responsibility of reducing the huge federal budget deficit—now estimated to be as high as $230 billion for fiscal year 1986—their top priority would be to cut defense spending. Asked to vote on each of the four principal means of cutting the deficit, 61% in the latest Gallup survey approve of cuts in the defense budget, 41% favor cuts in government spending for social programs, 23% would raise income taxes, and 11% would cut "entitlement" programs such as Social Security and Medicaid.

The administration and Congress agree that tackling the deficit is one of the nation's highest priorities and that the budget cuts for 1986 should total about $50 billion. That is the figure cited recently by Paul Volcker, chairman of the Federal Reserve Board, as the least amount necessary to be effective. How savings of this magnitude are to be achieved—deciding which programs will be cut and which will not—remains the thorniest issue still to be resolved.

The survey found general agreement on the priority of the measures that should be taken to reduce the deficit, with majorities in all major populations favoring cuts in defense spending. Nevertheless, there is considerable divergence in the views of many.

Sharp divisions are found along political party lines. Republicans, for example, favor defense cuts (53%) and cuts in spending for social programs (57%) by similar margins. On the other hand, 71% of Democrats favor defense cuts, but only 28% approve of cuts in social programs. Similarly, an increase in income taxes is favored by 20% of Republicans and 30% of Democrats. And while cuts in entitlements are not popular with members of either party, they are relatively more appealing to Republicans (17%) than to Democrats (7%). Political independents take positions between those of Republicans and Democrats on three of the four measures.

In terms of geography, southerners (48%) tend to favor cuts in social programs more than do persons from other regions (39%). However, southerners (53%) are less likely to want defense spending cuts than are those in other parts of the nation (65%).

JANUARY 27
SATISFACTION INDEX

Interviewing Date: 12/7–10/84
Survey #247-G

How satisfied or dissatisfied are you with the way things are going in this country at this time? To indicate this would you use this card, which goes from 0 to 10. The more satisfied you are with the way things are going in this country, the higher the number you should pick; the more dissatisfied you are, the lower the number you should pick.

The way things are going in the nation?

	Percent satisfied
National	52%*

By Sex

Male	55%
Female	48

By Ethnic Background

White	56%
Black	20

By Age

18–29 years	58%
30–49 years	51
50–64 years	48
65 years and over	50

By Income

$40,000 and over	62%
$30,000–$39,999	63
$20,000–$29,999	62
$10,000–$19,999	47
Under $10,000	34

By Politics

Republicans	74%
Democrats	34
Independents	52

Selected National Trend

1984

September	48%
February	50

1983

August	35

*The top five positions on the scale are combined.

The way the nation is governed?

	Percent satisfied
National	54%*

By Sex

Male	58%
Female	50

By Ethnic Background

White	58%
Black	21

By Age

18–29 years	53%
30–49 years	55
50–64 years	55
65 years and over	50

By Income

$40,000 and over	62%
$30,000–$39,999	58
$20,000–$29,999	62
$10,000–$19,999	53
Under $10,000	38

By Politics

Republicans	76%
Democrats	36
Independents	52

*The top five positions on the scale are combined.

The way democracy is working?

	Percent satisfied
National	59%*

By Sex

Male	60%
Female	57

By Ethnic Background

White	61%
Black	37

By Age

18–29 years	60%
30–49 years	56
50–64 years	65
65 years and over	55

By Income

$40,000 and over	80%
$30,000–$39,999	64
$20,000–$29,999	63
$10,000–$19,999	59
Under $10,000	43

By Politics

Republicans	73%
Democrats	49
Independents	57

*The top five positions on the scale are combined.

The ability of the United States to care for the poor?

	Percent satisfied
National	33%*

By Sex

Male	35%
Female	31

By Ethnic Background

White	35%
Black	17

By Age

18–29 years	29%
30–49 years	31
50–64 years	38
65 years and over	30

By Income

$40,000 and over	35%
$30,000–$39,999	32
$20,000–$29,999	38
$10,000–$19,999	33
Under $10,000	25

By Politics

Republicans	54%
Democrats	22
Independents	29

*The top five positions on the scale are combined.

Note: President Ronald Reagan begins his second term in office with the public's mood far more upbeat than it was when he began his first term in January 1981. Fifty-two percent of Americans currently express satisfaction with the way things are going in the nation, three times the 17% who did so four years ago, and higher than at any time since the measurement began in 1979. The low point in the six-year trend was recorded in August 1979, during President Jimmy Carter's administration, when only 12% of survey respondents expressed satisfaction.

Although satisfaction with the national state of affairs has grown among all population groups during President Reagan's tenure, there are marked differences in the current levels among certain groups. For example, only 20% of blacks, compared to 56% of whites, say they are satisfied with the way things are going in the country today. Among people whose family income is less than $10,000 per year, only 34% express satisfaction with the direction the nation is taking, compared to 59% of those whose income is $10,000 or more.

A slightly lower proportion of women (48%) than men (55%) express satisfaction. As might be expected, the findings divide sharply along political lines, with a far higher proportion of Republicans (74%) than Democrats (34%) saying they are satisfied with the way things are going.

The latest survey also indicates that 59% of the public is satisfied with the way democracy is working in the United States, and 54% express satisfaction with the way the nation is governed. Far fewer (33%) say they are satisfied with the ability of the United States to care for the poor. These findings help explain why some groups, including blacks and persons from low-income households, are not optimistic about the overall course the nation is taking. Much smaller proportions of blacks than whites, for example, express satisfaction with the way democracy is working, the way the nation is governed, and the ability of the United States to care for the poor. Pronounced differences are also found on the basis of income.

JANUARY 31
PRESIDENT REAGAN

Interviewing Date: 1/11–14/85
Survey #248-G

Now let me ask you about some specific problems. As I read off each problem, would you tell me whether you approve or disapprove of the way President Ronald Reagan is handling that problem:

Overall job performance?

Approve 62%
Disapprove 29
No opinion 9

Selected National Trend

	Percent approving
1984	
November–December	62%
June–July	53
February	55

Foreign policy?

Approve 52%
Disapprove 33
No opinion 15

Selected National Trend

	Percent approving
1984	
November–December	50%
June–July	39
February	40

Relations with the Soviet Union?

Approve 54%
Disapprove 31
No opinion 15

Selected National Trend

	Percent approving
1984	
November–December	52%
February	43

Disarmament negotiations?

Approve 52%
Disapprove 32
No opinion 16

Economic conditions?

Approve 51%
Disapprove 41
No opinion 8

Selected National Trend

	Percent approving
1984	
November–December	57%
June–July	48
February	49

Note: President Ronald Reagan begins his second term with a strong vote of confidence from the American people. In its first survey in 1985, the Gallup Poll finds 62% of the public approving of Reagan's overall performance in office, while less than half that proportion (29%) disapprove. The president's current rating matches that accorded him in a late November/early December poll after his landslide reelection victory. Not since May 1981 have a significantly larger number of Americans approved of Reagan's general handling of his presidential duties.

Compared to his predecessors at similar points in their presidential careers—in January of their second or elective terms—Reagan's current approval rating surpasses that received by Richard Nixon in January 1973, when 51% approved; Nixon, like Reagan, had won reelection the previous November by a landslide margin. The president's current approval rating is topped by those given Lyndon Johnson, Dwight Eisenhower, and Harry Truman in January 1965, 1957, and 1949, respectively. Johnson won the approval of 71% of the public, Eisenhower of 73%, and Truman of 69% on those occasions.

Presidential Performance Ratings

(At Start of Second or Elective Term)

	January	Approve	Dis-approve	No opinion
Reagan	1985	62%	29%	9%
Nixon	1973	51	37	12
Johnson	1965	71	15	14
Eisenhower	1957	73	14	13
Truman	1949	69	17	14

Compared to his 62% overall approval rating, Reagan currently earns somewhat lower ratings for his handling of foreign policy (52% approve), relations with the Soviet Union (54%), and the nuclear disarmament negotiations with the USSR (52%). The president's current 52% approval rating for his nuclear disarmament efforts, however, represents the first time he has topped the 50% mark and is marginally better than the 47% approval score he received late last year. The current survey was conducted soon after the January 7–8 meeting between U.S. Secretary of State George Shultz and Soviet Foreign Minister Andrei Gromyko, which set the stage for resumption of the disarmament negotiations. Reagan's stronger rating for handling this vital aspect of foreign policy reflects the public's favorable reaction to this event.

In the latest survey, President Reagan receives a somewhat lower rating for his handling of the economy (51% approve) than he did last November/December, when 57% approved. His current rating on economic conditions is similar to those he received throughout 1984, with the single exception of the postelection rating.

FEBRUARY 3
DEATH PENALTY

Interviewing Date: 1/11–14/85
Survey #248-G

Are you in favor of the death penalty for persons convicted of murder?

Yes 72%
No 20
No opinion 8

By Sex

Male

Yes 78%
No 16
No opinion 6

Female

Yes 67%
No 24
No opinion 9

By Ethnic Background
White

Yes 75%
No 18
No opinion 7

Nonwhite

Yes 56%
No 34
No opinion 10

Black

Yes 57%
No 35
No opinion 8

By Education
College Graduate

Yes 74%
No 22
No opinion 4

College Incomplete

Yes 76%
No 16
No opinion 8

High-School Graduate

Yes 74%
No 19
No opinion 7

Less Than High-School Graduate

Yes 65%
No 23
No opinion 12

By Region
East

Yes 66%
No 25
No opinion 9

Midwest

Yes 73%
No 19
No opinion 8

South

Yes 74%
No 19
No opinion 7

West

Yes 77%
No 16
No opinion 7

By Age
18–29 Years

Yes 71%
No 24
No opinion 5

30–49 Years

Yes 73%
No 20
No opinion 7

50 Years and Over

Yes 73%
No 17
No opinion 10

By Politics
Republicans

Yes 82%
No 13
No opinion 5

Democrats

Yes 65%
No 25
No opinion 10

Independents

Yes 72%
No 21
No opinion 7

By Occupation

Professional and Business

Yes 74%
No 21
No opinion 5

Clerical and Sales

Yes 78%
No 15
No opinion 7

Manual Workers

Yes 72%
No 20
No opinion 8

Nonlabor Force

Yes 67%
No 21
No opinion 12

Selected National Trend

	Yes	No	No opinion
1981	66%	25%	9%
1978	62	27	11
1976	65	28	7
1972	57	32	11
1971	49	40	11
1969	51	40	9
1966	42	47	11
1965	45	43	12
1960	51	36	13
1953	68	25	7

1937	65	35	*
1936	61	39	*

*Not included in these surveys

Asked of the 72% who favor the death penalty: Why do you favor the death penalty for persons convicted of murder?

Revenge: an "eye for an eye" 30%
Acts as deterrent 22
Murderers deserve punishment 18
Costly to keep them in prison 11
Keeps them from killing again 9
Removes potential risk to community ... 7
All other 13
No opinion 2
                                    ———
                                   112%*

Asked of the 20% who oppose the death penalty: Why do you oppose the death penalty for persons convicted of murder?

Wrong to take a life 40%
Wrongful convictions 15
Punishment should be left to God 15
Doesn't deter crime 5
Possibility of rehabilitation 5
Unfairly applied 3
All other 7
No opinion 16
                                    ———
                                   106%*

*Multiple responses were given.

Asked of the 72% who favor the death penalty: Suppose new evidence showed that the death penalty does not act as a deterrent to murder—that it does not lower the murder rate. Would you favor or oppose the death penalty?

Would still favor death penalty 51%
Would now oppose it 15
No opinion 6

Asked of the 20% who oppose the death penalty: Suppose new evidence showed that the death penalty acts as a deterrent to murder—

that it lowers the murder rate. Would you favor or oppose the death penalty?

Would still oppose death penalty 13%
Would now favor it 4
No opinion 3

As I read off each of these statements would you tell me whether you agree or disagree with it:

A poor person is more likely than a person of average or above average income to receive the death penalty for the same crime?

Agree 64%
Disagree 31
No opinion 5

By Ethnic Background
White

Agree 63%
Disagree 32
No opinion 5

Nonwhite

Agree 67%
Disagree 25
No opinion 8

Black

Agree 69%
Disagree 23
No opinion 8

By Income
$40,000 and Over

Agree 68%
Disagree 27
No opinion 5

$30,000–$39,999

Agree 66%
Disagree 31
No opinion 3

$20,000–$29,999

Agree 61%
Disagree 35
No opinion 4

$10,000–$19,999

Agree 65%
Disagree 29
No opinion 6

Under $10,000

Agree 58%
Disagree 32
No opinion 10

A black person is more likely than a white person to receive the death penalty for the same crime?

Agree 39%
Disagree 53
No opinion 8

By Ethnic Background
White

Agree 37%
Disagree 56
No opinion 7

Nonwhite

Agree 53%
Disagree 38
No opinion 9

Black

Agree 56%
Disagree 37
No opinion 7

What do you think should be the penalty for murder—the death penalty or life imprisonment, with absolutely no possibility of parole?

Death penalty . . , .56%
Life imprisonment 34
Neither (volunteered) 4
No opinion 6

By Ethnic Background
White

Death penalty 58%
Life imprisonment 31
Neither (volunteered) 4
No opinion 7

Nonwhite

Death penalty 43%
Life imprisonment 48
Neither (volunteered) 4
No opinion 7

Black

Death penalty 44%
Life imprisonment 46
Neither (volunteered) 4
No opinion 6

Do you feel that the death penalty acts as a deterrent to the commitment of murder, that it lowers the murder rate, or not?

Yes 62%
No 31
No opinion 7

Those Who Favor Death Penalty

Yes 78%
No 18
No opinion 4

Those Who Oppose Death Penalty

Yes 19%
No 74
No opinion 7

Apart from your own opinion about the death penalty, what form of punishment do you consider to be the most humane—the electric chair, the gas chamber, lethal injection, firing squad, or hanging?

Lethal injection 56%
Electric chair 16
Gas chamber 8
Firing squad 3
Hanging 1
None (volunteered) 7
No opinion 9

Note: Public support for the death penalty is at the highest point recorded in nearly half a century of scientific polling, with seven in ten Americans (72%) favoring capital punishment for persons convicted of murder. At the same time, however, the survey shows that support for the death penalty would decline dramatically (from 72% to 56%) if life imprisonment, without any possibility of parole, were a certainty for murderers. A similar decline (from 72% to 51%) among supporters would occur, the survey indicates, if new evidence were to show conclusively that the death penalty does not act as a deterrent to murder.

Those in the current survey who favor capital punishment for murder most often give these reasons: revenge, or an "eye for an eye"; these persons deserve punishment; it is costly to keep them in prison; the death penalty acts as a deterrent; it keeps them from killing again; it removes the potential risk to society if they are released. Those who oppose the death penalty most often cite these reasons: it is wrong to take a life; the person may be wrongly convicted; punishment should be left to God; the death penalty does not deter crime; there is always the possibility of rehabilitation; and the penalty is unfairly applied.

The current survey also reveals that many Americans hold the belief that the death penalty is unfairly applied. Two-thirds (64%) think poor persons are more likely than average or above average income people to receive the death penalty for the same crime, and four in ten (39%) believe blacks are more likely than whites to be sentenced to death for the same crime. Lethal injection, viewed by the public as the most humane method of execution, is named by 56%; this form of execution is followed by 16% who say the electric chair; 8%, the gas chamber; 3%, the firing squad; and 1%, hanging.

From the end of a de facto ten-year moratorium on capital punishment in 1977 through 1983, only eleven Americans were put to death. Since 1983, the rate of execution has greatly increased; currently there are more than 1,400 inmates on death row. Thirty-nine states now have death penalty statutes on the books, but the debate continues among penal experts over whether the death penalty discourages potential killers and whether it can be imposed fairly.

FEBRUARY 7
SATISFACTION INDEX

Interviewing Date: 12/7–10/84
Survey #247-G

Now, here are some questions concerning how satisfied or dissatisfied you are with various things in your life. To indicate this, would you use this card. [Respondents were handed a card with "extremely satisfied" at 10 down to "extremely dissatisfied" at 0.] If you are extremely satisfied with something, you would call off the highest number, 10. If you are extremely dissatisfied, you would mention the lowest number, 0. If you are neither extremely satisfied nor extremely dissatisfied, you would mention some number in between 0 and 10— the higher the number (6–10), the more satisfied; the lower the number (0–5), the more dissatisfied. Considering everything, how satisfied or dissatisfied are you with:

Your present housing?

Satisfied 82%
Dissatisfied 17
No opinion 1

By Ethnic Background
White

Satisfied 85%
Dissatisfied 14
No opinion 1

Nonwhite

Satisfied 65%
Dissatisfied 34
No opinion 1

Black

Satisfied 68%
Dissatisfied 32
No opinion .... *

*Less than 1%

Your standard of living?

Satisfied 76%
Dissatisfied 23
No opinion 1

By Ethnic Background
White

Satisfied 78%
Dissatisfied 21
No opinion 1

Nonwhite

Satisfied 62%
Dissatisfied 36
No opinion 2

Black

Satisfied 60%
Dissatisfied 38
No opinion 2

Your household income?

Satisfied 58%
Dissatisfied 39
No opinion 3

By Ethnic Background
White

Satisfied 60%
Dissatisfied 37
No opinion 3

Nonwhite

Satisfied 37%
Dissatisfied 60
No opinion 3

Black

Satisfied 33%
Dissatisfied 63
No opinion 4

Your family life?

Satisfied 90%
Dissatisfied 8
No opinion 2

By Ethnic Background
White

Satisfied 90%
Dissatisfied 9
No opinion 1

Nonwhite

Satisfied 91%
Dissatisfied 5
No opinion 4

Black

Satisfied 90%
Dissatisfied 5
No opinion 5

Your health today?

Satisfied 86%
Dissatisfied 13
No opinion 1

By Ethnic Background
White

Satisfied 86%
Dissatisfied 13
No opinion 1

Nonwhite

Satisfied 90%
Dissatisfied 9
No opinion 1

Black

Satisfied 87%
Dissatisfied 12
No opinion 1

Your job/the work you do?

Satisfied 70%
Dissatisfied 20
No opinion 10

By Ethnic Background
White

Satisfied 72%
Dissatisfied 18
No opinion 10

Nonwhite

Satisfied 57%
Dissatisfied 34
No opinion 9

Black

Satisfied 51%
Dissatisfied 39
No opinion 10

Your free time—the time when you are not working at your job?

Satisfied 80%
Dissatisfied 17
No opinion 3

By Ethnic Background
White

Satisfied 81%
Dissatisfied 17
No opinion 2

Nonwhite

Satisfied 75%
Dissatisfied 20
No opinion 5

Black

Satisfied 75%
Dissatisfied 19
No opinion 6

The way things are going in your personal life?

Satisfied 79%
Dissatisfied 17
No opinion 4

By Ethnic Background

White

Satisfied 81%
Dissatisfied 16
No opinion 3

Nonwhite

Satisfied 67%
Dissatisfied 26
No opinion 7

Black

Satisfied 61%
Dissatisfied 30
No opinion 9

Note: Although most Americans, regardless of race, exhibit a high degree of satisfaction with their lives, the findings of a new Gallup Poll indicate there still are two Americas—one black, one white—in the United States today. Despite marked gains in the last two decades, substantially fewer blacks than whites currently express satisfaction with their standard of living, income, housing, and jobs.

Less racial polarization is found in some categories than in others. For example, the survey found similar assessments of health, with 86% of whites and 87% of blacks expressing satisfaction.

Also, 81% of whites and 75% of blacks say they are satisfied with their leisure time. Similar proportions of whites (90%) and blacks (90%) also express satisfaction with their family life.

Sharp differences, however, continue to separate the races on the economically related dimensions of their lives: 60% of whites but only 33% of blacks say they are satisfied with family income; 72% of whites and 51% of blacks are content with their jobs; 85% of whites and 68% of blacks are satisfied with housing; and 78% of whites, but only 60% of blacks, are satisfied with their standard of living.

The relatively low level of satisfaction among blacks on these income-related items may explain why satisfaction with the way things are going in their personal lives continues to be lower among blacks than whites. In the survey, 81% of whites but only 61% of blacks say they are happy with their personal lives in general.

Satisfaction Levels
(Percent Satisfied)

	1984		1963	
	White	Black	White	Black
Family income	60%	33%	68%	38%
Housing	85	68	76	43
Job	72	51	90	54

Despite the continuing wide gap in satisfaction levels, blacks have made considerable progress since the early 1960s. These moves may be seen in the racial comparisons for 1984 and 1963 of items covered in both surveys, according to the table above.

FEBRUARY 10
WEALTH AND POVERTY

Interviewing Date: 12/7–10/84
Survey #247-G

Do you feel that the distribution of money and wealth in this country today is fair, or do you feel that the money and wealth in this country should be more evenly distributed among a larger percentage of the people?

Fair now 31%
More evenly distributed 60
No opinion 9

By Income
$40,000 and Over
Fair now 50%
More evenly distributed 45
No opinion 5

$30,000–$39,999
Fair now 36%
More evenly distributed 54
No opinion 10

$20,000–$29,999
Fair now 32%
More evenly distributed 63
No opinion 5

$10,000–$19,999
Fair now 29%
More evenly distributed 62
No opinion 9

Under $10,000
Fair now 16%
More evenly distributed 72
No opinion 12

Poor*
Fair now 15%
More evenly distributed 74
No opinion 11

Nonpoor*
Fair now 34%
More evenly distributed 58
No opinion 8

*Throughout this survey, the poor are considered to be those living in households with total annual incomes below the official 1984 U.S. poverty line, as well as households on the margin of poverty. Following the definition used by the U.S. Census Bureau, the survey counted households as "marginally poor" if their annual income was less than 125% of the current poverty line.

Would you say that the percentage of Americans living below the poverty line is increasing from year to year, or decreasing from year to year?

Increasing 70%
Decreasing 18
No opinion 12

By Income
$40,000 and Over
Increasing 74%
Decreasing 17
No opinion 9

$30,000–$39,999
Increasing 67%
Decreasing 20
No opinion 13

$20,000–$29,999
Increasing 72%
Decreasing 19
No opinion 9

$10,000–$19,999
Increasing 71%
Decreasing 17
No opinion 12

Under $10,000
Increasing 69%
Decreasing 16
No opinion 15

Poor
Increasing 72%
Decreasing 17
No opinion 11

Nonpoor

Increasing 70%
Decreasing 18
No opinion 12

Just your best estimate, what percentage of Americans would you say are living below the poverty line today?

0%–14% 16%
15%–20% 19
21%–30% 17
31%–49% 14
50% or more 15
No opinion 19
    Average (mean)   30

Poor

0%–14% 8%
15%–20% 9
21%–30% 17
31%–49% 11
50% or more 34
No opinion 21
    Average (mean)   41

Nonpoor

0%–14% 17%
15%–20% 21
21%–30% 17
31%–49% 15
50% or more 12
No opinion 18
    Average (mean)   28

In your opinion, which is more often to blame if a person is poor—lack of effort on his own part, or circumstances beyond his control?

Lack of effort 33%
Circumstances 34
Both (volunteered) 31
No opinion 2

By Income
$40,000 and Over

Lack of effort 38%
Circumstances 26
Both (volunteered) 34
No opinion 2

$30,000–$39,999

Lack of effort 42%
Circumstances 27
Both (volunteered) 29
No opinion 2

$20,000–$29,999

Lack of effort 33%
Circumstances 36
Both (volunteered) 30
No opinion 1

$10,000–$19,999

Lack of effort 27%
Circumstances 38
Both (volunteered) 32
No opinion 3

Under $10,000

Lack of effort 29%
Circumstances 41
Both (volunteered) 26
No opinion 4

Poor

Lack of effort 46%
Circumstances 27
Both (volunteered) 22
No opinion 5

Nonpoor

Lack of effort 32%
Circumstances 34
Both (volunteered) 32
No opinion 2

Do you, yourself, happen to be involved with a charity or social service activities, such as helping the poor, the sick, or the elderly?

Involved 31%
Not involved 68
Don't know 1

By Income
$40,000 and Over

Involved 46%
Not involved 53
Don't know 1

$30,000–$39,999

Involved 37%
Not involved 62
Don't know 1

$20,000–$29,999

Involved 34%
Not involved 65
Don't know 1

$10,000–$19,999

Involved 24%
Not involved 75
Don't know 1

Under $10,000

Involved 24%
Not involved 73
Don't know 3

Poor

Involved 21%
Not involved 78
Don't know 1

Nonpoor

Involved 33%
Not involved 66
Don't know 1

Selected National Trend

	Those involved
1981	29%
1977	27

Note: The American people perceive poverty in the United States to be more extensive than the estimates of the federal government indicate; they think the problem is getting worse, and favor a more even distribution of wealth among the population. These are the highlights of a major Gallup survey covering three key areas: public perceptions of poverty; the outlook of persons now living near the poverty line; and the public's views about steps that might be taken to alleviate the problem.

Although the federal government estimates that 15.2% of Americans are officially poor, survey respondents believe about twice this percentage (30%) lives below the poverty line. The survey also shows that a large majority (70%) believes the number of Americans living below the poverty line is increasing. Some experts, however, think poverty is declining, particularly if in-kind services such as food stamps, rent supplements, and Medicaid are taken into account.

In an effort to understand what the public sees as the basic causes of poverty, respondents were asked whether they thought lack of effort or circumstances were more to blame for a person's being poor. Public opinion is evenly divided between those who blame lack of effort (33%) and those blaming circumstances or the social environment (34%). Another 31% believe poverty is due to a combination of these factors. Interestingly, the current figures almost exactly parallel those recorded two decades ago. As might be expected, persons classified as poor in the current survey are more likely than the nonpoor to believe circumstances are more often to blame than lack of effort.

FEBRUARY 14

VIGILANTISM

Interviewing Date: 1/25–28/85
Survey #249-G

Have you, yourself, or has anyone else in your immediate family, ever been personally assaulted or mugged?

Yes, self 12%
Yes, other family member(s) 14
Net, any family member 24
Not assaulted 76

By Ethnic Background
White

Yes, self 11%
Yes, other family member(s) 13
Net, any family member 23
Not assaulted 77

Black

Yes, self 16%
Yes, other family member(s) 21
Net, any family member 34
Not assaulted 66

Did you happen to see, hear, or read about a recent incident in a New York City subway in which a man shot and wounded four teenagers who demanded money from him?

                                         Yes
National 92%

All persons in the survey were asked: Do you feel that incidents like these—taking the law into one's own hands, often called vigilantism—are sometimes justified because of the circumstances, or are never justified?

Sometimes 72%
Never 17
Always (volunteered) 8
No opinion 3

Self or Family Member Assaulted

Sometimes 76%
Never 15
Always (volunteered) 7
No opinion 2

No Family Member Assaulted

Sometimes 71%
Never 18
Always (volunteered) 8
No opinion 3

Note: As national attention continues to focus on the case of Bernhard Goetz, the "subway vigilante" who shot and wounded four youths who demanded money from him in a New York City subway last December, the Gallup Poll finds a large majority of Americans holding the view that incidents such as these are sometimes justified by the circumstances. A total of 72% of Americans holds this view, while an additional 8% of hardliners volunteer that taking the law into one's hands—sometimes called vigilantism—is always justified. Only 17% in the survey maintain that such action is never justified.

As many as 92% of Americans have heard or read about the Goetz case, one of the highest awareness scores recorded in the fifty-year history of the Gallup Poll. Even among persons whose formal education ended before high-school graduation, as many as 84% have heard or read about the incident.

Little difference is found between the views of men and women, blacks and whites, and younger and older persons. Interestingly, not much difference is found between the opinions of persons who have been assaulted (or those from homes where other family members have been victims) and those who have not. An alarming one-fourth of Americans nationwide (24%) say that they or other members of their families have been personally assaulted or mugged at some point in their lives, with a higher proportion of blacks (34%) than whites (23%) having been victims.

As for Goetz, a New York grand jury recently indicted him for illegal possession of handguns; it failed to charge him with attempted murder. If convicted on the weapons charge, Goetz could be sentenced to serve up to nine years in jail.

FEBRUARY 17
PRESIDENT REAGAN

Interviewing Date: 1/25–28/85
Survey #249-G

Do you approve or disapprove of the way Ronald Reagan is handling his job as president?

Approve 64%
Disapprove 28
No opinion 8

Selected National Trend

	Approve	Dis-approve	No opinion
1985			
January 11–14	62%	29%	9%
1984			
December 7–10	59	32	9
November 30–			
December 3	62	30	8
November 9–12	61	31	8

How do you think Ronald Reagan will go down in history—as an outstanding president, above average, below average, or poor?

Outstanding 15%
Above average 40
Average (volunteered) 27
Below average 9
Poor 5
No opinion 4

By Sex
Male

Outstanding 16%
Above average 41
Average (volunteered) 24
Below average 9
Poor 6
No opinion 4

Female

Outstanding 14%
Above average 40
Average (volunteered) 29
Below average 9
Poor 4
No opinion 4

By Ethnic Background
White

Outstanding 16%
Above average 43
Average (volunteered) 27
Below average 8
Poor 3
No opinion 3

Nonwhite

Outstanding 9%
Above average 21
Average (volunteered) 29
Below average 16
Poor 16
No opinion 9

Black

Outstanding 7%
Above average 22
Average (volunteered) 29
Below average 17
Poor 17
No opinion 8

By Education
College Graduate

Outstanding 14%
Above average 48
Average (volunteered) 23
Below average 10
Poor 2
No opinion 3

College Incomplete

Outstanding 17%
Above average 43

Average (volunteered) 26
Below average 7
Poor 4
No opinion 3

High-School Graduate

Outstanding 16%
Above average 44
Average (volunteered) 28
Below average 5
Poor 4
No opinion 3

Less Than High-School Graduate

Outstanding 13%
Above average 25
Average (volunteered) 29
Below average 13
Poor 11
No opinion 9

By Region
East

Outstanding 14%
Above average 36
Average (volunteered) 32
Below average 9
Poor 5
No opinion 4

Midwest

Outstanding 15%
Above average 46
Average (volunteered) 23
Below average 7
Poor 4
No opinion 5

South

Outstanding 18%
Above average 38
Average (volunteered) 24
Below average 8
Poor 7
No opinion 5

West

Outstanding 12%
Above average 40
Average (volunteered) 30
Below average 10
Poor 5
No opinion 3

By Age
18–29 Years

Outstanding 9%
Above average 47
Average (volunteered) 28
Below average 11
Poor 3
No opinion 2

30–49 Years

Outstanding 15%
Above average 40
Average (volunteered) 26
Below average 9
Poor 5
No opinion 5

50 Years and Over

Outstanding 19%
Above average 36
Average (volunteered) 27
Below average 7
Poor 6
No opinion 5

By Income
$40,000 and Over

Outstanding 15%
Above average 56
Average (volunteered) 22
Below average 5
Poor 1
No opinion 1

$30,000–$39,999

Outstanding 14%
Above average 50

Average (volunteered) 24
Below average 7
Poor 3
No opinion 2

$20,000–$29,999

Outstanding 18%
Above average 37
Average (volunteered) 30
Below average 8
Poor 4
No opinion 3

$10,000–$19,999

Outstanding 13%
Above average 36
Average (volunteered) 28
Below average 9
Poor 8
No opinion 6

Under $10,000

Outstanding 15%
Above average 28
Average (volunteered) 27
Below average 14
Poor 8
No opinion 8

By Politics

Republicans

Outstanding 25%
Above average 52
Average (volunteered) 18
Below average 2
Poor 2
No opinion 1

Democrats

Outstanding 8%
Above average 28
Average (volunteered) 34
Below average 15
Poor 10
No opinion 5

Independents

Outstanding 11%
Above average 43
Average (volunteered) 30
Below average 7
Poor 4
No opinion 5

Note: A 55% majority of Americans thinks Ronald Reagan will go down in history as an outstanding or above average president, while 27% predict he will be viewed as an average leader. Only 14% think Reagan will go into the history books as a below average or poor chief executive. These findings are recorded at a time when Reagan receives a 64% job approval rating from the American public, the highest rating given him in nearly four years.

Views are highly favorable to the Reagan presidency in all regions of the country and among all major population groups, with the exception of blacks, who have been consistently critical of the Reagan administration. While only 11% of whites say Reagan will go down in history as a below average or poor president, 34% of blacks hold this view. But perhaps as remarkable is the finding that many blacks think history will treat Reagan well, with 29% saying he will be regarded by history as an above average (22%) or outstanding (7%) president. Not surprisingly, sharp differences are found by political affiliation, with 77% of Republicans expecting Reagan to be viewed as above average or outstanding. But even among Democrats, positive expectations (36%) outweigh negative ones (25%) by a considerable margin.

Public's Presidential Assessments

	Reagan Jan. 1985	Carter Dec. 1980	Ford Dec. 1976
Outstanding	15%	3%	5%
Above average	40	11	20
Average (volunteered)	27	37	50
Below average	9	31	15
Poor	5	15	6
No opinion	4	3	4

As shown above, President Reagan fares much better in public expectations than did President Jimmy Carter at a comparable period. Near the end of Carter's presidency in December 1980, when only 34% of the public approved of Carter's performance in office and after he had been defeated by Ronald Reagan in the November election, 14% said Carter would go down in history as an above average or outstanding president, while 37% said average, and 46% said below average or poor. Also, toward the close of Gerald Ford's tenure in December 1976, when his job performance rating stood at 53% approval, 25% of the public judged he would be regarded as an above average or outstanding president, 50% as average, and 21% as below average or poor. That survey was conducted shortly after Carter's election victory over incumbent Ford.

FEBRUARY 21
COST OF LIVING

Interviewing Date: 1/11–14; 25–28/85
Survey #248-G; 249-G

Asked of nonfarm families: What is the smallest amount of money a family of four (husband, wife, and two children) needs each week to get along in this community?

	Median average
National	$302

Selected National Trend

	Median average
1984	$300
1982	296
1980	250
1976	177
1973	149
1970	126
1966	99
1959	79
1952	60
1948	50
1937	30

Asked of nonfarm families: What is the smallest amount of money your family needs each week to get along in this community?

	Median average
National	$298

By Size of Household

Single person	$152
Two-person family	250
Three-person family	301
Four-person family	302
Five-person family or more	375

Note: Americans believe it now takes at least $302 per week for a husband, wife, and two children to make ends meet, the highest figure recorded in Gallup surveys since 1937, but statistically unchanged from the amounts recorded in each of the last three years. The sharply lower inflation rate during this period is reflected in this trend.

The annual Gallup audits of the public's perceptions of living costs have paralleled the Consumer Price Index compiled by the U.S. Bureau of Labor Statistics. According to this index, living costs for 1984 were only 4% higher than during the comparable 1983 period.

In 1937, when the Gallup Poll first surveyed public perceptions of weekly living costs for a family of four, the median response was $30, or one-tenth the current amount. By 1947, the figure had climbed to $43. It did not hit three-digit proportions until 1967, when the median estimate was $101. It took only twelve years, until 1978, for living costs to pass $200. The $300 mark was reached last year, merely six years later.

FEBRUARY 24
"STAR WARS" PROPOSAL

Interviewing Date: 1/25–28/85
Survey #249-G

How closely have you followed the discussions over the administration's so-called "Star Wars" proposal—that is, its proposal to develop a space-based defense against nuclear attack—very closely, fairly closely, or not at all?

Very closely 16%
Fairly closely 51
Not at all 30
No opinion 3

Asked of those who heard or read about the "Star Wars" proposal: Would you like to see the United States go ahead with the development of such a program, or not?

Yes, develop 52%
No, don't develop 38
No opinion 10

By Sex
Male

Yes, develop 60%
No, don't develop 34
No opinion 6

Female

Yes, develop 43%
No, don't develop 43
No opinion 14

By Ethnic Background
White

Yes, develop 54%
No, don't develop 36
No opinion 10

Nonwhite

Yes, develop 40%
No, don't develop 53
No opinion 7

Black

Yes, develop 38%
No, don't develop 55
No opinion 7

By Education
College Graduate

Yes, develop 53%
No, don't develop 43
No opinion 4

College Incomplete

Yes, develop 56%
No, don't develop 33
No opinion 11

High-School Graduate

Yes, develop 52%
No, don't develop 37
No opinion 11

Less Than High-School Graduate

Yes, develop 45%
No, don't develop 41
No opinion 14

By Region
East

Yes, develop 51%
No, don't develop 42
No opinion 7

Midwest

Yes, develop 54%
No, don't develop 37
No opinion 9

South

Yes, develop 54%
No, don't develop 35
No opinion 11

West

Yes, develop 49%
No, don't develop 39
No opinion 12

By Age

18–24 Years

Yes, develop 50%
No, don't develop 42
No opinion 8

25–29 Years

Yes, develop 55%
No, don't develop 39
No opinion 6

30–49 Years

Yes, develop 50%
No, don't develop 40
No opinion 10

50 Years and Over

Yes, develop 55%
No, don't develop 34
No opinion 11

By Politics

Republicans

Yes, develop 68%
No, don't develop 21
No opinion 11

Democrats

Yes, develop 39%
No, don't develop 52
No opinion 9

Independents

Yes, develop 48%
No, don't develop 43
No opinion 9

Also asked of the aware group: In your opinion, would the U.S. development of this system increase or decrease the likelihood of reaching a nuclear arms agreement with the Soviet Union?

Increase likelihood for agreement 47%
Decrease likelihood 32
No difference (volunteered) 13
No opinion 8

Also asked of the aware group: In your opinion, would developing this system make the world safer from nuclear destruction, or less safe?

Make world safer 50%
Make world less safe 32
No difference (volunteered) 11
No opinion 7

The following table shows the relationship between views on development of the plan and opinion on its effect on the arms talks and the chances for peace:

Effect on Reaching Arms Agreement

	Should U.S. develop "Star Wars"?	
	Yes	No
Increase likelihood	68%	19%
Decrease likelihood	17	57
No difference (volunteered)	11	15
No opinion	4	9

Effect on World Peace

Make world safer	80%	13%
Make world less safe	9	69
No difference (volunteered)	8	12
No opinion	3	6

Note: A majority of Americans who have followed the discussions over the administration's "Star Wars" proposal favors the development of such a system, with the belief that it would increase the likelihood of reaching a nuclear arms agreement with the Soviet Union and improve the chances for peace. Two-thirds (67%) say they have followed the discussions over the proposal very or fairly closely. Of this group, 52% would like to see the United States go ahead with development, while 38% are opposed.

If the proposal is developed, 47% of respondents believe that the system will increase the likelihood of reaching a nuclear arms agreement with the Soviet Union, and 50% believe its development will make the world safer from nuclear destruction. Conversely, 32% say development would decrease the likelihood, and 32% also think the world will be less safe.

The administration's Strategic Defense Initiative, popularly known as "Star Wars" since President Ronald Reagan announced the plan in 1983, is a space-based defense against nuclear weapons. The administration argues that the time has come to move away from reliance on weapons of mass destruction to a defensive system in order to deter a nuclear war. Critics contend that it would intensify the arms race, that development costs would be enormous, and they question the feasibility of the entire "Star Wars" concept.

FEBRUARY 28
MOST IMPORTANT PROBLEM

Interviewing Date: 1/25–28/85
Survey #249-G

What do you think is the most important problem facing this country today?

Threat of war; international tensions 27%
Unemployment 20
Excessive government spending;
  budget deficit 18
High cost of living; taxes 12
Economy (general) 6
Poverty; hunger 6
Crime 4
Moral, religious decline in society 2
All others 18
No opinion 3
                   116%*

Selected National Trend

	Aug. 1984	Feb. 1984	Nov. 1983
Threat of war; international tensions	22%	28%	37%
Unemployment	23	28	32
Excessive government spending; budget deficit	16	12	5
High cost of living; taxes	18	10	11
Economy (general)	8	5	3
Poverty; hunger	3	**	**
Crime	4	4	2
Moral, religious decline in society ...	3	7	6
All others	14	14	10
No opinion	3	5	3
	114%*	113%*	109%*

*Multiple responses were given.
**Less than 1%

All those who named a problem were then asked: Which political party do you think can do a better job of handling the problem you have just mentioned—the Republican party or the Democratic party?

Republican party 39%
Democratic party 29
No difference (volunteered) 24
No opinion 8

Selected National Trend

	Aug. 1984	Feb. 1984	Nov. 1983
Republican party	39%	30%	28%
Democratic party	37	32	35
No difference (volunteered)	16	26	24
No opinion	8	12	13

Note: Fear of war, the arms race with the Soviet Union, and international tensions in general continue to be the dominant concerns of the American people. Unemployment is named next most often, with government spending, including the burgeoning federal budget deficit, the third-ranked public concern.

In the latest Gallup Poll, fear of war and international unrest are cited by 27% as the most important problems facing the nation, with unemployment named by 20% and government spending by 18%. The latter has shown a strong upward trend during the last year; in a February 1984 survey, it was cited by only 12% as the nation's top problem.

The current level of public concern over the international situation is about the same as recorded throughout 1984, except in an August survey, when it was slightly lower. Unemployment, while still a serious economic problem, has declined slowly in the public's view as the nation's top concern. The current figure of 20% is the lowest recorded since the 1981–82 recession. In sharp contrast, in October 1982, 62% named unemployment the major problem facing the nation; international tensions were mentioned in that survey by merely 6%, less than one-fourth the current level.

The high cost of living, named by 12% in the current survey, continues to trouble many Americans. Other problems include the economy in general (6%), poverty and hunger (6%), crime (4%), and a perceived moral and religious decline in American society (2%).

For the first time since the spring of 1981, shortly after the start of President Ronald Reagan's first term, a significantly higher proportion of the public now believes the Republican party (39%), rather than the Democratic party (29%), can better handle the problem they consider most important. Throughout 1984, respondents were evenly divided between the two parties. For each of the two preceding years, the Democratic party was the public's consistent choice. The Democrats' strongest recent showing occurred in April 1983, when they were 2 to 1 over the GOP as better able to handle the most important problems facing the country, 41% to 20%. In May 1981, the Republican party led the Democratic party on this key measurement, 36% to 21%.

MARCH 3
NATIONAL DEFENSE/GOVERNMENT SPENDING

Interviewing Date: 1/25–28/85
Survey #249-G

There is much discussion as to the amount of money the government in Washington should spend for national defense and military purposes. How do you feel about this? Do you think we are spending too little, too much, or about the right amount?

Too little 11%
Too much 46
About right 36
No opinion 7

By Politics
Republicans

Too little 15%
Too much 29
About right 49
No opinion 7

Democrats

Too little 7%
Too much 60
About right 27
No opinion 6

Independents

Too little 10%
Too much 49
About right 35
No opinion 6

Selected National Trend

	Too little	Too much	About right	No opinion
1983	11%	37%	36%	7%
1981	51	15	22	12
1976	22	36	32	10

1971	11	50	31	8
1969	8	52	31	9
1960	21	18	45	16

How do you feel about spending for social programs? Do you think we are spending too little, too much, or about the right amount?

Too little 42%
Too much 22
About right 30
No opinion 7

By Politics
Republicans

Too little 27%
Too much 32
About right 36
No opinion 5

Democrats

Too little 55%
Too much 13
About right 26
No opinion 6

Independents

Too little 44%
Too much 23
About right 26
No opinion 7

Note: While the Reagan administration's proposed budget for fiscal 1986 clearly calls for major cuts in social programs and further increases for defense, the public would do just the opposite: cut defense and increase spending for social programs. In the latest Gallup Poll, public opinion is 4 to 1 that too much (46%) rather than too little (11%) is now being spent for national defense and military purposes. When it comes to social programs, however, the public leans 2 to 1 (42% to 22%) that too little is earmarked for this purpose. Support for reduced defense spending is now at the highest point since 1971, when 50% thought it was excessive.

The public's views on defense and social spending are conditioned to a great extent by their political persuasion. Democrats are far more inclined than Republicans to favor increased social spending and to endorse defense cuts. At the same time, however, only 15% of Republicans concur with the administration's view that too little is now spent for defense, with most saying the current defense budget is either about right (49%) or too high (29%).

These findings are recorded at a time when there is broad agreement between the administration and Congress that reducing the federal budget deficit is one of the nation's highest priorities and that the budget cuts should total about $50 billion. The debate now centers on which programs should be cut. Earlier survey findings showed that if the American people had the responsibility for reducing the huge federal budget deficit, their top priority would be to cut defense spending. Asked to vote on each of the four principal means of cutting the deficit, 61% in a December Gallup survey approved of cuts in the defense budget, 41% favored cuts in spending for social programs, 23% would raise income taxes, and 11% would cut "entitlement" programs such as Social Security and Medicaid.

MARCH 6
BIRTH CONTROL PILLS

Interviewing Date: 1/14–2/10/85
Special Telephone Survey

In your opinion, are there substantial risks with using the birth control pill?

Yes 70%
No 25
Don't know 5

By Sex
Male

Yes 62%
No 31
Don't know 7

Female

Yes	76%
No	21
Don't know	3

For women under age 35, how would you compare the health risks from childbearing with the health risks from taking birth control pills? Would you say childbirth is:

Much less risky than pill	24%
Somewhat less risky	20
About as risky as pill	19
Somewhat more risky than pill	12
Much more risky	6
Don't know	19

By Sex

Male

Much less risky than pill	23%
Somewhat less risky	17
About as risky as pill	19
Somewhat more risky than pill	13
Much more risky	8
Don't know	20

Female

Much less risky than pill	24%
Somewhat less risky	22
About as risky as pill	18
Somewhat more risky than pill	10
Much more risky	6
Don't know	20

Note: Contrary to accepted medical evidence, a large majority of Americans associates substantial health risks with the use of birth control pills, with many believing their use to be more dangerous than childbearing itself. A recent Gallup survey commissioned by the American College of Obstetricians and Gynecologists found many American adults misinformed about the safety of a variety of birth control methods. For example, 76% of the women and 62% of the men interviewed say there are substantial risks involved in using the birth control pill. These fears are groundless, according to a 1983 study by the Alan Guttmacher Institute, which found that "use of the pill probably prevents five times as many hospitalizations as it causes, and probably prevents more deaths than it causes."

Asked to compare the health risk of using oral contraceptives with childbearing, nearly half (46%) of the women surveyed believe the risks of the pill are greater than those of childbearing. Only about one woman in six (16%) sees childbearing as a greater threat to health, while the remainder (38%) are either unsure of the relative risks or view them as essentially equivalent. Almost a fourth of all women think that childbearing is much less risky than use of the pill, and a like proportion of unmarried women under age 35 also hold this view.

Again, medical evidence refutes the public's belief that use of the pill entails greater risks than does childbearing. According to sponsors of the survey, "more women are saved from death by birth control pills than die of their complications. For each 100,000 women who use the pill, there will be about 5 deaths, compared to about 10 maternal deaths per 100,000 births."

MARCH 7
COST OF LIVING

Interviewing Date: 1/11–14; 25–28/85
Survey #248-G; 249-G

Asked of nonfarm families: On the average, about how much does your family spend on food, including milk, each week?

	Median average
National	$75

By Region

East	$81
Midwest	$66
South	$75
West	$76

By Income

$20,000 and over	$83
Under $20,000	$61

By Size of Household

Single person	$41
Two-person family	$61
Three-person family	$76
Four-person family	$98
Five-person family or more	$101

Selected National Trend

	Median average
1984	$70
1981	$62
1978	$50
1975	$47
1971	$35
1959	$29
1949	$25
1937	$11

Note: The average American family now spends about $75 per week on food. This figure, although not significantly higher than the amounts recorded in each of the last three years, represents the largest family food budget reported since the Gallup Poll began its audits on this topic nearly a half century ago.

Since 1937, the weekly amount spent on food has increased almost sevenfold, from $11 in the first audit to the current $75. During the period between 1949 and 1969, the figure grew from $25 to $33 per week, an increase of only 32%. However, from 1970 to the present, food expenditures have more than doubled, from $34 to $75 per week.

Persons in the survey whose annual family income is $20,000 or more report spending about one-third again as much on food as do those with lower incomes. However, food bills represent a larger portion of total expenditures of families in the lower income category than is true of upper income households.

MARCH 10
NATIONAL DEFENSE

Interviewing Date: 2/15–18/85
Survey #250-G

At the present time, which nation do you feel is stronger in terms of nuclear weapons, the United States or the Soviet Union—or do you think they are about equal in nuclear strength?

United States	24%
Soviet Union	23
About equal	44
No opinion	9

By Education
College Graduate

United States	24%
Soviet Union	20
About equal	50
No opinion	6

College Incomplete

United States	21%
Soviet Union	21
About equal	50
No opinion	8

High-School Graduate

United States	24%
Soviet Union	22
About equal	44
No opinion	10

Less Than High-School Graduate

United States	25%
Soviet Union	26
About equal	37
No opinion	12

Selected National Trend

	United States	Soviet Union	About equal	No opinion
March 1983	15%	42%	35%	8%
April–May 1982	17	40	32	11

In your opinion, which of the following increases the chances of nuclear war more— a continuation of the nuclear arms buildup here and in the Soviet Union, or the United States falling behind the Soviet Union in nuclear weaponry?

Continued arms buildup 41%
United States falling behind 43
No opinion 16

By Education
College Graduate

Continued arms buildup 52%
United States falling behind 38
No opinion 10

College Incomplete

Continued arms buildup 44%
United States falling behind 45
No opinion 11

High-School Graduate

Continued arms buildup 39%
United States falling behind 46
No opinion 15

Less Than High-School Graduate

Continued arms buildup 34%
United States falling behind 43
No opinion 23

Selected National Trend

	Continued arms buildup	United States falling behind	No opinion
March 1983	38%	47%	15%
August 1982*	43	46	11

*This survey was conducted by the Gallup Organization for the *Wall Street Journal*.

Note: With U.S. and Soviet negotiators resuming arms talks in Geneva on March 12, a new Gallup survey finds a strong plurality of Americans believing that the two nations are about equal in nuclear weaponry, the largest proportion to do so in the last three years. In the mid-February poll, 44% express the view that the superpowers are at parity in nuclear strength, with opinion evenly divided between those who say the United States (24%) or the Soviet Union (23%) holds a nuclear advantage. As recently as March 1983, Americans were far more inclined to believe the Soviets (42%), rather than the United States (15%), enjoyed a nuclear edge, with substantially fewer (35%) saying there was nuclear parity between the two nations.

Reflecting Americans' growing perception that the United States has succeeded in reducing or eliminating any nuclear advantage the Soviet Union may have had, the latest survey also finds a shift toward the view that continuation of the arms race increases the chance of nuclear war more than does the Reagan administration falling behind the Soviets in nuclear strength. Currently the public splits evenly on this issue, with 43% thinking U.S. nuclear inferiority would constitute a greater threat to peace, and 41% saying a continued nuclear arms buildup would be a greater hazard. A year ago, the former was considered a bigger risk than the latter by a small but significant 47% to 38% margin. The latest findings also may reflect the results of another Gallup survey, reported earlier, that public support for reduced U.S. defense spending is now at the highest point since 1971, with 46% believing that too much, rather than too little (11%), is now being spent for national defense and military purposes.

MARCH 14
"RIGHT TO DIE" RULING

Interviewing Date: 1/25–28/85
Survey #249-G

The New Jersey Supreme Court recently ruled that all life-sustaining medical treatment may be withheld or withdrawn from terminally ill patients, provided that is what the patients want or would want if they were able to express their wishes. Would you like to see such a ruling in the state in which you live, or not?

Yes 81%
No 13
No opinion 6

By Sex
Male
Yes 84%
No 11
No opinion 5

Female
Yes 78%
No 15
No opinion 7

By Ethnic Background
White
Yes 82%
No 12
No opinion 6

Nonwhite
Yes 70%
No 19
No opinion 11

Black
Yes 68%
No 22
No opinion 10

By Education
College Graduate
Yes 92%
No 6
No opinion 2

College Incomplete
Yes 86%
No 11
No opinion 3

High-School Graduate
Yes 80%
No 14
No opinion 6

Less Than High-School Graduate
Yes 68%
No 19
No opinion 13

By Region
East
Yes 77%
No 14
No opinion 9

Midwest
Yes 80%
No 13
No opinion 7

South
Yes 76%
No 17
No opinion 7

West
Yes 90%
No 7
No opinion 3

By Age
18–29 Years
Yes 80%
No 16
No opinion 4

30–49 Years
Yes 86%
No 9
No opinion 5

50–64 Years

Yes 82%
No 12
No opinion 6

65 Years and Over

Yes 68%
No 20
No opinion 12

By Politics
Republicans

Yes 82%
No 13
No opinion 5

Democrats

Yes 74%
No 17
No opinion 9

Independents

Yes 87%
No 9
No opinion 4

By Religion
Protestants

Yes 80%
No 13
No opinion 7

Catholics

Yes 77%
No 15
No opinion 8

Note: By an overwhelming majority, the American people endorse a recent ruling of the New Jersey Supreme Court that all life-support systems may be withheld from terminally ill patients, if that is what they want or would want if they could express their wishes. A recent national Gallup Poll found 81% in favor of having their own state adopt a "right-to-die" code similar to the New Jersey high court ruling, while 13% are opposed. The survey found heavy support in all major population groups, with only slightly greater opposition among blacks, persons age 65 and older, and those whose formal education ended before graduation from high school. Nevertheless, opposition among these population segments does not exceed 25%.

In January the New Jersey Supreme Court ruled that all forms of life support, including food, may be withheld from incompetent as well as competent, terminally ill patients. If patients' wishes cannot be determined, their family and physicians must decide whether the burdens of life-sustaining treatment outweigh the benefits of life.

This ruling is expected to have broad national impact. It is the first by a state high court to confirm patients' right to refuse medical treatment, even at the risk of death, as well as the first to eliminate the distinction between feeding patients and other forms of life support. The major concern of critics is that the ruling could be applied capriciously; for example, for economic reasons.

MARCH 17
REAGAN ADMINISTRATION POLICIES

Interviewing Date: 2/15–18/85
Survey #250-G

I am going to read off some foreign and domestic problems that the Reagan administration has been faced with since taking office. As I read off each problem, one at a time, would you tell me whether you feel it has gotten much better, somewhat better, somewhat worse, or much worse as a result of the Reagan policies:

Inflation?

Better 64%
Worse 20
Same 13
No opinion 3

By Politics
Republicans

Better 77%
Worse 11
Same 10
No opinion 2

Democrats

Better 50%
Worse 31
Same 16
No opinion 3

Independents

Better 70%
Worse 16
Same 11
No opinion 3

Unemployment?

Better 49%
Worse 30
Same 17
No opinion 4

By Politics
Republicans

Better 69%
Worse 15
Same 13
No opinion 3

Democrats

Better 31%
Worse 46
Same 19
No opinion 4

Independents

Better 51%
Worse 24
Same 20
No opinion 5

Energy situation?

Better 39%
Worse 22
Same 28
No opinion 11

By Politics
Republicans

Better 47%
Worse 13
Same 30
No opinion 10

Democrats

Better 31%
Worse 32
Same 27
No opinion 10

Independents

Better 40%
Worse 21
Same 28
No opinion 11

Environmental situation?

Better 22%
Worse 34
Same 33
No opinion 11

By Politics
Republicans

Better 30%
Worse 23
Same 37
No opinion 10

Democrats

Better 16%
Worse 43
Same 31
No opinion 10

Independents

Better 21%
Worse 35
Same 30
No opinion 14

Ability of the nation to defend itself militarily?

Better 62%
Worse 10
Same 20
No opinion 8

By Politics
Republicans

Better 73%
Worse 8
Same 13
No opinion 6

Democrats

Better 54%
Worse 13
Same 24
No opinion 9

Independents

Better 62%
Worse 9
Same 21
No opinion 8

Increasing respect for the United States abroad?

Better 44%
Worse 30
Same 18
No opinion 8

By Politics
Republicans

Better 61%
Worse 19
Same 14
No opinion 6

Democrats

Better 30%
Worse 40
Same 21
No opinion 9

Independents

Better 44%
Worse 30
Same 20
No opinion 6

Chances for balancing the national budget?

Better 23%
Worse 46
Same 23
No opinion 8

By Politics
Republicans

Better 35%
Worse 36
Same 24
No opinion 5

Democrats

Better 14%
Worse 57
Same 21
No opinion 8

Independents

Better 20%
Worse 45
Same 26
No opinion 9

Chances for reducing the size of the federal government?

Better 29%
Worse 31
Same 26
No opinion 14

Republicans

Better	40%
Worse	23
Same	25
No opinion	12

Democrats

Better	20%
Worse	40
Same	27
No opinion	13

Independents

Better	28%
Worse	28
Same	27
No opinion	17

Chances for reducing the federal taxes of the average citizen?

Better	27%
Worse	43
Same	24
No opinion	6

By Politics

Republicans

Better	39%
Worse	29
Same	26
No opinion	6

Democrats

Better	16%
Worse	58
Same	20
No opinion	6

Independents

Better	28%
Worse	40
Same	25
No opinion	7

Chances for world peace?

Better	35%
Worse	29
Same	30
No opinion	6

By Politics

Republicans

Better	52%
Worse	16
Same	28
No opinion	4

Democrats

Better	20%
Worse	40
Same	32
No opinion	8

Independents

Better	36%
Worse	30
Same	28
No opinion	6

Chances for nuclear disarmament?

Better	22%
Worse	38
Same	31
No opinion	9

By Politics

Republicans

Better	31%
Worse	27
Same	36
No opinion	6

Democrats

Better	14%
Worse	49
Same	26
No opinion	11

Better 22%
Worse 38
Same 30
No opinion 10

Note: With President Ronald Reagan now well into his second term, Americans give his administration positive ratings on its record of achievement in the key problem areas of inflation, defense, unemployment, and building respect for the United States abroad. On inflation, 64% currently see an improvement, while 20% disagree. In 1982, 37% said inflation was better, 48% worse; the inflation rate is now about half that of mid-1982.

About half (49%) say the unemployment situation has improved since Reagan took office in 1981, while far fewer (30%) see the situation as having worsened. In striking contrast, a June 1982 survey found the public thinking 81% to 8% that unemployment had gotten worse, rather than better. Since that first Reagan report card, the unemployment rate has gone from 9.5%, then the highest in forty years, to 7.3% last month.

The administration receives generally mixed reviews from the public on the energy situation, improving the chances for world peace (women's views contribute heavily to the downside on this rating), and reducing the size of government. Negative ratings are recorded on reducing personal income taxes, despite the fact that personal income taxes have been cut by 25% since Reagan took office. (One explanation might be a perceived relationship between the tax cuts and the present budget deficit.) The administration also scores relatively poorly on balancing the national budget, reducing environmental problems, and nuclear disarmament.

Reagan Report Card

	Percent saying better		
	Feb. 1985	June 1982	Point difference
Inflation	64%	37%	+27
Defense	62	54	+ 8
Unemployment	49	8	+41
Respect for United States	44	35	+ 9
Energy situation	39	25	+14
Chances for peace ...	35	24	+11
Reduce government size	29	43	−14
Reduce personal taxes	27	39	−12
Balance budget	23	31	− 8
Environmental situation	22	20	+ 2

The pluses and minuses in the latest report card on Reagan are dramatized by comparing the results of the 1985 and 1982 surveys. As seen above, the Reagan administration has registered gains on seven of the problems, most notably unemployment and inflation, but has lost ground on reducing the size of the government, reducing personal income taxes, and balancing the budget.

MARCH 21
IDEAL FAMILY SIZE

Interviewing Date: 2/15–18/85
Survey #250-G

What do you think is the ideal number of children for a family to have?

One 4%
Two 56
Three 21
Four 8
Five 1
Six or more 2
None 2
No opinion 6

Selected National Trend
(Those Saying Four or More Children)

1985 ....11%
1983 14
1980 16
1978 17
1977 13
1974 19
1973 20

```
1971  ..............................23
1968  ..............................41
1966  ..............................35
1957  ..............................37
1953  ..............................41
1947  ..............................47
1945  ..............................49
1941  ..............................41
1936  ..............................34
```

The following table shows the trend since 1968—the first year for which this detailed information is available—in the proportions of Catholics and Protestants favoring four or more children:

Selected National Trend

		Total U.S.	Protestants	Catholics
1985	......	11%	10%	9%
1983	......	14	13	19
1980	......	16	17	19
1978	......	17	16	21
1977	......	13	13	19
1974	......	19	18	20
1973	......	20	20	23
1971	......	23	22	28
1968	......	41	37	50

Note: The appeal of large families continues to decline, with merely 11% in the latest Gallup Poll saying the ideal number of children is four or more. This is the smallest proportion favoring families of this size since Gallup began recording the public's preferences in 1936. As recently as 1968, 41% thought the ideal American family would include four children or more. In the current survey, a 56% majority believes the model number of children is two, while 21% prefer three, 4% one, and 2% none. Two-child families have been preferred since the early 1970s.

Roman Catholics historically have favored larger families than have Protestants. In the 1968 survey, for example, 50% of Catholics, compared to 37% of Protestants, cited four or more children as the ideal. Now, however, statistically identical proportions of Catholics (9%) and Protestants (10%) share this view.

In Gallup's first sounding of public sentiment on family size in 1936, 34% said four or more

children represented the ideal. By 1945 the figure had risen to 49%, presaging the postwar "baby boom." The proportion favoring large families declined gradually between 1947 and 1968, and subsequently dropped sharply.

Americans' views on the ideal number of children generally have paralleled and, in many instances, anticipated actual population trends. Today's high cost of rearing children, the uncertainty about the world situation, and the presence in the labor force of a majority of the mothers of young children are undoubtedly factors in the long-term trend toward small families.

MARCH 24
IDEAL PLACE TO LIVE

Interviewing Date: 2/15–18/85
Survey #250-G

If you could live anywhere you wished, which one of these places would you prefer?

Large city (1,000,000+ population) 7%
Medium-sized city (100,000 to 999,999) ..15
Small city (50,000 to 99,999) 16
Large town (10,000 to 49,999) 13
Small town (2,500 to 9,999) 23
Rural area, on a farm 17
Rural area, not on a farm 8
Don't know 1

Asked of the 38% who replied that they would like to live in a large, medium, or small city: Where in the city—within the city itself, or in the suburbs outside the city?

	Total	Large city respondents	Medium city respondents	Small city respondents
Within city	34%	62%	33%	22%
In suburbs	64	38	66	74
Don't know	2	*	1	4

*Less than 1%

If you had the chance, would you like to move away from this community (city), or not?

	Yes, would like to move away
National	34%

By Ethnic Background

White	32%
Black	49
Hispanic	47

By Education

College graduate	31%
College incomplete	33
High-school graduate	35
Less than high-school graduate	37

By Region

East	39%
Midwest	35
South	29
West	35

By Age

18–29 years	44%
30–49 years	37
50–64 years	27
65 years and over	17

By Occupation

Professional and business	32%
Other white collar	38
Blue collar	40

By Community Size

One million and over	41%
500,000–999,999	28
50,000–499,999	30
2,500–49,999	36
Under 2,500; rural	27

Note: Given the opportunity, almost half of American adults would move to towns with fewer than 10,000 inhabitants or to rural areas, according to the latest Gallup Poll. Now the vast majority lives in or near cities with much larger populations. Furthermore, two-thirds of those expressing a preference for city life would rather live in the suburbs than within city limits. With the exception of those who opt for a large city, 62% of whom would like to live within the core city, the suburbs are more appealing than the center cities, as shown in the table.

The current poll shows that 7% would prefer to live in a large city, 15% in a medium-sized city, 16% in a small city, 13% in a large town, and 23% in a small town. The nostalgic appeal of life in the country still draws many, with 17% expressing the wish to live on a farm (in fact, only 3% of the populace does so), and an additional 8% would like to live in a rural area, but not on a farm.

Despite the lure of country living, another survey question reveals that a mass migration to rural and small town America is unlikely, with only 34% saying they would like to move away from the communities and cities where they now live. The desire to get out of town is strongly conditioned by demographic factors such as age and race and also is related to community size, geographic region, education, and occupation.

In the survey, 44% of persons 18 to 29 years old say they would like to move away, with that figure dropping sharply and progressively as age rises. Among persons 65 and older, merely 17% say they would like to move. Similarly, almost half of blacks (49%) and Hispanics (47%), compared to 32% of whites, would like to move.

Residents of cities with 1 million population or more (41%) are more desirous of leaving than are those living in smaller cities and towns (30%). Somewhat fewer southerners (29%) want to move away than do those living in other regions of the nation (36%). Also, respondents from families in which the chief wage earner is employed in business or the professions (32%) are slightly less anxious to leave than are those working in other white-collar jobs (38%) or in blue-collar occupations (40%). Similarly, dissatisfaction with their present communities is less apt to be expressed by persons in better educated and higher income groups.

MARCH 28
PERSONAL FINANCES

Interviewing Date: 3/8–11/85
Survey #251-G

We are interested in how people's financial situation may have changed. Would you say that you are financially better off now than you were a year ago, or are you financially worse off now?

Better 48%
Worse 25
Same (volunteered) 26
No opinion 1

By Sex
Male

Better 51%
Worse 23
Same (volunteered) 25
No opinion 1

Female

Better 45%
Worse 26
Same (volunteered) 28
No opinion 1

By Ethnic Background
White

Better 49%
Worse 23
Same (volunteered) 27
No opinion 1

Nonwhite

Better 38%
Worse 37
Same (volunteered) 25
No opinion .... *

Black

Better 34%
Worse 42
Same (volunteered) 24
No opinion .... *

By Education
College Graduate

Better 61%
Worse 16
Same (volunteered) 22
No opinion 1

College Incomplete

Better 52%
Worse 22
Same (volunteered) 25
No opinion 1

High-School Graduate

Better 46%
Worse 25
Same (volunteered) 28
No opinion 1

Less Than High-School Graduate

Better 37%
Worse 32
Same (volunteered) 30
No opinion 1

By Region
East

Better 48%
Worse 22
Same (volunteered) 29
No opinion 1

Midwest

Better 43%
Worse 29
Same (volunteered) 28
No opinion .... *

South

Better	47%
Worse	25
Same (volunteered)	26
No opinion	2

West

Better	55%
Worse	22
Same (volunteered)	23
No opinion	*

By Age

18–29 Years

Better	58%
Worse	27
Same (volunteered)	14
No opinion	1

30–49 Years

Better	52%
Worse	22
Same (volunteered)	25
No opinion	1

50 Years and Over

Better	36%
Worse	25
Same (volunteered)	38
No opinion	1

By Income

$40,000 and Over

Better	66%
Worse	16
Same (volunteered)	18
No opinion	*

$30,000–$39,999

Better	67%
Worse	10
Same (volunteered)	21
No opinion	2

$20,000–$29,999

Better	51%
Worse	24
Same (volunteered)	25
No opinion	*

$10,000–$19,999

Better	43%
Worse	27
Same (volunteered)	29
No opinion	1

Under $10,000

Better	26%
Worse	39
Same (volunteered)	35
No opinion	*

By Politics

Republicans

Better	58%
Worse	16
Same (volunteered)	25
No opinion	1

Democrats

Better	37%
Worse	33
Same (volunteered)	29
No opinion	1

Independents

Better	50%
Worse	24
Same (volunteered)	25
No opinion	1

*Less than 1%

Selected National Trend

	Better	Worse	Same (volunteered)	No opinion
1984				
Nov.–Dec.	43%	24%	32%	1%
July	40	25	30	1

1983				
June	28	29	32	1
1982				
November	28	37	34	1
February	28	47	24	1
1981				
June	33	35	30	1

Now looking ahead, do you expect that at this time near year you will be financially better off than now, or worse off than now?

Better 57%
Worse 12
Same (volunteered) 26
No opinion 5

By Sex
Male

Better 60%
Worse 11
Same (volunteered) 24
No opinion 5

Female

Better 54%
Worse 12
Same (volunteered) 28
No opinion 6

By Ethnic Background
White

Better 57%
Worse 12
Same (volunteered) 26
No opinion 5

Nonwhite

Better 56%
Worse 12
Same (volunteered) 24
No opinion 8

Black

Better 55%
Worse 12
Same (volunteered) 25
No opinion 8

By Education
College Graduate

Better 65%
Worse 8
Same (volunteered) 24
No opinion 3

College Incomplete

Better 65%
Worse 8
Same (volunteered) 23
No opinion 4

High-School Graduate

Better 57%
Worse 11
Same (volunteered) 28
No opinion 4

Less Than High-School Graduate

Better 46%
Worse 18
Same (volunteered) 28
No opinion 8

By Region
East

Better 54%
Worse 11
Same (volunteered) 28
No opinion 7

Midwest

Better 52%
Worse 15
Same (volunteered) 30
No opinion 3

South

Better	59%
Worse	11
Same (volunteered)	26
No opinion	4

West

Better	64%
Worse	11
Same (volunteered)	20
No opinion	5

By Age
18–29 Years

Better	79%
Worse	7
Same (volunteered)	12
No opinion	2

30–49 Years

Better	65%
Worse	9
Same (volunteered)	21
No opinion	5

50 Years and Over

Better	33%
Worse	18
Same (volunteered)	42
No opinion	7

By Income
$40,000 and Over

Better	72%
Worse	7
Same (volunteered)	20
No opinion	1

$30,000–$39,999

Better	74%
Worse	7
Same (volunteered)	17
No opinion	2

$20,000–$29,999

Better	60%
Worse	9
Same (volunteered)	28
No opinion	3

$10,000–$19,999

Better	50%
Worse	14
Same (volunteered)	29
No opinion	7

Under $10,000

Better	41%
Worse	19
Same (volunteered)	31
No opinion	9

By Politics
Republicans

Better	65%
Worse	7
Same (volunteered)	24
No opinion	4

Democrats

Better	49%
Worse	17
Same (volunteered)	28
No opinion	6

Independents

Better	58%
Worse	11
Same (volunteered)	27
No opinion	4

Selected National Trend

	Better	Worse	Same (volunteered)	No opinion
1984				
Nov.–Dec.	50%	17%	28%	5%
July	52	12	28	8
1983				
June	43	19	28	10

1982				
November	41	22	27	10
February	42	31	21	6
1981				
June	44	25	23	8

The following is the trend of the two questions combined:

Selected National Trend

(Overall Financial Outlook)

	Opti-mists	Pessi-mists	Neutral	No opinion
1985				
March 8–11	52%	14%	29%	5%
1984				
Nov.–Dec.	48	18	29	5
July	47	15	30	8
1983				
June	34	24	32	10
1982				
November	32	25	33	10
February	31	33	29	7
1981				
June	36	27	28	9

Note: While the national economy is giving off mixed signals, American consumers' financial outlook is now more optimistic than at any other time during President Ronald Reagan's four-plus years in office. The current level of optimism also tops any since 1976, when these measurements began.

In the latest Gallup Poll, 57% say they expect to be financially better off a year from now, while 26% think their situation will be about the same, and 12% foresee a downturn. Asked to rate their current financial status vis-à-vis a year ago, 48% see an improvement, 26% perceive no change, and 25% claim to be worse off. When both questions—looking ahead and looking back—are combined into an overall index, economic optimists are found to outnumber pessimists by almost a 4-to-1 ratio, 52% to 14%.

More than one-third of the public (37%) now fall into the category of super optimists, a dramatic improvement from the 18% recorded two years ago and 28% last year. Studies have shown that these people, who say they are now better off than in the past and expect to be still better off in the future, are likely to be buyers of big-ticket discretionary items, such as houses, cars, and major appliances, and to be heavy users of credit.

Not surprisingly, the degree to which people are optimistic about their economic future is influenced by demographic factors such as age, education, and family income. For example, 83% of 18 to 24 year olds say they will be better off a year from now, while only 19% of those 65 and over share this optimism. Similarly, greater optimism is found among persons with some college training and those whose annual family income is $20,000 or more.

The survey found a strong political coloration to Americans' economic forecasts, with Republicans more likely than Democrats to have an optimistic outlook. Nevertheless, almost half of Democrats (49%), compared to 65% of Republicans, expect to be better off next year than they are now.

No significant difference is found by race, for blacks in the survey are as likely as whites to say they expect to be better off next year. Also, financial optimism is national in scope, with roughly similar proportions from each region optimistic about the coming year.

MARCH 31
NICARAGUA

Interviewing Date: 3/8–11/85
Survey #251-G

Can you tell me which side the United States is backing in Nicaragua—the Sandinista government or the rebel forces?

Sandinista government 14%
Rebel forces (correct) 38
Don't know 48

Asked of the informed group (the 38% who responded correctly): Do you think the United States should continue to help the rebel forces in Nicaragua, or stay completely out of the situation?

Continue to help	42%
Stay completely out	50
Not sure	8

By Politics
Republicans

Continue to help	60%
Stay completely out	33
Not sure	7

Democrats

Continue to help	29%
Stay completely out	64
Not sure	7

Independents

Continue to help	38%
Stay completely out	52
Not sure	10

Also asked of the informed group: As I read several kinds of aid, please tell me whether you would favor or oppose the United States providing each type of aid for the rebel forces in Nicaragua:

Moral, diplomatic support?

	Favor
National	47%

By Politics

Republicans	63%
Democrats	35
Independents	44

Economic assistance?

National	41%

By Politics

Republicans	58%
Democrats	27
Independents	39

Military supplies?

National	36%

By Politics

Republicans	55%
Democrats	23
Independents	32

U.S. military advisers?

National	31%

By Politics

Republicans	45%
Democrats	19
Independents	30

U.S. troops?

National	8%

By Politics

Republicans	12%
Democrats	3
Independents	9

Also asked of the informed group: How likely do you think it is that the U.S. involvement in Nicaragua could turn into another situation like Vietnam—that is, that the United States could become more and more deeply involved as time goes on? Would you say this is very likely, fairly likely, fairly unlikely, or very unlikely?

Very likely	28%
Fairly likely	31
Fairly unlikely	22
Very unlikely	16
No opinion	3

By Politics

Republicans

Very likely	15%
Fairly likely	29
Fairly unlikely	31
Very unlikely	23
No opinion	2

Democrats

Very likely	35%
Fairly likely	36
Fairly unlikely	16
Very unlikely	9
No opinion	4

Independents

Very likely	31%
Fairly likely	28
Fairly unlikely	21
Very unlikely	16
No opinion	4

Also asked of the informed group: If the rebel forces in Nicaragua fail to overthrow the Sandinista government in Nicaragua, how likely do you think it is that the Sandinista type of government will spread to other Central American nations—very likely, fairly likely, fairly unlikely, or very unlikely?

Very likely	32%
Fairly likely	37
Fairly unlikely	18
Very unlikely	7
No opinion	6

By Politics

Republicans

Very likely	37%
Fairly likely	39
Fairly unlikely	13
Very unlikely	4
No opinion	7

Democrats

Very likely	27%
Fairly likely	35
Fairly unlikely	21
Very unlikely	9
No opinion	8

Independents

Very likely	34%
Fairly likely	34
Fairly unlikely	20
Very unlikely	8
No opinion	4

The following table compares the views on the two previous questions of those who favor and those who oppose continued U.S. aid to the rebel forces, based on the informed group:

Another Vietnam?

		Favor U.S. action	
		Continue	
		to help	Stay out
	Total	rebels	completely
Very, fairly likely	59%	38%	76%
Very, fairly unlikely	38	60	20
No opinion	3	2	4

Sandinista government will spread (domino effect)?

		Favor U.S. action	
		Continue	
		to help	Stay out
	Total	rebels	completely
Very, fairly likely	69%	82%	58%
Very, fairly unlikely	25	16	33
No opinion	6	2	9

Note: Despite President Ronald Reagan's vigorous support for the guerrilla forces seeking to overthrow the Sandinista regime in Nicaragua, one-half of informed Americans believe the United States should cease its activities there. A 76%

majority of these people fears that our further intervention in Nicaragua could turn into another Vietnam, with the United States becoming more and more deeply involved with the passage of time.

On the other hand, informed Americans who say we should continue to help the Nicaraguan rebels (42%) are far less apt to foresee a Vietnam-like situation developing, with a 60% majority saying this is unlikely to occur. Nevertheless, almost four in ten (38%) concede that an American involvement of this kind could develop.

Not surprisingly, there is a strong political dimension to the public's views on Nicaragua, with 60% of informed Republicans but only half that proportion of informed Democrats (29%) saying we should continue to help the *contras*. Informed independents lean 52% to 38% against further U.S. intervention.

The survey also queried the informed group about what types of assistance the U.S. government should provide the Nicaraguan rebels. Moral and diplomatic aid, which we are now providing, was the leading choice, mentioned by 47%. Other forms of aid and the percentages favoring each are: economic assistance (41%), military supplies (36%), sending U.S. military advisers (31%), and sending U.S. troops (8%). Sending troops receives comparatively little support regardless of political affiliation, with only 12% of informed Republicans, 3% of informed Democrats, and 9% of informed independents favoring this action.

A 69% majority of the informed public, including majorities of each political persuasion, believes it likely that the Sandinista type of government, unless checked, may spread to other Central American nations. In a similar survey four years ago, an 82% majority of informed Americans thought that a domino effect would probably occur if the Duarte government of El Salvador, which the United States supports, fell to the Communist insurgents. The 13 percentage-point decline since then, in the proportion fearing the spread of leftist governments in the region if America's protégés are allowed to lose, suggests some loss of public credulity in the domino theory.

APRIL 4
PARTY BETTER FOR PEACE AND PROSPERITY

Interviewing Date: 3/8–11/85
Survey #251-G

Looking ahead for the next few years, which political party do you think would be more likely to keep the United States out of World War III—the Republican party or the Democratic party?

Republican 39%
Democratic 33
No difference; no opinion 28

Selected National Trend

	Republican party	Democratic party	No difference; no opinion
September 1984	38%	38%	24%
August 1984	36	40	24
April 1984	30	42	28
September 1983	26	39	35
April 1981	29	34	37
August 1976	29	32	39
September 1972	32	28	40
October 1968	37	24	39
October 1964	22	45	33
October 1960	40	25	35
October 1956	46	16	38
January 1952	36	15	49
September 1951	28	21	51

Which political party—the Republican party or the Democratic party—do you think will do a better job of keeping the country prosperous?

Republican 48%
Democratic 32
No difference; no opinion 20

Selected National Trend

	Republican party	Democratic party	No difference; no opinion
September 1984	49%	33%	18%
August 1984	48	36	16

April 1984	44	36	20
September 1983	33	40	27
April 1981	40	31	29
August 1976	23	47	30
September 1972	38	35	27
October 1968	34	37	29
October 1964	21	53	26
October 1960	31	46	23
October 1956	39	39	22
January 1952	31	35	34
September 1951	29	37	34

Note: The Republican party not only is widely perceived as more likely than the Democratic party to keep the nation prosperous but also now it leads the Democrats as more likely to keep the nation at peace. This is the first time the GOP has held a clear-cut lead on both these crucial issues since Gallup began these measurements in 1951.

In the latest Gallup Poll, 48% say the Republican party will do a better job of keeping the United States prosperous, while 32% name the Democratic party, and 20% see little difference between the parties or do not offer an opinion. The Republicans have had a significant advantage over the Democrats in only two other years since 1951, during President Ronald Reagan's first term in 1981 and last year. Prior to 1981, the Democratic party enjoyed a near monopoly on the prosperity issue.

Until recently the Republicans' newly acquired advantage as the party of prosperity had been at least partially offset by the Democrats' edge as the party of peace. This began to unravel last September, when the parties were tied on the peace issue, with each chosen by 38% of the public. Currently, 39% see the Republican party as stronger in this regard, 33% cite the Democratic party, and 28% see no difference or have no opinion. With only a few exceptions, the Democrats have led on this issue for the last decade, with the lead changing hands periodically before then. The last time the GOP held an outright advantage as better able to keep the nation out of war was during the closing months of President Richard Nixon's successful reelection campaign in 1972. Perceptions of the Republican party as peacemaker may have been enhanced by the resumption of disarmament negotiations between the United States and the Soviet Union in Geneva on March 12.

APRIL 7
PRESIDENT REAGAN

Interviewing Date: 3/8–11/85
Survey #251-G

Do you approve or disapprove of the way Ronald Reagan is handling his job as president?

Approve 56%
Disapprove 37
No opinion 7

By Sex
Male

Approve 58%
Disapprove 34
No opinion 8

Female

Approve 53%
Disapprove 40
No opinion 7

By Ethnic Background
White

Approve 60%
Disapprove 33
No opinion 7

Nonwhite

Approve 28%
Disapprove 61
No opinion 11

Black

Approve 19%
Disapprove 70
No opinion 11

By Education

College Graduate

Approve 61%
Disapprove 35
No opinion 4

College Incomplete

Approve 65%
Disapprove 29
No opinion 6

High-School Graduate

Approve 58%
Disapprove 35
No opinion 7

Less Than High-School Graduate

Approve 41%
Disapprove 48
No opinion 11

By Region

East

Approve 53%
Disapprove 41
No opinion 6

Midwest

Approve 56%
Disapprove 39
No opinion 5

South

Approve 57%
Disapprove 33
No opinion 10

West

Approve 57%
Disapprove 36
No opinion 7

By Age

18–29 Years

Approve 58%
Disapprove 33
No opinion 9

30–49 Years

Approve 57%
Disapprove 37
No opinion 6

50 Years and Over

Approve 52%
Disapprove 40
No opinion 8

By Politics

Republicans

Approve 88%
Disapprove 8
No opinion 4

Democrats

Approve 28%
Disapprove 66
No opinion 6

Independents

Approve 55%
Disapprove 35
No opinion 10

Selected National Trend

	Approve	Dis-approve	No opinion
1985			
February 15–18	60%	31%	9%
January 25–28	64	28	8
January 11–14	62	29	9
1984			
December	59	32	9
October	58	33	9
August	54	38	8
June	54	36	10

April	54	36	10
February	55	36	9

Now let me ask you about some specific problems. As I read off each problem, would you tell me whether you approve or disapprove of the way President Ronald Reagan is handling that problem:

Economic conditions in this country?

Approve 51%
Disapprove 44
No opinion 5

By Politics
Republicans

Approve 78%
Disapprove 18
No opinion 4

Democrats

Approve 27%
Disapprove 69
No opinion 4

Independents

Approve 51%
Disapprove 43
No opinion 6

Selected National Trend

	Approve
1985	
January 11–14	51%
1984	
June–July	48
February	49
January	48

Foreign policy?

Approve 45%
Disapprove 39
No opinion 16

By Politics
Republicans

Approve 70%
Disapprove 19
No opinion 11

Democrats

Approve 25%
Disapprove 57
No opinion 18

Independents

Approve 45%
Disapprove 40
No opinion 15

Selected National Trend

	Approve
1985	
January 11–14	52%
1984	
June–July	39
February	40
January	38

Situation in Nicaragua?

Approve 26%
Disapprove 43
No opinion 31

By Politics
Republicans

Approve 41%
Disapprove 26
No opinion 33

Democrats

Approve 13%
Disapprove 58
No opinion 29

Independents

Approve 25%
Disapprove 46
No opinion 29

Selected National Trend

	Approve
*1984**	
November–December	34%
May	28
February	29
January	28

*In 1984 the question concerned the situation in Central America.

Relations with the Soviet Union?

Approve	53%
Disapprove	34
No opinion	13

By Politics

Republicans

Approve	78%
Disapprove	12
No opinion	10

Democrats

Approve	31%
Disapprove	55
No opinion	14

Independents

Approve	53%
Disapprove	32
No opinion	15

Selected National Trend

	Approve
1985	
January 11–14	54%
1984	
November–December	52
May	46
February	43

Nuclear disarmament negotiations with the Soviet Union?

Approve	49%
Disapprove	35
No opinion	16

By Politics

Republicans

Approve	70%
Disapprove	18
No opinion	12

Democrats

Approve	32%
Disapprove	51
No opinion	17

Independents

Approve	49%
Disapprove	35
No opinion	16

Selected National Trend

	Approve
January 11–14, 1985	52%
November–December 1984	47

Note: President Ronald Reagan completed the first three months of his second term with six in ten Americans (60%) approving of his performance in office. This strong showing virtually matches the 61% average approval rating the president earned late last year, following his landslide re-election victory.

In the latest Gallup Poll, Reagan's approval rating was slightly below his average for the quarter, with 56% approving and 37% disapproving of his handling of his presidential duties. It is too early to tell whether this single measurement represents a temporary drop in Reagan's standing with the public, or marks the start of a gradual decline in his popularity from the exuberant level of the postelection period.

Other questions in the latest survey suggest that President Reagan's modest drop in overall popularity may be related to a decline in the public's assessment of his conduct of foreign policy. Currently, Reagan's handling of foreign policy is positively rated by 45%, down from 52% approval in mid-January. Also, the president wins the support of only 26% of Americans for his handling of the situation in Nicaragua. In a November-December poll on the broader subject of Central American affairs, Reagan received a higher 34% approval score.

In the current survey, 51% approve of the president's handling of economic conditions, unchanged from January. For his overall handling of relations with the Soviet Union, 53% now give Reagan a favorable grade, statistically identical to the 54% approval rating accorded him in January. Almost half the public (49%) currently approves of his handling of the disarmament negotiations with the Soviet Union, again statistically similar to the 52% approval recorded in January. (The first of the Geneva disarmament talks was held the day after the latest survey was completed.)

If, in fact, Reagan's current approval rating turns out to be only a temporary setback in a record that has remained near the 60% level for the last six months, he will have avoided the fate that befell each of his reelected postwar predecessors and those beginning their first elective terms. Each of the four men who fit this description, Presidents Richard Nixon, Lyndon Johnson, Dwight Eisenhower, and Harry Truman, became progressively less popular as the year wore on, as shown in the table below:

Presidential Approval Ratings

(First Year of Second or Elective Term)

		Quarterly Averages			
		1st	2nd	3rd	4th
Nixon	1973	60%	47%	35%	29%
Johnson	1965	70	67	64	64
Eisenhower	1957	72	65	60	57
Truman	1949	63	57	51	NA

APRIL 11
THE FUTURE

Interviewing Date: 2/15–18/85 (U.S. only)
Survey #250-G

> Asked in the United States: Do you think for people like yourself that the world in ten years' time will be a better place to live than it is now, a worse place, or just about the same as it is today?

Better	30%
Worse	30
Same	35
No opinion	5

By Sex
Male

Better	35%
Worse	27
Same	35
No opinion	3

Female

Better	25%
Worse	33
Same	36
No opinion	6

By Ethnic Background
White

Better	30%
Worse	29
Same	37
No opinion	4

Black

Better	29%
Worse	40
Same	24
No opinion	7

By Education
College Graduate

Better	34%
Worse	23
Same	39
No opinion	4

College Incomplete

Better	32%
Worse	28
Same	37
No opinion	3

High-School Graduate

Better	29%
Worse	32
Same	36
No opinion	3

Less Than High-School Graduate

Better	26%
Worse	36
Same	31
No opinion	7

By Region

East

Better	28%
Worse	31
Same	34
No opinion	7

Midwest

Better	32%
Worse	28
Same	37
No opinion	3

South

Better	29%
Worse	29
Same	37
No opinion	5

West

Better	31%
Worse	34
Same	32
No opinion	3

By Age

18–29 Years

Better	30%
Worse	35
Same	32
No opinion	3

30–49 Years

Better	33%
Worse	29
Same	34
No opinion	4

50 Years and Over

Better	27%
Worse	28
Same	38
No opinion	7

By Income

$20,000 and Over

Better	32%
Worse	27
Same	38
No opinion	3

Under $20,000

Better	26%
Worse	35
Same	33
No opinion	6

Asked in sixteen nations*: Do you think for people like yourself that the world in ten years' time will be a better place to live than it is now, a worse place, or just about the same as it is today?

	Better	Worse	Same	No opinion**
Uruguay	54%	23%	15%	9%
Greece	46	29	15	10
Argentina†	44	27	12	8
Brazil	27	48	17	8
Turkey	26	38	12	24
Switzerland	23	33	40	4
Philippines	21	29	42	8
Canada	19	35	41	4
Great Britain	18	45	31	6
Portugal	16	37	9	38
Belgium	15	31	37	17
Netherlands	15	26	53	6
Australia	14	41	38	7

South Africa†† ..	13	52	28	7
Japan	12	53	18	17
West Germany ...	4	31	46	19

*The international results are based on in-person interviews conducted by affiliates of Gallup International Research Institutes earlier this year with an average of over 1,000 citizens of each country.
**Some rows do not add to 100% because of rounding.
†Buenos Aires only
††Whites only

Note: Of the citizens of seventeen nations surveyed, Americans are among the most optimistic in their perceptions of what the world will be like ten years from now. In a recent Gallup International survey, Americans are evenly divided between those who think the world will be a better place to live in (30%) and those who think it will be worse (30%). A 35% plurality thinks conditions will not have changed much in ten years' time.

In terms of optimism, Americans rank fourth on the list of seventeen nations, topped only by the residents of Uruguay, Greece, and Argentina. In those nations, 54%, 46%, and 44%, respectively, see the world as a better place to live in ten years from now. At the bottom of the list, in terms of those who think the world will be a worse place to live in, are the Japanese (53% are pessimistic), white South Africans (52%), Brazilians (48%), and British (45%).

There is considerable variation in the attitudes of Americans from different backgrounds. Men, for example, are somewhat more optimistic (35%) than women (25%). Blacks and whites share the same degree of optimism found in the United States as a whole, but blacks more often express pessimism (40%) than do whites (29%). Greater optimism may be found among persons who attended college and in households with above average family incomes.

Age, however, does not seem to be an important factor, with Americans of all ages sharing nearly the same point of view about the future. Similarly, persons from all regions of the nation

have the same basic outlook toward the world in ten years' time.

APRIL 14
ALCOHOLIC BEVERAGES

Interviewing Date: 2/15–18/85
Survey #250-G

Do you have occasion to use alcoholic beverages such as liquor, wine, or beer, or are you a total abstainer?

	Those who drink
National	67%

By Sex

Male	72%
Female	62

By Education

College graduate	80%
College incomplete	74
High-school graduate	69
Less than high-school graduate	49

By Region

East	72%
Midwest	70
South	56
West	73

By Age

18–29 years	74%
30–49 years	74
50 years and over	54

By Religion

Protestants	60%
Southern Baptists	45
Methodists	63
Catholics	78

Selected National Trend

	Those who drink
1984	64%
1983	65
1982	65
1981	70
1979	69
1977	71
1974	68
1969	64
1966	65
1964	63
1960	62
1958	55
1957	58
1956	60
1952	60
1950	60
1947	63
1945	67
1939	58

Has drinking* ever been a cause of trouble in your family?

	Yes
National	21%

By Sex

Male	19%
Female	23

By Education

College graduate	17%
College incomplete	21
High-school graduate	22
Less than high-school graduate	24

By Region

East	18%
Midwest	22
South	23
West	23

By Age

18–29 years	24%
30–49 years	24
50 years and over	15

By Religion

Protestants	21%
Southern Baptists	23
Methodists	21
Catholics	20

*The word "liquor" was used instead of "drinking" in surveys before 1984. However, a split-ballot comparison of the two words in the latest survey shows no statistical difference in the results.

Selected National Trend

	Yes
1984	17%
1981	22
1978	24
1976	17
1974	12
1966	12
1950	14

Asked of those who drink alcoholic beverages: Do you sometimes drink more than you think you should?

	Yes
National	32%

By Sex

Male	38%
Female	25

By Education

College graduate	32%
College incomplete	29
High-school graduate	30
Less than high-school graduate	38

By Region

East	25%
Midwest	35
South	34
West	34

By Age

18–29 years	43%
30–49 years	33
50 years and over	16

By Religion

Protestants	32%
Catholics	31

Selected National Trend

	Yes
1978	23%
1974	18

Also asked of those who drink alcoholic beverages: Do you plan to cut down or quit drinking within the next year?

Yes, cut down	14%
Yes, quit	2
No	83
Don't know	1

Note: Two Americans in three (67%) currently drink alcoholic beverages. In last year's survey, the figure was 64%. The proportion of drinkers appears to have levelled off after a downtrend during the last three years.

The new survey also shows the proportion who say that drinking has been a cause of trouble in their families. Currently, 21% cite drinking as a family problem, compared to 17% in a July 1984 survey. The latest figure is nearly double the 12% recorded in 1974.

A growing number of adults admit they sometimes drink more than they should, with 32% of drinkers now acknowledging they occasionally overindulge, compared to 23% in 1978, and 18% in 1974.

Many drinkers would like either to cut down their drinking (14%) or quit entirely (2%). Among those who say they sometimes drink too much, 31% plan to cut down, and 4% plan to quit. The main reasons given include health and diet considerations, expense, overindulgence, hangovers, advice of others, and the fact that drinking interferes with their work and other activities. Nine in ten (93%) of those who plan to cut back or quit think they will be successful in their efforts, but 6% are not sure whether or not they will succeed, and 1% expect to fail.

APRIL 18
UNITED NATIONS

Interviewing Date: 2/15–18/85 (U.S. only)
Survey #250-G

Asked in the United States: In general, do you feel the United Nations is doing a good job or a poor job in trying to solve the problems it has had to face?

Good job	38%
Poor job	44
No opinion	18

By Sex
Male

Good job	36%
Poor job	51
No opinion	13

Female

Good job	39%
Poor job	38
No opinion	23

By Ethnic Background
White

Good job	38%
Poor job	44
No opinion	18

Nonwhite

Good job	34%
Poor job	46
No opinion	20

Black

Good job 31%
Poor job 49
No opinion 20

By Education
College Graduate

Good job 32%
Poor job 56
No opinion 12

College Incomplete

Good job 41%
Poor job 41
No opinion 18

High-School Graduate

Good job 41%
Poor job 43
No opinion 16

Less Than High-School Graduate

Good job 35%
Poor job 41
No opinion 24

By Region
East

Good job 36%
Poor job 47
No opinion 17

Midwest

Good job 35%
Poor job 45
No opinion 20

South

Good job 42%
Poor job 40
No opinion 18

West

Good job 39%
Poor job 45
No opinion 16

By Age
18–24 Years

Good job 47%
Poor job 34
No opinion 19

25–29 Years

Good job 41%
Poor job 33
No opinion 26

30–49 Years

Good job 40%
Poor job 46
No opinion 14

50–64 Years

Good job 34%
Poor job 51
No opinion 15

65 Years and Over

Good job 26%
Poor job 51
No opinion 23

By Income
$40,000 and Over

Good job 37%
Poor job 52
No opinion 11

$30,000–$39,999

Good job 44%
Poor job 45
No opinion 11

$20,000–$29,999

Good job 39%
Poor job 42
No opinion 19

$10,000–$19,999

Good job 39%
Poor job 41
No opinion 20

Under $10,000

Good job 35%
Poor job 41
No opinion 24

By Politics
Republicans

Good job 41%
Poor job 42
No opinion 17

Democrats

Good job 40%
Poor job 43
No opinion 17

Independents

Good job 33%
Poor job 50
No opinion 17

Selected National Trend

	Good job	Poor job	No opinion
1983	36%	51%	13%
1982	36	49	15
1980	31	53	16
1975	33	51	16
1971	35	43	22
1970	44	40	16
1967	49	35	16
1956	51	37	12

Asked in sixteen nations*: In general, do you feel the United States is doing a good job or a poor job in trying to solve the problems it has had to face?

	Good job	Poor job	No opinion**
Philippines	64%	15%	21%
Netherlands	66	23	12
Switzerland	49	24	27
Belgium	34	17	49
Australia	49	34	17
Portugal	17	14	69
Brazil	27	23	50
Argentina†	32	32	36
Canada	36	39	26
Greece	31	36	33
West Germany	25	31	44
Japan	16	28	56
Great Britain	26	47	27
Turkey	22	43	35
Uruguay	25	49	27
South Africa††	13	65	22

*The international results are based on in-person interviews conducted by affiliates of Gallup International Research Institutes earlier this year with an average of over 1,000 citizens of each country.
**Some rows do not add to 100% because of rounding.
†Buenos Aires only
††Whites only

Note: Although marginally more Americans still hold negative than positive opinions about the performance of the United Nations, public opinion about the world body is gradually improving. In the latest Gallup Poll, 38% believe the United Nations is doing a good job in trying to solve the problems it faces, 44% say it is doing a poor job, and 18% express no opinion.

While the current positive rating is statistically indistinguishable from the 36% who expressed this view in both 1982 and 1983, the new figure nevertheless represents a modest improvement from 1980, when merely 31% thought the United Nations was doing a good job compared to 53% who criticized its efforts.

Americans have held more negative than positive views about the world body since 1970, when a slim 44% to 40% plurality gave it a favorable rating. In earlier surveys, roughly half the public perceived the United Nations as doing a satisfactory job.

The views of Americans are about midway down a list of seventeen nations in which the same question was asked, ranked in order of the ratio of positive to negative opinions. As shown on the table, in five countries—the Philippines, the Netherlands, Switzerland, Belgium, and Australia—favorable attitudes toward the United Nations significantly outnumber unfavorable ones. In Portugal, Brazil, Argentina, Canada, the United States, Greece, and West Germany, positive and negative assessments are fairly evenly divided. However, in Japan, Great Britain, Turkey, and Uruguay, public opinion runs about 2 to 1 negative. And white South Africans vote 5 to 1 in opposition to the world body.

APRIL 21

WEALTH AND POVERTY—UNITED STATES AND GREAT BRITAIN*

Interviewing Date: 12/7–10/84 (U.S. Only)
Survey #247-G

Do you feel that the distribution of money and wealth in this country today is fair, or do you feel that the money and wealth in this country should be more evenly distributed among a larger percentage of the people?

	United States	Great Britain
Fair now	31%	20%**
More evenly distributed	60	73
No opinion	9	8

Would you say that the percentage of Americans (British) living below the poverty line is increasing from year to year, or decreasing from year to year?

	United States	Great Britain
Increasing	70%	73%
Decreasing	18	9
No opinion	12	18

Just your best estimate, what percentage of Americans (British) would you say are living below the poverty line today?

	United States	Great Britain
0–14%	16% ⎫	18% ⎫
15%–20%	19 ⎬ 52%	18 ⎬ 54%
21%–30%	17 ⎭	18 ⎭
31%–49%	14	12
50% or more	15	17
No opinion	19	17

In your opinion, which is more often to blame if a person is poor—lack of effort on his own part, or circumstances beyond his control?

	United States	Great Britain
Lack of effort	33%	21%**
Circumstances	34	49
Both (volunteered)	31	28
No opinion	2	3

*The British results are based on a nationwide survey conducted March 6–11, 1985.

**Total adds to more than 100% because of rounding.

Note: The assessments of the British and Americans about the extent of poverty in their respective nations, and what should be done about it, are remarkably similar. As determined by recent Gallup surveys in both countries, large majorities—73% in Britain and 60% in the United States—believe that money and wealth in their own nations should be more evenly distributed.

Furthermore, respondents in both countries share the same view—73% in Britain and 70% in the United States—that the percentage living below the poverty line is increasing. Both agree—54% of the British and 52% of Americans—that the proportion of people below the poverty line is three in ten or less.

Disagreement, however, is found when it comes to the cause of poverty. The British are more than 2 to 1 of the belief that circumstances, rather than lack of effort, are more often to blame if a person is poor. Americans, on the other hand, are evenly divided on this issue, with equal proportions citing circumstances and lack of effort.

APRIL 25
POLITICAL AFFILIATION

Interviewing Date: January–March 1985
Various Surveys*

*In politics, as of today, do you consider yourself a Republican, a Democrat, or an independent?***

Republican	35%
Democrat	37
Independent	28

By Sex
Male

Republican	35%
Democrat	35
Independent	30

Female

Republican	36%
Democrat	39
Independent	25

By Ethnic Background
White

Republican	39%
Democrat	33
Independent	28

*Based on more than 6,000 interviews
**Those saying they have no party preference or who named other parties (3% in the latest surveys) are excluded.

Black

Republican	10%
Democrat	72
Independent	18

Hispanic

Republican	23%
Democrat	47
Independent	30

By Education
College Graduate

Republican	37%
Democrat	33
Independent	30

College Incomplete

Republican	42%
Democrat	29
Independent	29

High-School Graduate

Republican	35%
Democrat	37
Independent	28

Less Than High-School Graduate

Republican	28%
Democrat	48
Independent	24

By Region
East

Republican	33%
Democrat	39
Independent	28

Midwest

Republican	37%
Democrat	30
Independent	33

South

Republican 35%
Democrat 41
Independent 24

West

Republican 38%
Democrat 36
Independent 26

By Age
18–29 Years

Republican 38%
Democrat 31
Independent 31

30–49 Years

Republican 32%
Democrat 37
Independent 31

50 Years and Over

Republican 36%
Democrat 42
Independent 22

By Income
$20,000 and Over

Republican 41%
Democrat 32
Independent 27

Under $20,000

Republican 29%
Democrat 43
Independent 28

By Occupation
Professional and Business

Republican 43%
Democrat 29
Independent 28

Other White Collar

Republican 34%
Democrat 39
Independent 27

Blue Collar Workers

Republican 30%
Democrat 40
Independent 30

Skilled Workers Only

Republican 35%
Democrat 34
Independent 31

Unskilled Workers Only

Republican 26%
Democrat 44
Independent 30

By Labor Union Household
Labor Union Members

Republican 28%
Democrat 44
Independent 28

Nonlabor Union Members

Republican 37%
Democrat 36
Independent 27

Selected National Trend

	Republican	Democrat	Independent
1984	31%	40%	29%
1983	25	44	31
1982	26	45	29
1981	28	42	30
1980	24	46	30
1979	22	45	33
1978	23	48	29
1977	21	48	31
1976	23	47	30
1975	22	45	33
1972	28	43	29

1968	. . . .	27	46	27
1964	. . . .	25	53	22
1960	. . . .	30	47	23
1954	. . . .	34	46	20
1952	. . . .	34	41	25
1950	. . . .	33	45	22
1949	. . . .	32	48	20
1946	. . . .	40	39	21
1944	. . . .	39	41	20
1940	. . . .	38	42	20
1937	. . . .	34	50	16

Note: The grass-roots political realignment occasioned by President Ronald Reagan's reelection last November remained intact throughout the first quarter of 1985. As they had during the election period, nearly equal proportions of voting-age Americans in the latest surveys claim affiliation with the Democratic and Republican parties. In four in-person Gallup surveys this year 35% classify themselves as Republicans, 37% as Democrats, and 28% as independents. During the October-December quarter of 1984 the figures were Republicans, 35%; Democrats, 38%; and independents, 27%.

Currently the GOP also leads among whites, 18- to 29-year olds, persons who attended but did not graduate from college, those with family incomes of $20,000 or more per year, and mid-westerners. In addition, the two parties are now at a virtual standoff, not only nationally and among voters of both sexes, but also among high-school graduates, skilled blue collar workers, in non-union households, and among westerners.

A comparison of party affiliation during the first quarters of 1985 and 1984, as shown below, reveals significant GOP gains in almost every major population group. In the 1984 quarter the Republicans could claim a small plurality over the Democrats only among college graduates and persons from households in which the chief wage earner was employed in business or the professions.

Affiliation by Party

(Quarterly in 1984)

	Republican	Democrat	Independent
Fourth quarter	35%	38%	27%
Third quarter	32	39	29
Second quarter	28	42	30
First quarter	28	41	31

While the two major parties have been roughly equal in grass-roots strength for the last six months, it is still too soon to tell whether the present division of party allegiance represents a basic realignment of political loyalties, or reflects only a temporary setback for the Democrats. Nevertheless, the Democrats' present 2-percentage point advantage is the narrowest observed since 1946, when 40% of voters described themselves as Republicans and 39% as Democrats.

Gallup surveys during the last half century have shown that political party allegiance tends to ebb and flow with the fortunes of the party controlling the White House. Thus, Republican affiliation rose to 28% at the time of President Reagan's election in 1980. After the onset of the recession, however, it declined steadily to the 23% level until mid-1983, when there was clear evidence of economic recovery. The proportion of the electorate claiming Republican allegiance has been on a slow but steady upturn since then.

Republican Gains

(First Quarter 1984–First Quarter 1985)

	Point change
National	+7

By Sex

Male	+6
Female	+10

By Ethnic Background

White	+8
Black	+7
Hispanic	+4

By Education

College graduate .... +1
College incomplete .... +8
High-school graduate .... +8
Less than high-school graduate .... +10

By Region

East .... +6
Midwest .... +9
South .... +9
West .... +6

By Age

18–29 years .... +10
30–49 years .... +5
50 years and over .... +7

By Income

$20,000 and over .... +8
Under $20,000 .... +7

By Occupation

Professional and business .... +8
Other white collar .... +9
Blue collar workers .... +8
Skilled workers only .... +12
Unskilled workers only .... +5

By Labor Union Household

Labor union members .... +7
Nonlabor union members .... +7

APRIL 28
PRESIDENTIAL TRIAL HEATS

Interviewing Date: 2/15–18/85
Survey #250-G

Suppose the 1988 presidential election were being held today. If George Bush were the Republican candidate and Edward (Teddy) Kennedy were the Democratic candidate, which would you like to see win? [Those who named other candidates or were undecided were then asked: As of today, do you lean

more to Bush, the Republican, or to Kennedy, the Democrat?]

Bush 41%
Kennedy 47
Other; undecided 12

By Sex
Male

Bush 43%
Kennedy 46
Other; undecided 11

Female

Bush 39%
Kennedy 48
Other; undecided 13

By Ethnic Background
White

Bush 45%
Kennedy 43
Other; undecided 12

Black

Bush 11%
Kennedy 78
Other; undecided 11

By Education
College Graduate

Bush 50%
Kennedy 40
Other; undecided 10

College Incomplete

Bush 47%
Kennedy 41
Other; undecided 12

High-School Graduate

Bush 43%
Kennedy 44
Other; undecided 13

Less Than High-School Graduate

Bush 29%
Kennedy 61
Other; undecided 10

50 Years and Over

Bush 43%
Kennedy 44
Other; undecided 13

By Region

East

Bush 33%
Kennedy 55
Other; undecided 12

By Income

$40,000 and Over

Bush 59%
Kennedy 32
Other; undecided 9

Midwest

Bush 46%
Kennedy 42
Other; undecided 12

$30,000–$39,999

Bush 47%
Kennedy 40
Other; undecided 13

South

Bush 45%
Kennedy 41
Other; undecided 14

$20,000–$29,999

Bush 45%
Kennedy 44
Other; undecided 11

West

Bush 40%
Kennedy 51
Other; undecided 9

$10,000–$19,999

Bush 32%
Kennedy 56
Other; undecided 12

By Age

18–29 Years

Bush 44%
Kennedy 46
Other; undecided 10

Under $10,000

Bush 28%
Kennedy 56
Other; undecided 16

30–49 Years

Bush 38%
Kennedy 50
Other; undecided 12

By Politics

Republicans

Bush 75%
Kennedy 16
Other; undecided 9

Democrats

Bush 13%
Kennedy 77
Other; undecided .10

Independents

Bush 40%
Kennedy 44
Other; undecided .16

By Religion
Protestants

Bush 44%
Kennedy 44
Other; undecided .12

Catholics

Bush 36%
Kennedy 51
Other; undecided .13

By Occupation
Professional and Business

Bush 50%
Kennedy 41
Other; undecided 9

Other White Collar

Bush 37%
Kennedy 45
Other; undecided .18

Blue Collar Workers

Bush 36%
Kennedy 53
Other; undecided .11

By Labor Union Household
Labor Union Members

Bush 34%
Kennedy 57
Other; undecided 9

Nonlabor Union Members

Bush 43%
Kennedy 44
Other; undecided .13

Note: In an early sounding for the 1988 presidential election, potential Democratic candidate Senator Edward Kennedy is the public's narrow choice over Vice-President George Bush, a front-runner for the Republican nomination; Kennedy receives 47% of the votes to Bush's 41%, with 12% undecided. In a similar mock election in April 1982 before President Ronald Reagan had announced his reelection plans, Kennedy led Bush by a slightly larger 52% to 41% margin. That contest, unlike the current one, was conducted only among registered voters.

The closeness of the current Kennedy-Bush trial heat is accentuated by the fact that among whites the race is a statistical draw, with Bush receiving 45% of the white vote and Kennedy, 43%. The nearly monolithic black vote, 78% for Kennedy to 11% for Bush, suffices to give the Massachusetts senator his narrow overall margin. Similarly, the votes of 18 to 29 year olds and those age 50 and older are very evenly divided. Kennedy's 50% to 38% lead among 30 to 49 year olds, therefore, contributes importantly to his overall edge over the vice-president. As might be expected, Bush makes his strongest showing among the college-educated and upper-income groups and in households headed by business and professional workers.

The race is a statistical tie among men, high-school graduates, Protestants, members of non-union households and middle-income families, and among midwesterners and southerners. Consequently, Kennedy owes his modest national lead over Bush to his strength among constituents of the old-line Democratic coalition: blue collar workers, Catholics, the less well educated, members of labor union households, lower-income groups, and, as noted earlier, blacks. Kennedy also enjoys slightly greater appeal among women than among men, and somewhat more strength in the eastern and western regions than elsewhere in the country. Each possible candidate receives the votes of about three-fourths of his own party members, with independents' votes fairly evenly split.

MAY 2
PRESIDENT REAGAN

Interviewing Date: 4/12–15/85
Survey #252-G

Do you approve or disapprove of the way Ronald Reagan is handling his job as president?

Approve 52%
Disapprove 37
No opinion 11

Reagan Performance Ratings
for the Last Six Months

	Approve	Dis-approve	No opinion
1985			
March 8–11	56%	37%	7%
February 15–18	60	31	9
January 25–28	64	28	8
January 11–14	62	29	9
1984			
December 7–10	59	32	9
November 30–			
December 3	62	30	8
November 9–12	61	31	8
October 26–29	58	33	9
September 28–			
October 1	54	35	11

The following table compares President Reagan's job approval scores among men and women:

Percent Approval

	Men	Women	Point difference
1985			
March 8–11	58%	53%	5
February 15–18	61	58	3
January 25–28	64	63	1
January 11–14	67	57	10

1984			
December 7–10	64	55	9
November 30–			
December 3	67	56	11
November 9–12	64	58	6
October 26–29	60	57	3
September 28–			
October 1	57	51	6

Note: In a period marked by sharp debate over funding for the MX missile, aid to the Nicaraguan *contras*, and the trade imbalance with Japan, President Ronald Reagan's standing with the American people has declined to the lowest level since before his reelection last November. In the latest Gallup Poll, 52% approve of the way Reagan is handling his presidential duties, while 37% disapprove, and 11% are undecided. The president's job rating has been gradually declining since late January, when 64% approved and 28% disapproved.

On four different occasions last year, the public's assessment of Reagan's performance fell to 52% approval, most recently last July. At no time in 1984 did it drop below this mark.

The president's 4-point drop in approval since the previous mid-March survey is accompanied by a similar increase in the proportion of undecided voters, with no change in his disapproval score. This suggests that some people may have switched from being moderate Reagan supporters to fence sitters awaiting future developments before recommitting themselves.

Women have given President Reagan lower competency ratings than have men in every Gallup survey conducted since he took office, and 9% fewer women than men voted for him in the 1984 election. Until the last survey, there was evidence that the "gender gap" had diminished. In the three previous polls, for instance, the president's approval ratings among women averaged only 3 points lower than those of men.

In the new survey, however, an 11-point difference separates the views of men and women, with 58% of men, but only 47% of women, approving of his job performance. The return of a gender gap of this magnitude means that since late January, Reagan has suffered a 16-point decline in popularity among women, compared to only 6 points among men. Heavy media coverage of the MX missile and Nicaragua stories at the time of the survey may have reawakened women's apprehensions about U.S. military involvement abroad, which has been among their chief concerns.

MAY 5
FEDERAL BUDGET DEFICIT

Interviewing Date: 4/12–15/85
Survey #252-G

In your opinion, is the current federal budget deficit a very serious problem for the country, a fairly serious problem, not a serious problem, or is this something you haven't thought much about?

Very serious problem 58%
Fairly serious 23
Not serious 5
Not thought much about; no opinion 14

By Sex
Male

Very serious problem 60%
Fairly serious 24
Not serious 7
Not thought much about; no opinion 9

Female

Very serious problem 56%
Fairly serious 22
Not serious 3
Not thought much about; no opinion 19

By Ethnic Background
White

Very serious problem 59%
Fairly serious 23
Not serious 4
Not thought much about; no opinion 14

Nonwhite

Very serious problem 52%
Fairly serious 19
Not serious 10
Not thought much about; no opinion 19

Black

Very serious problem 54%
Fairly serious 18
Not serious 11
Not thought much about; no opinion 17

By Education
College Graduate

Very serious problem 66%
Fairly serious 28
Not serious 3
Not thought much about; no opinion 3

College Incomplete

Very serious problem 62%
Fairly serious 26
Not serious 6
Not thought much about; no opinion 6

High-School Graduate

Very serious problem 55%
Fairly serious 24
Not serious 5
Not thought much about; no opinion 16

Less Than High-School Graduate

Very serious problem 52%
Fairly serious 15
Not serious 4
Not thought much about; no opinion 29

By Region
East

Very serious problem 51%
Fairly serious 24
Not serious 6
Not thought much about; no opinion 19

Midwest

Very serious problem 60%
Fairly serious 24
Not serious 3
Not thought much about; no opinion 13

South

Very serious problem 58%
Fairly serious 21
Not serious 6
Not thought much about; no opinion 15

West

Very serious problem 63%
Fairly serious 23
Not serious 4
Not thought much about; no opinion 10

By Age
18–29 Years

Very serious problem 46%
Fairly serious 27
Not serious 8
Not thought much about; no opinion 19

30–49 Years

Very serious problem 57%
Fairly serious 27
Not serious 4
Not thought much about; no opinion 12

50 Years and Over

Very serious problem 68%
Fairly serious 15
Not serious 4
Not thought much about; no opinion 13

By Income
$50,000 and Over

Very serious problem 64%
Fairly serious 25
Not serious 4
Not thought much about; no opinion 7

$35,000–$49,999

Very serious problem 64%
Fairly serious 25
Not serious 3
Not thought much about; no opinion 8

$25,000–$34,999

Very serious problem 54%
Fairly serious 31
Not serious 4
Not thought much about; no opinion 11

$15,000–$24,999

Very serious problem 55%
Fairly serious 22
Not serious 5
Not thought much about; no opinion 18

$10,000–$14,999

Very serious problem 60%
Fairly serious 21
Not serious 6
Not thought much about; no opinion 13

Under $10,000

Very serious problem 53%
Fairly serious 16
Not serious 7
Not thought much about; no opinion 24

By Politics
Republicans

Very serious problem 53%
Fairly serious 27
Not serious 6
Not thought much about; no opinion 14

Democrats

Very serious problem 62%
Fairly serious 21
Not serious 5
Not thought much about; no opinion 12

Independents

Very serious problem	60%
Fairly serious	23
Not serious	4
Not thought much about; no opinion	13

At present the federal budget is running at the rate of over $200 billion per year. Basically, there are only a few ways this deficit can be reduced. Please tell me whether you approve or disapprove of each of the following ways to reduce the deficit:

Raise income taxes?

Approve	18%
Disapprove	76
No opinion	6

By Sex
Male

Approve	22%
Disapprove	75
No opinion	3

Female

Approve	14%
Disapprove	78
No opinion	8

By Ethnic Background
White

Approve	17%
Disapprove	77
No opinion	6

Nonwhite

Approve	19%
Disapprove	75
No opinion	6

Black

Approve	20%
Disapprove	74
No opinion	6

By Education
College Graduate

Approve	28%
Disapprove	69
No opinion	3

College Incomplete

Approve	20%
Disapprove	75
No opinion	5

High-School Graduate

Approve	14%
Disapprove	79
No opinion	7

Less Than High-School Graduate

Approve	12%
Disapprove	81
No opinion	7

By Region
East

Approve	16%
Disapprove	78
No opinion	6

Midwest

Approve	15%
Disapprove	77
No opinion	8

South

Approve	20%
Disapprove	74
No opinion	6

West

Approve	19%
Disapprove	77
No opinion	4

By Age

18–29 Years

Approve 19%
Disapprove 78
No opinion 3

30–49 Years

Approve 14%
Disapprove 80
No opinion 6

50 Years and Over

Approve 21%
Disapprove 71
No opinion 8

By Income

$50,000 and Over

Approve 25%
Disapprove 72
No opinion 3

$35,000–$49,999

Approve 20%
Disapprove 76
No opinion 4

$25,000–$34,999

Approve 15%
Disapprove 79
No opinion 6

$15,000–$24,999

Approve 14%
Disapprove 81
No opinion 5

$10,000–$14,999

Approve 18%
Disapprove 78
No opinion 4

Under $10,000

Approve 19%
Disapprove 70
No opinion 11

By Politics

Republicans

Approve 18%
Disapprove 76
No opinion 6

Democrats

Approve 20%
Disapprove 73
No opinion 7

Independents

Approve 16%
Disapprove 80
No opinion 4

Selected National Trend

	Approve
December 1984	23%
January 1983	18

Make cuts in government spending for social programs?

Approve 39%
Disapprove 55
No opinion 6

By Sex

Male

Approve 47%
Disapprove 47
No opinion 6

Female

Approve 31%
Disapprove 63
No opinion 6

By Ethnic Background

White

Approve	43%
Disapprove	51
No opinion	6

Nonwhite

Approve	17%
Disapprove	78
No opinion	5

Black

Approve	16%
Disapprove	79
No opinion	5

By Education

College Graduate

Approve	53%
Disapprove	44
No opinion	3

College Incomplete

Approve	39%
Disapprove	55
No opinion	6

High-School Graduate

Approve	36%
Disapprove	57
No opinion	7

Less Than High-School Graduate

Approve	30%
Disapprove	62
No opinion	8

By Region

East

Approve	32%
Disapprove	62
No opinion	6

Midwest

Approve	39%
Disapprove	52
No opinion	9

South

Approve	45%
Disapprove	50
No opinion	5

West

Approve	37%
Disapprove	58
No opinion	5

By Age

18–29 Years

Approve	35%
Disapprove	61
No opinion	4

30–49 Years

Approve	42%
Disapprove	51
No opinion	7

50 Years and Over

Approve	37%
Disapprove	56
No opinion	7

By Income

$50,000 and Over

Approve	57%
Disapprove	39
No opinion	4

$35,000–$49,999

Approve	43%
Disapprove	54
No opinion	3

$25,000–$34,999

Approve 47%
Disapprove 47
No opinion 6

$15,000–$24,999

Approve 39%
Disapprove 54
No opinion 7

$10,000–$14,999

Approve 32%
Disapprove 61
No opinion 7

Under $10,000

Approve 26%
Disapprove 67
No opinion 7

By Politics
Republicans

Approve 54%
Disapprove 38
No opinion 8

Democrats

Approve 26%
Disapprove 69
No opinion 5

Independents

Approve 39%
Disapprove 55
No opinion 6

Selected National Trend

	Approve
December 1984	41%
January 1983	41

Make cuts in defense spending?

Approve 66%
Disapprove 28
No opinion 6

By Sex
Male

Approve 66%
Disapprove 29
No opinion 5

Female

Approve 65%
Disapprove 27
No opinion 8

By Ethnic Background
White

Approve 65%
Disapprove 29
No opinion 6

Nonwhite

Approve 71%
Disapprove 22
No opinion 7

Black

Approve 74%
Disapprove 19
No opinion 7

By Education
College Graduate

Approve 75%
Disapprove 22
No opinion 3

College Incomplete

Approve 68%
Disapprove 27
No opinion 5

High-School Graduate

Approve 59%
Disapprove 33
No opinion 8

Less Than High-School Graduate

Approve 66%
Disapprove 25
No opinion 9

By Region
East

Approve 71%
Disapprove 24
No opinion 5

Midwest

Approve 65%
Disapprove 24
No opinion 11

South

Approve 57%
Disapprove 38
No opinion 5

West

Approve 75%
Disapprove 21
No opinion 4

By Age
18–29 Years

Approve 65%
Disapprove 29
No opinion 6

30–49 Years

Approve 64%
Disapprove 30
No opinion 6

50 Years and Over

Approve 68%
Disapprove 25
No opinion 7

By Income
$50,000 and Over

Approve 73%
Disapprove 22
No opinion 5

$35,000–$49,999

Approve 69%
Disapprove 27
No opinion 4

$25,000–$34,999

Approve 60%
Disapprove 34
No opinion 6

$15,000–$24,999

Approve 64%
Disapprove 32
No opinion 4

$10,000–$14,999

Approve 69%
Disapprove 26
No opinion 5

Under $10,000

Approve 64%
Disapprove 25
No opinion 11

By Politics
Republicans

Approve 56%
Disapprove 36
No opinion 8

Democrats

Approve 76%
Disapprove 19
No opinion 5

Independents

Approve 65%
Disapprove 30
No opinion 5

Selected National Trend

	Approve
December 1984	61%
January 1983	57

Make cuts in "entitlement" programs such as Social Security, Medicaid, and the like?

Approve 9%
Disapprove 87
No opinion 4

By Sex
Male

Approve 10%
Disapprove 86
No opinion 4

Female

Approve 7%
Disapprove 89
No opinion 4

By Ethnic Background
White

Approve 9%
Disapprove 87
No opinion 4

Nonwhite

Approve 5%
Disapprove 91
No opinion 4

Black

Approve 6%
Disapprove 91
No opinion 3

By Education
College Graduate

Approve 18%
Disapprove 79
No opinion 3

College Incomplete

Approve 8%
Disapprove 88
No opinion 4

High-School Graduate

Approve 8%
Disapprove 87
No opinion 5

Less Than High-School Graduate

Approve 3%
Disapprove 94
No opinion 3

By Region
East

Approve 6%
Disapprove 90
No opinion 4

Midwest

Approve 10%
Disapprove 84
No opinion 6

South

Approve 10%
Disapprove 86
No opinion 4

West

Approve 9%
Disapprove 89
No opinion 2

By Age
18–29 Years

Approve 6%
Disapprove 90
No opinion 4

30–49 Years

Approve 10%
Disapprove 86
No opinion 4

50 Years and Over

Approve 9%
Disapprove 87
No opinion 4

By Income
$50,000 and Over

Approve 20%
Disapprove 76
No opinion 4

$35,000–$49,999

Approve 10%
Disapprove 88
No opinion 2

$25,000–$34,999

Approve 9%
Disapprove 87
No opinion 4

$15,000–$24,999

Approve 9%
Disapprove 86
No opinion 5

$10,000–$14,999

Approve 5%
Disapprove 92
No opinion 3

Under $10,000

Approve 5%
Disapprove 90
No opinion 5

By Politics
Republicans

Approve 14%
Disapprove 80
No opinion 6

Democrats

Approve 4%
Disapprove 94
No opinion 2

Independents

Approve 10%
Disapprove 87
No opinion 3

Selected National Trend

	Approve
December 1984	11%
January 1983	12

Note: Congressional debate on the 1986 federal budget begins at a time of growing perception that the current deficit poses a very serious threat to the nation. The public increasingly is giving highest priority to cuts in defense spending to reduce the deficit.

In the latest Gallup Poll, 58% characterize the current deficit as a very serious national problem, and an additional 23% see it as fairly serious. Only 5% perceive the deficit as not serious, while 14% say they have not given the matter much thought or do not express an opinion. The latest figures represent a small but significant shift since December toward the view that the current deficit is very serious, rather than fairly serious. In the earlier survey, 54% called it very serious, and 29%, fairly serious.

The new poll also finds two-thirds of Americans (66%) favoring cuts in defense spending, up from 61% last December and 57% in January 1983. On the other hand, public support for each of three other deficit-reduction measures has fallen or remained static since the earlier surveys. Currently, 39% favor cuts in government spending for social programs, not significantly changed from the 41% recorded in both 1984 and 1983. Raising income taxes is now favored by 18%, a significant reduction from 23% in December, but unchanged from 1983. And by far the least popular means of reducing the deficit, cutting entitlement programs, has steadily declined in public favor, from 12% in 1983 to 11% last year to 9% at present.

While the survey found general agreement on the priority of the measures that should be taken to reduce the deficit, with majorities in all major population groups favoring cuts in defense spending, there is considerable divergence along party and regional lines. Republicans, for example, favor defense cuts (56%) and cuts in spending for social programs (54%) by similar margins. On the other hand, 76% of Democrats favor defense cuts, but only 26% approve of cuts in social programs. And while cuts in entitlements are not popular with members of either party, they are relatively more appealing to Republicans (14%) than to Democrats (4%). Political independents take positions between those of Republicans and Democrats on three of the four measures. Southerners (45%) tend to favor cuts in social programs more than do persons from other regions (36%). However, southerners (57%) are less likely to want defense spending cuts than are those in other parts of the nation (70%).

In March, Senate Republican leaders reached a compromise agreement with the Reagan administration on a budget for fiscal 1986 that would trim roughly $52 billion from the projected deficit. The plan, which faces stormy debate in Congress, also would reduce projected deficits by $295 billion through fiscal 1988. Key elements of the compromise are reducing cost-of-living increases for Social Security and other retirement programs,

and limiting defense outlays to a 3% rise, in addition to inflation adjustments, instead of the 6% increase requested in the original White House plan. If approved, the entire compromise package would meet the goal of reducing the federal deficit to 2% of the gross national product.

MAY 9
SEAT BELTS

Interviewing Date: 4/12–15/85
Survey #252-G

Thinking about the last time you got into a car, did you use a seat belt, or not?

	Yes, used belt
National	40%

By Sex

Male	39%
Female	41

By Education

College graduate	58%
College incomplete	46
High-school graduate	34
Less than high-school graduate	29

By Region

East	53%
Midwest	38
South	28
West	46

By Age

18–24 years	35%
25–29 years	34
30–49 years	44
50–64 years	36
65 years and over	44

By Occupation

Professional and business	50%
Clerical and sales	38
Blue collar workers	33

Selected National Trend

	Yes, used belt
1984	25%
1982	17
1977	22
1973	28

Would you favor or oppose a law that would fine a person $25 if he or she did not wear a seat belt when riding in an automobile?

Favor	35%
Oppose	59
No opinion	6

By Sex

Male

Favor	34%
Oppose	62
No opinion	4

Female

Favor	37%
Oppose	56
No opinion	7

By Education

College Graduate

Favor	43%
Oppose	52
No opinion	5

College Incomplete

Favor	38%
Oppose	56
No opinion	6

High-School Graduate

Favor	32%
Oppose	63
No opinion	5

Less Than High-School Graduate

Favor	31%
Oppose	62
No opinion	7

By Region

East

Favor	43%
Oppose	49
No opinion	8

Midwest

Favor	33%
Oppose	63
No opinion	4

South

Favor	34%
Oppose	61
No opinion	5

West

Favor	30%
Oppose	64
No opinion	6

By Age

18–24 Years

Favor	37%
Oppose	59
No opinion	4

25–29 Years

Favor	39%
Oppose	57
No opinion	4

30–49 Years

Favor	37%
Oppose	57
No opinion	6

50–64 Years

Favor 34%
Oppose 62
No opinion 4

65 Years and Over

Favor 30%
Oppose 62
No opinion 8

By Occupation

Professional and Business

Favor 40%
Oppose 56
No opinion 4

Clerical and Sales

Favor 35%
Oppose 65
No opinion .... *

Blue Collar Workers

Favor 35%
Oppose 59
No opinion 6

*Less than 1%

Selected National Trend

	Favor	Oppose	No opinion
1982	19%	75%	6%
1977	17	78	5
1973	23	71	6

Note: As might be expected, persons who report using a seat belt are far more favorably disposed toward a fine for nonuse than those who did not use a seat belt the last time they rode in a car. As shown in the following table, seat belt users are evenly divided between those who favor (46%) and oppose (47%) such a law. On the other hand, nonusers are opposed to the proposed law by more than a 2-to-1 ratio, with 28% in favor and 68% opposed.

When Last in Car

	Total	Used belt	Did not use belt
$25 fine			
Favor	35%	46%	28%
Oppose	59	47	68
No opinion	6	7	4

Note: A dramatic rise in the use of auto seat belts has occurred since last year, with 40% of adults now reporting that they wore a seat belt the last time they rode in a car, compared to 25% in 1984 and 17% in 1982. The latest Gallup Poll also reveals growing public support for a law that would fine people $25 for not using seat belts, although a majority still opposes such a law.

Although sharp increases in use are recorded since 1982 in all major population groups, marked differences remain. Persons who attended college and those from households in which the chief wage earner is employed in business or the professions are considerably more likely than their counterparts to be seat belt users. Similarly, in the East—which includes New York and New Jersey—53% of residents currently report using seat belts, three times the 17% figure recorded in 1982. Southerners (28%) continue to trail those from other regions (46%). And younger adults (under 30 years), who were at or near the national average in the earlier surveys, now significantly lag behind 30 to 49 year olds in seat belt use.

At present only two states, New York and New Jersey, have mandatory seat belt laws on the books. New York, the first state to require their use, recently reported a 27% decline in the number of drivers and passengers killed in motor vehicle accidents in the first three months its law has been in effect. In addition, five states have enacted seat belt legislation that will take effect in coming months.

U.S. Transportation Secretary Elizabeth Dole issued an order last year requiring all new automobiles to have passive restraints, such as air bags or automatic seat belts, by 1989. The requirement would be waived if states containing two-thirds of the U.S. population pass mandatory seat belt use laws by then.

MAY 12
IDEAL LIFE-STYLE FOR WOMEN

Interviewing Date: 4/12–15/85
Survey #252-G

Asked of women: Let's talk about the ideal life for you personally. Which one of the alternatives on this card do you feel would provide the most interesting and satisfying life for you personally? [Respondents were handed a card listing five alternative life-styles.]

Married with children
  With full-time job 38%
  With no full-time job 34
Married with no children
  With full-time job 6
  With no full-time job 3
Unmarried with full-time job 9
No opinion 10

By Ethnic Background
White

Married with children
  With full-time job 38%
  With no full-time job 34
Married with no children
  With full-time job 6
  With no full-time job 3
Unmarried with full-time job 9
No opinion 10

Nonwhite

Married with children
  With full-time job 56%
  With no full-time job 12
Married with no children
  With full-time job 3
  With no full-time job 6
Unmarried with full-time job 10
No opinion 13

Black

Married with children
  With full-time job 56%
  With no full-time job 14
Married with no children
  With full-time job 2
  With no full-time job 7
Unmarried with full-time job 11
No opinion 10

By Education
College Graduate

Married with children
  With full-time job 44%
  With no full-time job 24
Married with no children
  With full-time job 12
  With no full-time job 4
Unmarried with full-time job 7
No opinion 9

College Incomplete

Married with children
  With full-time job 39%
  With no full-time job 35
Married with no children
  With full-time job 4
  With no full-time job 1
Unmarried with full-time job 13
No opinion 8

High-School Graduate

Married with children
  With full-time job 33%
  With no full-time job 43
Married with no children
  With full-time job 3
  With no full-time job 4
Unmarried with full-time job 9
No opinion 8

Less Than High-School Graduate

Married with children
  With full-time job 43%
  With no full-time job 25

Married with no children
  With full-time job 7
  With no full-time job 2
Unmarried with full-time job 9
No opinion 14

By Region
East

Married with children
  With full-time job 36%
  With no full-time job 32
Married with no children
  With full-time job 5
  With no full-time job 3
Unmarried with full-time job 11
No opinion 13

Midwest

Married with children
  With full-time job 41%
  With no full-time job 38
Married with no children
  With full-time job 6
  With no full-time job 3
Unmarried with full-time job 5
No opinion 7

South

Married with children
  With full-time job 32%
  With no full-time job 36
Married with no children
  With full-time job 7
  With no full-time job 4
Unmarried with full-time job 12
No opinion 9

West

Married with children
  With full-time job 47%
  With no full-time job 28
Married with no children
  With full-time job 6
  With no full-time job 2
Unmarried with full-time job 8
No opinion 9

By Age
18–29 Years

Married with children
  With full-time job 44%
  With no full-time job 25
Married with no children
  With full-time job 9
  With no full-time job 2
Unmarried with full-time job 14
No opinion 6

30–49 Years

Married with children
  With full-time job 43%
  With no full-time job 34
Married with no children
  With full-time job 5
  With no full-time job 3
Unmarried with full-time job 8
No opinion 7

50 Years and Over

Married with children
  With full-time job 30%
  With no full-time job 40
Married with no children
  With full-time job 6
  With no full-time job 3
Unmarried with full-time job 8
No opinion 13

By Income
$50,000 and Over

Married with children
  With full-time job 56%
  With no full-time job 30
Married with no children
  With full-time job 3
  With no full-time job 2
Unmarried with full-time job 1
No opinion 8

$35,000–$49,999

Married with children
  With full-time job 47%
  With no full-time job 33

Married with no children
  With full-time job 1
  With no full-time job 2
Unmarried with full-time job 9
No opinion 8

$25,000–$34,999

Married with children
  With full-time job 40%
  With no full-time job 38
Married with no children
  With full-time job 5
  With no full-time job 2
Unmarried with full-time job 8
No opinion 7

$15,000–$24,999

Married with children
  With full-time job 38%
  With no full-time job 29
Married with no children
  With full-time job 10
  With no full-time job 4
Unmarried with full-time job 10
No opinion 9

$10,000–$14,999

Married with children
  With full-time job 25%
  With no full-time job 47
Married with no children
  With full-time job 8
  With no full-time job 3
Unmarried with full-time job 9
No opinion 8

Under $10,000

Married with children
  With full-time job 37%
  With no full-time job 26
Married with no children
  With full-time job 6
  With no full-time job 4
Unmarried with full-time job 13
No opinion 14

Selected National Trend

1982

Married with children
  With full-time job 40%
  With no full-time job 39
Married with no children
  With full-time job 5
  With no full-time job 2
Unmarried with full-time job 6
No opinion 8

1980

Married with children
  With full-time job 33%
  With no full-time job 41
Married with no children
  With full-time job 6
  With no full-time job 4
Unmarried with full-time job 8
No opinion 8

1975

Married with children
  With full-time job 32%
  With no full-time job 44
Married with no children
  With full-time job 6
  With no full-time job 3
Unmarried with full-time job 9
No opinion 6

Note: Although the traditional role of wife and mother is still considered to be the ideal life-style by the vast majority of American women, that ideal increasingly includes a full-time job outside the home. Currently, 72% of women view marriage with children as the most interesting and satisfying life for them personally. Within this group, 38% also would like to have a full-time job, while 34% would prefer being a stay-at-home wife and mother.

Since 1975, when the Gallup Poll first asked this question, there has been little change in the overall appeal of marriage and children. But the proportion of women choosing outside jobs has gradually increased from 32% in 1975 to 38%

today, while the proportion preferring to remain at home has steadily declined from 44% a decade ago to 34% at present.

The stereotypical career woman—single and in pursuit of a full-time career—has as little appeal today as in 1975, with merely 9% of women in each survey opting for this way of life. Similarly, childless marriages, with or without employment, are the choice of only 9% in each survey.

The growing role of employment for women parallels their increasing presence in the job market. In 1975, the federal government estimated that 46% of women age 16 and over were in the labor force; by 1984, that figure had risen to 54%.

MAY 14
RELIGION—SPIRITUAL EXPERIENCES

Interviewing Date: 4/12–15/85
Survey #252-G

Have you ever been aware of, or influenced by, a presence or a power—whether you call it God or not—which is different from your everyday self?

	Yes
National	43%

By Sex

Male	38%
Female	47

By Ethnic Background

White	44%
Nonwhite	35
Black	36

By Education

College graduate	50%
College incomplete	47
High-school graduate	39
Less than high-school graduate	37

By Region

East	40%
Midwest	41
South	43
West	47

By Age

18–24 years	35%
25–29 years	39
30–49 years	47
50–64 years	40
65 years and over	44

By Religion

Protestants (all)	48%
Southern Baptists	52
Methodists	48
Lutherans	43
Catholics	37

Religion very important in life	50%
Religion fairly important	38
Religion not very important	24

Asked of those who responded in the affirmative: Would you describe this?

Presence of God	21%
Guidance, help from God	11
Indescribable feeling	11
Calming, comforting	10
Contentment, peace, well-being	7
At time of illness	6
Answer to prayer	6
Like E.S.P., intuition	5
Guardian	4
Gave me strength	3
Conscience	3
A light	2
All others	6
Don't know	5

Also asked of those who replied in the affirmative: What effect has this had on you or your life?

Strengthened my belief in God 15%
Gave me strength for living 14
Made me a better person 10
Had positive effect (general) 8
Made me appreciate life more 8
Had no effect 7
Made me more understanding of others ... 6
Made me a happier person 5
Gave me peace of mind 4
Helped me make decision 4
Helped in discerning right from wrong ... 4
Gave me hope 3
Improved family life 3
Made me thankful 2
Made me reassess my life 2
Gave me more self-confidence 2
Made me feel more religious 2
All others 6
Don't know 10
                                   ———
                                   115%*

*Multiple responses were given.

Note: A remarkable 43% of Americans say they
have had unusual and inexplicable spiritual or religious experiences, as determined by a recent
nationwide Gallup survey. These experiences cover
a wide range—from nature-inspired feelings of
awe, to answered prayers, to out-of-body
experiences—and generally have made a profound
and positive impact on people's lives.

When the same question was asked by the Gallup affiliate in Great Britain, 33% replied affirm-
atively, a figure that almost exactly matches the
percentage recorded in an earlier survey conducted
by the Religious Experience Research Unit at
Manchester College, Oxford (now the Alistair
Hardy Research Center, Oxford).

MAY 16
PREMARITAL SEX

Interviewing Date: 4/12–15/85
Survey #252-G

> There's a lot of discussion about the way
> morals and sexual attitudes are changing in
> this country. What is your opinion about this:

*Do you think it is wrong for a man and a
woman to have sexual relations before marriage, or not?*

Wrong 39%
Not wrong 52
No opinion 9

By Sex
Male

Wrong 32%
Not wrong 57
No opinion 11

Female

Wrong 44%
Not wrong 48
No opinion 8

By Ethnic Background
White

Wrong 40%
Not wrong 51
No opinion 9

Nonwhite

Wrong 28%
Not wrong 59
No opinion 13

Black

Wrong 26%
Not wrong 61
No opinion 13

By Education
College Graduate

Wrong 30%
Not wrong 62
No opinion 8

College Incomplete

Wrong 32%
Not wrong 58
No opinion 10

High-School Graduate

Wrong 41%
Not wrong 49
No opinion 10

Less Than High-School Graduate

Wrong 46%
Not wrong 43
No opinion 11

By Region
East

Wrong 40%
Not wrong 51
No opinion 9

Midwest

Wrong 36%
Not wrong 53
No opinion 11

South

Wrong 48%
Not wrong 44
No opinion 8

West

Wrong 24%
Not wrong 67
No opinion 9

By Age
18–24 Years

Wrong 17%
Not wrong 74
No opinion 9

25–29 Years

Wrong 19%
Not wrong 76
No opinion 5

30–49 Years

Wrong 35%
Not wrong 55
No opinion 10

50–64 Years

Wrong 47%
Not wrong 40
No opinion 13

65 Years and Over

Wrong 67%
Not wrong 24
No opinion 9

By Income
$50,000 and Over

Wrong 29%
Not wrong 62
No opinion 9

$35,000–$49,999

Wrong 40%
Not wrong 52
No opinion 8

$25,000–$34,999

Wrong 36%
Not wrong 54
No opinion 10

$15,000–$24,999

Wrong 35%
Not wrong 55
No opinion 10

$10,000–$14,999

Wrong 44%
Not wrong 49
No opinion 7

Under $10,000

Wrong 40%
Not wrong 49
No opinion 11

By Politics

Republicans

Wrong 45%
Not wrong 47
No opinion 8

Democrats

Wrong 37%
Not wrong 53
No opinion 10

Independents

Wrong 33%
Not wrong 58
No opinion 9

By Religion

Protestants

Wrong 46%
Not wrong 44
No opinion 10

Catholics

Wrong 33%
Not wrong 58
No opinion 9

By Occupation

Professional and Business

Wrong 32%
Not wrong 60
No opinion 8

Clerical and Sales

Wrong 33%
Not wrong 58
No opinion 9

Manual Workers

Wrong 36%
Not wrong 55
No opinion 9

Nonlabor Force

Wrong 55%
Not wrong 35
No opinion 10

Selected National Trend

	Wrong	Not wrong	No opinion
1973	48%	43%	9%
1969	68	21	11

Persons in the current survey who say religion is very important in their lives tend to believe that premarital sex is wrong (54%) rather than not wrong (36%). On the other hand, large majorities of those who say religion is only fairly important (66%), or not important (80%), say sex before marriage is acceptable:

Importance of Religion in Life

	Total	Very important	Fairly important	Not very important
Premarital sex	(100%)	(54%)	(30%)	(15%)
Wrong	39%	54%	25%	13%
Not wrong	52	36	66	80
No opinion	9	10	9	7

Note: For the first time in the almost two decades the topic has been studied, a majority of adults considers premarital sex acceptable. As recently as 1969, a commanding two-thirds' majority thought sex before marriage was wrong. Now, in the latest Gallup Poll, 52% say premarital sex is not wrong, while 39% say it is wrong. When the question was first asked in 1969, 68% said it was wrong and 21%, not wrong.

Although a pronounced shift toward greater acceptance has occurred in all major population segments, majorities of persons age 50 and older and those whose formal education ended at the grade-school level continue to disapprove of premarital sex. In addition to age and education, significant differences are found on the basis of gender, religious preference, and geographic region. Men, for instance, are less likely than women to consider premarital sex unacceptable, with 32% of men compared to 44% of women saying it is wrong. Similarly, while Protestants are evenly divided on the issue, with 46% believing premarital sex is wrong and 44% not wrong, Catholics lean strongly to the liberal viewpoint, with 33% saying it is wrong and 58% not wrong. Majorities in every region except the South take the position that premarital sex is not wrong. Southerners are closely divided, with 48% saying it is wrong and 44% not wrong.

MAY 19
LABOR UNIONS

Interviewing Date: 4/12–15/85
Survey #252-G

Do you approve or disapprove of labor unions?

Approve 58%
Disapprove 27
No opinion 15

By Sex
Male

Approve 59%
Disapprove 30
No opinion 11

Female

Approve 57%
Disapprove 24
No opinion 19

By Ethnic Background
White

Approve 55%
Disapprove 29
No opinion 16

Black

Approve 74%
Disapprove 16
No opinion 10

By Education
College Graduate

Approve 58%
Disapprove 33
No opinion 9

College Incomplete

Approve 53%
Disapprove 31
No opinion 16

High-School Graduate

Approve 60%
Disapprove 25
No opinion 15

Less Than High-School Graduate

Approve 58%
Disapprove 23
No opinion 19

By Region
East

Approve 60%
Disapprove 24
No opinion 16

Midwest

Approve 63%
Disapprove 23
No opinion 14

South

Approve 51%
Disapprove 33
No opinion 16

West

Approve 59%
Disapprove 28
No opinion 13

By Age

18–29 Years

Approve 62%
Disapprove 23
No opinion 15

30–49 Years

Approve 56%
Disapprove 30
No opinion 14

50 Years and Over

Approve 57%
Disapprove 28
No opinion 15

By Income

$25,000 and Over

Approve 55%
Disapprove 32
No opinion 13

Under $25,000

Approve 60%
Disapprove 24
No opinion 16

By Politics

Republicans

Approve 48%
Disapprove 36
No opinion 16

Democrats

Approve 67%
Disapprove 22
No opinion 11

Independents

Approve 57%
Disapprove 26
No opinion 17

By Occupation

Professional and Business

Approve 55%
Disapprove 34
No opinion 11

Other White Collar

Approve 56%
Disapprove 29
No opinion 15

Skilled Blue Collar

Approve 58%
Disapprove 25
No opinion 17

Unskilled Blue Collar

Approve 66%
Disapprove 18
No opinion 16

By Labor Union Household

Labor Union Members

Approve 81%
Disapprove 12
No opinion 7

Nonlabor Union Members

Approve 52%
Disapprove 31
No opinion 17

Selected National Trend

	Approve	Dis-approve	No opinion
1981	55%	35%	10%
1979	55	33	12
1978	59	31	10
1973	59	26	15
1967	66	23	11
1965	70	19	11
1963	67	23	10
1961	63	22	15
1959	68	19	13

1957	76	14	10
1953	75	18	7
1949	62	22	16
1947	64	25	11
1941	61	30	9
1939	68	24	8
1936	72	20	8

Note: The long slide in public approval of labor unions, from 70% in 1965 to 55% in 1979 and 1981, appears to have come to a halt, with 58% in the latest Gallup survey expressing approval. The change is more pronounced on the disapproval side, with 27% currently saying they disapprove of labor unions, compared to 35% in the 1981 survey.

Key factors in the improved ratings given unions today are the views of members of labor union households themselves. Although the present 52% approval rating among nonunion members is not significantly changed from 1981, approval among union people has increased by 8 percentage points, as shown below.

Approval of Labor Union Households

	National	Labor union members	Nonunion members
April 1985	58%	81%	52%
1981	55	73	50
1979	55	77	48
1965	70	90	64

At least part of Americans' disaffection with the union movement may be traced to their general disapproval of strikes, which have declined in recent years. According to the U.S. Department of Labor, the number of work stoppages involving 1,000 or more workers dropped from 235 in 1979 to 187 in 1980, 96 in 1982, 81 in 1983, and 56 for the first eleven months of 1984.

MAY 23
MINIMUM WAGE FOR TEEN-AGERS

Interviewing Date: 4/12–15/85
Survey # 252-G

A proposal has been made that teen-agers 19 and under be allowed to receive a sub-minimum wage of $2.50 per hour for the summer months to provide work for more unemployed youth. Have you heard or read about this proposal?

Yes, have heard or read 57%
No, have not 43

Asked of those who replied in the affirmative: How do you, yourself, feel? Everything considered, do you favor or oppose lowering the minimum wage for teen-agers during the summer months?

Favor 51%
Oppose 45
No opinion 4

By Sex
Male

Favor 55%
Oppose 41
No opinion 4

Female

Favor 47%
Oppose 49
No opinion 4

By Ethnic Background
White

Favor 56%
Oppose 40
No opinion 4

Black

Favor 28%
Oppose 69
No opinion 3

By Education
College Graduate

Favor 62%
Oppose 33
No opinion 5

College Incomplete

Favor 51%
Oppose 46
No opinion 3

High-School Graduate

Favor 45%
Oppose 52
No opinion 3

Less Than High-School Graduate

Favor 49%
Oppose 47
No opinion 4

By Region
East

Favor 43%
Oppose 50
No opinion 7

Midwest

Favor 51%
Oppose 46
No opinion 3

South

Favor 56%
Oppose 43
No opinion 1

West

Favor 55%
Oppose 42
No opinion 3

By Age
18–24 Years

Favor 32%
Oppose 64
No opinion 4

25–29 Years

Favor 58%
Oppose 42
No opinion .... *

30–49 Years

Favor 50%
Oppose 45
No opinion 5

50 Years and Over

Favor 57%
Oppose 40
No opinion 3

By Income
$25,000 and Over

Favor 59%
Oppose 38
No opinion 3

Under $25,000

Favor 45%
Oppose 51
No opinion 4

By Politics
Republicans

Favor 70%
Oppose 27
No opinion 3

Democrats

Favor 39%
Oppose 58
No opinion 3

Independents

Favor 51%
Oppose 45
No opinion 4

By Labor Union Household

Labor Union Members

Favor 36%
Oppose 59
No opinion 5

Nonlabor Union Members

Favor 55%
Oppose 42
No opinion 3

*Less than 1%

Note: A proposal for lowering the minimum wage for teen-age workers this summer receives a mixed reaction from the adult public, with roughly equal proportions of those familiar with the proposal favoring and opposing it. This plan, similar to one now under active consideration by the Reagan administration, calls for a minimum wage of $2.50 per hour for workers age 19 and under. Currently, all workers must be paid at least $3.35 per hour, regardless of age. The object of the proposal would be to create summer jobs for chronically unemployed young people.

In a recent Gallup survey, adults who said they had heard or read about the proposal (57% of the total) were asked their opinions about it. A bare 51% majority votes in favor, while 45% are opposed. For subsamples of the size of the aware group, differences of this magnitude are not statistically meaningful.

Greater opposition is expressed by young adults, 18 to 29 years old, who are closest in age to the youth who would be directly affected if the proposal were enacted, than by persons age 50 and older. Blacks vote it down by more than a 2-to-1 ratio, with 28% in favor and 69% opposed. Aware whites, on the other hand, are somewhat more positive (56%) than negative (40%), about the proposal. (Unemployment among black teenagers is particularly acute, with more than four in ten unable to find jobs in March, according to the U.S. Labor Department.)

Opposition also is found in population groups that historically have been more affected by layoffs in times of high unemployment: members of blue collar and labor union households, those whose formal education ended at or below the high-school level, and persons with family incomes below the national median. Furthermore, a strong political coloration is apparent: Republicans overwhelmingly endorse the proposal, 70% to 27%, while Democrats vigorously oppose it, 58% to 39%. Independents fall exactly at the national level, 51% in favor, and 45% opposed.

When teen-agers themselves were questioned by the Gallup Youth Survey in 1981, they voted against a similar proposal by a lopsided 72% to 27% margin. Most of the 13 to 18 year olds in the survey opposed a lower minimum wage on the grounds that jobs were available for those who sought hard enough for them, and that it would not be worth their time to work for less than the $3.35 per hour minimum wage.

Newly appointed Labor Secretary William Brock, who is now considering modifications of the administration's proposal, has termed the lower minimum wage for teen-agers his "top legislative priority proposal for 1985." In reply to critics who charge that employers would replace older workers with cheaper young people, Brock is considering stiff legal penalties against such a practice. The proposal, as now written, faces strong opposition from organized labor and black leaders.

Under the Reagan plan, the lower wage would be in effect for a three-year test period through 1988. Teen-age workers would be paid the subminimum rate for summer or after-school work. Labor Department officials predict that the new wage scale might create as many as 400,000 jobs.

MAY 26
HANDGUNS

Interviewing Date: 4/12–15/85
Survey #252-G

Do you favor or oppose the registration of all handguns?

Favor 70%
Oppose 25
No opinion 5

By Sex

Male

Favor 64%
Oppose 33
No opinion 3

Female

Favor 77%
Oppose 16
No opinion 7

By Ethnic Background

White

Favor 69%
Oppose 25
No opinion 6

Black

Favor 81%
Oppose 16
No opinion 3

By Education

College Graduate

Favor 72%
Oppose 25
No opinion 3

College Incomplete

Favor 72%
Oppose 22
No opinion 6

High-School Graduate

Favor 68%
Oppose 26
No opinion 6

Less Than High-School Graduate

Favor 70%
Oppose 25
No opinion 5

By Region

East

Favor 78%
Oppose 16
No opinion 6

Midwest

Favor 74%
Oppose 21
No opinion 5

South

Favor 65%
Oppose 31
No opinion 4

West

Favor 62%
Oppose 32
No opinion 6

By Age

18–29 Years

Favor 73%
Oppose 21
No opinion 6

30–49 Years

Favor 69%
Oppose 24
No opinion 4

50 Years and Over

Favor 69%
Oppose 25
No opinion 6

Gun Owners Only

Favor 61%
Oppose 35
No opinion 4

Nongun Owners Only

Favor 78%
Oppose 16
No opinion 6

Handgun Owners Only

Favor 56%
Oppose 4
No opinion 3

Some communities have passed laws banning the sale and possession of handguns. Would you favor or oppose having such a law in this city/community?

Favor 40%
Oppose 56
No opinion 4

By Sex
Male

Favor 30%
Oppose 67
No opinion 3

Female

Favor 48%
Oppose 46
No opinion 6

By Ethnic Background
White

Favor 38%
Oppose 58
No opinion 4

Black

Favor 51%
Oppose 45
No opinion 4

By Education
College Graduate

Favor 41%
Oppose 57
No opinion 2

College Incomplete

Favor 39%
Oppose 56
No opinion 5

High-School Graduate

Favor 38%
Oppose 57
No opinion 5

Less Than High-School Graduate

Favor 40%
Oppose 55
No opinion 5

By Region
East

Favor 56%
Oppose 39
No opinion 5

Midwest

Favor 36%
Oppose 59
No opinion 5

South

Favor 30%
Oppose 66
No opinion 4

West

Favor 38%
Oppose 58
No opinion 4

By Age

18–29 Years

Favor 41%
Oppose 55
No opinion 4

30–49 Years

Favor 38%
Oppose 59
No opinion 3

50 Years and Over

Favor 41%
Oppose 54
No opinion 5

By Community Size

One Million and Over

Favor 51%
Oppose 44
No opinion 5

500,000–999,999

Favor 36%
Oppose 61
No opinion 3

50,000–499,999

Favor 43%
Oppose 54
No opinion 3

2,500–49,999

Favor 33%
Oppose 62
No opinion 5

Under 2,500; Rural

Favor 26%
Oppose 69
No opinion 5

Gun Owners Only

Favor 22%
Oppose 75
No opinion 3

Nongun Owners Only

Favor 53%
Oppose 41
No opinion 6

Handgun Owners Only

Favor 16%
Oppose 83
No opinion 1

Those Who Favor Handgun Registration

Favor 50%
Oppose 47
No opinion 3

Those Who Oppose Handgun Registration

Favor 13%
Oppose 86
No opinion 1

Note: A large and growing majority of Americans, including those who own handguns, favors registration of these weapons. Public support for the passage of local laws banning the sale and possession of handguns, however, appears to be waning.

In the Gallup Poll's latest sounding, 70% favor and 25% oppose handgun registration, representing a slight shift toward control since 1982, when 66% favored registration and 30% opposed it. The current proregistration majority includes 61% of persons from households possessing guns of any kind, and 56% of those from homes in which handguns in particular are owned. Nonowners favor registration by almost a 5-to-1 ratio, 78% to 16%.

The Gallup Poll periodically has assessed public opinion on many handgun control measures and consistently has found Americans throughout the nation and from all walks of life supportive of stricter handgun laws. However, while the public heavily endorses more stringent controls, it has stopped short of favoring an outright ban on the sale or possession of handguns.

The Chicago suburb of Morton Grove, Illinois, made national headlines in 1981 when it became the first municipality in the United States to enact an ordinance prohibiting both the sale and possession of handguns. The Morton Grove ordinance has withstood all legal challenges. In the current Gallup survey, 40% favor having their city or community pass a law or ordinance similar to Morton Grove's, while 56% are opposed. This represents a shift toward greater opposition since the question was first asked two years ago, when 44% favored and 48% opposed a local ban on the sale and possession of handguns.

Today, men oppose the handgun ban by a 2-to-1 margin, while women are very evenly divided. Majority opposition is found in every geographical region but the East, and in all but the very largest metropolitan areas. Whites oppose the measure, while blacks are closely divided. Nonowners and persons favoring registration are fairly evenly split.

MAY 30
RELIGION

Interviewing Date: Various Dates During 1984 and 1985
Various Surveys

At the present time, do you think religion as a whole is increasing its influence on American life, or losing its influence?

Selected National Trend*

	Increasing	Losing
1985	48%	39%
1984	42	39
1983	44	42
1981	38	46
1980	35	46
1978	37	48
1977	36	45
1976	44	45
1975	39	51

1974	31	56
1970	14	75
1969	14	70
1968	18	67
1967	23	57
1965	33	45
1962	45	31
1957	69	14

*"The same" or "no opinion" is excluded.

Do you believe that religion can answer all or most of today's problems, or that religion is largely old fashioned and out of date?

Selected National Trend

	Can answer	Out of date	No opinion
1985	61%	22%	17%
1984	56	21	23
1982	60	22	18
1981	65	15	20
1974	62	20	18
1957	81	7	12

Note: A growing number of respondents believe religion is increasing its influence on American life, with 48% currently holding this opinion compared to 39% who think religion is losing its influence. The proportion who sees religion gaining in impact on society is now more than three times that recorded in 1969, when 14% said religion was increasing its influence and 70% said losing. When this index was started in 1957, 69% saw religion gaining influence on American life, while far fewer (14%) said losing.

The uptrend in those saying religion is increasing its influence parallels a slight upturn in those who believe that religion can answer all or most of today's problems—from 56% in 1984 to 61% in the latest survey. These trends have not generally run parallel. The current figure, however, is 20 points lower than that recorded in the first measurement in 1957, when 81% thought religion could provide answers for contemporary problems.

Following are the latest findings on religious involvement and practice, as well as confidence in the church:

1) Ninety-one percent of Americans currently state a religious preference, statistically the same as recorded since the late 1970s.

2) Sixty-eight percent say they are members of a church or synagogue, statistically unchanged from the mid-1970s.

3) Forty percent of adults attend a church or synagogue in a typical week, with little change since the mid-1960s.

4) Fifty-six percent say religion is very important in their lives, representing little change over the last half decade.

5) Finally, the percentage which expresses a great deal, or quite a lot, of confidence in the church or organized religion—65% in the latest survey—has remained remarkably flat over the last decade.

JUNE 2
PERSONAL LIVES/OUTLOOK FOR THE NATION

Interviewing Date: 3/8–11/85
Survey #251-G

Here is a picture of a ladder. Suppose we say that the top of the ladder represents the best possible life for you, and the bottom represents the worst possible life for you. On which step of the ladder do you feel you personally stand at the present time? On which step would you say you stood five years ago? Just your best guess, on which step do you think you will stand in the future, say about five years from now?

The following figures represent weighed average ratings on the 11-point ladder scale, with 10 representing the best situation and 0 the worst:

Five years ago 5.7
Today 6.4
Five years hence 7.6

Selected National Trend

	Five years ago	Today	Five years hence
1982	5.9	6.3	6.5
1981	6.0	6.4	7.3
1976	5.7	6.7	7.7
1974	5.5	6.6	7.4
1972	5.5	6.4	7.6
1971	5.8	6.6	7.5
1964	6.0	6.9	7.9
1959	5.9	6.6	7.8

Looking at the ladder again, suppose the top represents the best possible situation for our country, the bottom the worst possible situation. Please show me on which step of the ladder you think the United States is at the present time. On which step would you say the United States was five years ago? Just your best guess, if things go pretty much as you now expect, where do you think the United States will be on the ladder, say about five years from now?

The following figures represent weighed average ratings on the 11-point ladder scale, with 10 representing the best situation and 0 the worst:

Five years ago 5.3
Today 5.9
Five years hence 6.6

Selected National Trend

	Five years ago	Today	Five years hence
1982	6.5	5.3	6.0
1981	6.0	5.1	6.3
1976	6.0	5.5	6.1
1974	6.3	4.8	5.8
1972	5.6	5.5	6.2
1971	6.2	5.4	6.2
1964	6.1	6.5	7.7
1959	6.5	6.7	7.4

Note: American adults, when asked to contemplate the quality of their lives in the next five years, exhibit a level of optimism not surpassed in almost a generation. Similarly, their outlook for the future of the United States is currently higher than it has been in more than twenty years.

In March, the Gallup Poll conducted a special survey in which respondents reported their hopes and aspirations, fears and anxieties, both for themselves and for the nation. In addition to their verbal descriptions, they were asked to rate their lives today, five years ago, and five years from now, using a scaling device created in the late 1950s by Hadley Cantril, one of the pioneers in the development of scientific polling techniques.

After concentrating on and describing their lives in the best possible light—what their future lives would look like if they are to be happy—as well as in the worst possible light, respondents were handed a card depicting a ladder. Simply put, in the current survey respondents give their present lives a 6.4 rating, roughly two-thirds of the way up the ladder; their lives five years ago a 5.7 rating, or somewhat below their present lives; and their lives five years from now a 7.6 rating, or well above both their present and past ratings.

The public's current optimism represents a sharp upturn from 1982, when perceptions of the future doubtless were clouded by the recession. The latest figures closely resemble those recorded in 1972, a prosperous year with low inflation and unemployment.

A comparison of personal and national findings shows that the public consistently has expressed greater optimism about their personal lives rather than about the nation as a whole. However, the latest ratings indicate a high degree of current satisfaction with the nation, and the strongest expression of optimism since the beginning of the Vietnam War era.

JUNE 6
ELECTORAL REFORMS

Interviewing Date: 5/17–20/85
Survey #253-G

It has been proposed that four individual regional primaries be held in different weeks of June during a presidential election year. Does this sound to you like a good idea, or a poor idea?

Good idea 40%
Poor idea 34
No opinion 26

By Education
College Graduate

Good idea 41%
Poor idea 34
No opinion 25

College Incomplete

Good idea 44%
Poor idea 35
No opinion 21

High-School Graduate

Good idea 40%
Poor idea 33
No opinion 27

Less Than High-School Graduate

Good idea 36%
Poor idea 33
No opinion 31

By Region
East

Good idea 39%
Poor idea 36
No opinion 25

Midwest

Good idea 42%
Poor idea 36
No opinion 22

South

Good idea 38%
Poor idea 31
No opinion 31

West

Good idea 40%
Poor idea 33
No opinion 27

By Age
18–29 Years

Good idea 45%
Poor idea 26
No opinion 29

30–49 Years

Good idea 42%
Poor idea 36
No opinion 22

50 Years and Over

Good idea 34%
Poor idea 37
No opinion 29

By Politics
Republicans

Good idea 38%
Poor idea 36
No opinion 26

Democrats

Good idea 42%
Poor idea 34
No opinion 24

Independents

Good idea 40%
Poor idea 31
No opinion 29

Selected National Trend

	Good idea	Poor idea	No opinion
1984	45%	30%	25%
1982	44	33	23

Note: A proposal for selecting presidential candidates in four regional primaries, instead of the present system of individual state ones, receives a mixed response from the public despite growing support from political party leaders. In the latest Gallup Poll, 40% favor the regional primaries plan, while 34% oppose it and 26% do not offer an opinion. The latest findings represent a modest decline since last year, when 45% backed the proposal and 30% opposed it.

Gallup surveys consistently have found the public to favor a variety of electoral reforms designed to improve the nominating process. In each of eight national surveys conducted since 1952, for example, a heavy majority has voted in favor of a single nationwide primary election to choose presidential candidates instead of by political party conventions, as at present.

Southern Democratic party officials recently expressed support for selecting their party's 1988 presidential nominee through this process of regional primaries. One of their principal objectives would be to reduce what they see as a disproportionate influence of the results of the Iowa caucuses and the New Hampshire primary, historically held early in each presidential year.

In the current poll, slim pluralities of Democrats and independents back the regional primary plan, while Republicans are evenly divided between those who favor and oppose it. Regional reactions also are mixed, with roughly equal proportions from each area supporting and opposing the proposal. Slightly greater backing is found among younger adults.

JUNE 9
PRESIDENT REAGAN

Interviewing Date: 5/17–20/85
Survey #253-G

Do you approve or disapprove of the way Ronald Reagan is handling his job as president?

Approve 55%
Disapprove 37
No opinion 8

By Sex

Male

Approve 57%
Disapprove 35
No opinion 8

Female

Approve 53%
Disapprove 38
No opinion 9

By Ethnic Background

White

Approve 60%
Disapprove 32
No opinion 8

Nonwhite

Approve 21%
Disapprove 68
No opinion 11

Black

Approve 18%
Disapprove 72
No opinion 10

By Education

College Graduate

Approve 63%
Disapprove 33
No opinion 4

College Incomplete

Approve 64%
Disapprove 30
No opinion 6

High-School Graduate

Approve 54%
Disapprove 39
No opinion 7

Less Than High-School Graduate

Approve 43%
Disapprove 43
No opinion 14

By Region

East

Approve 50%
Disapprove 41
No opinion 9

Midwest

Approve 54%
Disapprove 40
No opinion 6

South

Approve 57%
Disapprove 33
No opinion 10

West

Approve 59%
Disapprove 32
No opinion 9

By Age

18–29 Years

Approve 60%
Disapprove 33
No opinion 7

30–49 Years

Approve 56%
Disapprove 35
No opinion 9

50 Years and Over

Approve 50%
Disapprove 41
No opinion 9

By Income

$25,000 and Over

Approve 63%
Disapprove 31
No opinion 6

Under $25,000

Approve 49%
Disapprove 41
No opinion 10

By Politics

Republicans

Approve 87%
Disapprove 9
No opinion 4

Democrats

Approve 24%
Disapprove 66
No opinion 10

Independents

Approve 55%
Disapprove 34
No opinion 11

By Occupation

Professional and Business

Approve 64%
Disapprove 30
No opinion 6

Clerical and Sales

Approve 57%
Disapprove 37
No opinion 6

Manual Workers

Approve 51%
Disapprove 40
No opinion 9

Nonlabor Force

Approve 48%
Disapprove 40
No opinion 12

Selected National Trend

	Approve	Dis-approve	No opinion
1985			
April 12–15	52%	37%	11%
March 8–11	56	37	7
February 15–18	60	31	9
January 25–28	64	28	8
January 11–14	62	29	9
1984			
December 7–10	59	32	9
November 30– December 3	62	30	8
November 9–12	61	31	8

Do you approve or disapprove of President Reagan's visiting the Bitburg cemetery?

Approve 42%
Disapprove 42
No opinion 16

By Sex

Male

Approve 45%
Disapprove 39
No opinion 16

Female

Approve 40%
Disapprove 44
No opinion 16

By Ethnic Background

White

Approve 44%
Disapprove 40
No opinion 16

Nonwhite

Approve 26%
Disapprove 56
No opinion 18

Black

Approve 26%
Disapprove 57
No opinion 17

By Education
College Graduate

Approve 48%
Disapprove 36
No opinion 16

College Incomplete

Approve 46%
Disapprove 38
No opinion 16

High-School Graduate

Approve 44%
Disapprove 42
No opinion 14

Less Than High-School Graduate

Approve 33%
Disapprove 48
No opinion 19

By Region
East

Approve 38%
Disapprove 49
No opinion 13

Midwest

Approve 47%
Disapprove 40
No opinion 13

South

Approve 43%
Disapprove 38
No opinion 19

West

Approve 40%
Disapprove 41
No opinion 19

By Age
18–29 Years

Approve 47%
Disapprove 35
No opinion 18

30–49 Years

Approve 42%
Disapprove 41
No opinion 17

50 Years and Over

Approve 38%
Disapprove 48
No opinion 14

By Politics
Republicans

Approve 60%
Disapprove 25
No opinion 15

Democrats

Approve 26%
Disapprove 60
No opinion 14

Independents

Approve 40%
Disapprove 41
No opinion 19

Did you happen to see, hear, or read about President Reagan's embargo on trade with Nicaragua?

	Yes
National	54%

Asked of those who replied in the affirmative: Do you approve or disapprove of the embargo on trade with Nicaragua?

Approve	46%
Disapprove	37
No opinion	17

By Sex
Male

Approve	53%
Disapprove	37
No opinion	10

Female

Approve	37%
Disapprove	37
No opinion	26

By Ethnic Background
White

Approve	49%
Disapprove	32
No opinion	19

Nonwhite

Approve	19%
Disapprove	73
No opinion	8

Black

Approve	18%
Disapprove	75
No opinion	7

By Education
College Graduate

Approve	47%
Disapprove	37
No opinion	16

College Incomplete

Approve	46%
Disapprove	34
No opinion	20

High-School Graduate

Approve	47%
Disapprove	36
No opinion	17

Less Than High-School Graduate

Approve	42%
Disapprove	43
No opinion	15

By Region
East

Approve	44%
Disapprove	40
No opinion	16

Midwest

Approve	41%
Disapprove	41
No opinion	18

South

Approve	53%
Disapprove	30
No opinion	17

West

Approve 43%
Disapprove 39
No opinion 18

By Age
18–24 Years

Approve 42%
Disapprove 36
No opinion 22

25–29 Years

Approve 38%
Disapprove 36
No opinion 26

30–49 Years

Approve 48%
Disapprove 36
No opinion 16

50 Years and Over

Approve 46%
Disapprove 38
No opinion 16

By Politics
Republicans

Approve 65%
Disapprove 16
No opinion 19

Democrats

Approve 26%
Disapprove 58
No opinion 16

Independents

Approve 45%
Disapprove 38
No opinion 17

By Religion
Protestants

Approve 49%
Disapprove 34
No opinion 17

Catholics

Approve 46%
Disapprove 35
No opinion 19

Note: Although a substantial proportion of Americans faults President Ronald Reagan for both his visit to the Bitburg cemetery and his embargo on trade with Nicaragua, his overall standing with the public seems not to have suffered. In fact, the recent decline in the president's performance rating, from 64% approval in late January to 52% in mid-April, now appears to have ended. In the latest Gallup Poll, 55% approve of Reagan's overall performance in office, while 37% disapprove and 8% withhold judgment. The latest survey was conducted prior to the announcement of the president's tax proposal.

While the 3-percentage point improvement since April in Reagan's competency rating in itself is not statistically significant, it nonetheless marks the first rise in his ratings' trend in almost four months. While the president's approval ratings have fluctuated since March, the proportion disapproving has remained at a steady 37% in all three surveys conducted during this period, with an unusually high 11% undecided vote recorded in the April survey. The hypothesis was advanced at that time that some people may have switched from being moderate Reagan supporters to fence sitters, awaiting future developments before recommitting themselves. If that hypothesis still holds, the new survey findings suggest that these quondam fence sitters, in fact, are recommitting themselves, and in the president's favor.

The current reversal in Reagan's downward trend in approval since early this year also marks a return to the president's camp of certain population segments that had been among the heaviest defectors in the April survey. At that time, for example, an 11-percentage point difference separated the views of men and women, with 58% of men but only 47% of women approving of Reagan's job performance; this suggested a return of the now familiar "gender gap" that has plagued Reagan throughout his presidential tenure. With the new survey, the gap has returned to a more typical 4 points, with 57% of men and 53% of women approving of his conduct in office.

Public opinion about the controversial Bitburg affair is evenly divided, with 42% approving and an equal percentage disapproving of the president's May 5 visit to the German military cemetery. Somewhat greater approval is expressed by men, younger Americans of both sexes, college educated and upper income groups, and Republicans, than by their counterparts. However, even among these strong Reagan constituencies, significant proportions disapprove of the Bitburg visit, including 25% of Republicans.

For the Nicaragua question, more support is drawn from those in favor of the president's trade embargo: 46% approve, while 37% disapprove and 17% offer no opinion. Men outnumber women in their approval by 53% to 37%, but whites (49%) far outstrip nonwhites (19%) and blacks (18%) in support of the embargo against trade with Nicaragua. Categories are fairly even across lines of education, region, age, and religion, but Republicans sharply outnumber Democrats in their approval by 65% to 26%.

JUNE 13
INFLATION AND UNEMPLOYMENT

Interviewing Date: 5/17–20/85
Survey #253-G

The inflation rate is now running at about 4%. By this time next year, what do you think the inflation rate will be?

	May 1985*	Dec. 1983**	Nov. 1982†
9% or higher	5%	15%	24%
8%	9	10	16
7%	6	15	9
6%	18	12	17
5%	13	22	10
4% or lower	35	16	8
No opinion	14	10	16
Median average	5.4%	6.1%	7.3%

The current unemployment rate is now 7.3%. By this time next year, what do you think the unemployment rate will be?

	May 1985*	Dec. 1983**	Nov. 1982†
10% or higher	16%	17%	58%
9%	10	9	12
8%	20	21	10
7%	24	16	4
6%	12	9	2
5% or lower	6	19	1
No opinion	12	9	13
Median average	7.8%	7.6%	10.1%

*In mid-1986
**At the end of 1984
†At the end of 1983

Misery Index

	Inflation rate	Unemployment rate	Total
	Median Averages		
National	5.4%	7.8%	13.2%

By Ethnic Background

White	5.3%	7.7%	13.0%
Black	6.5	8.8	15.3

By Education

College	5.1%	7.5%	12.6%
High school or less	5.6	8.0	13.6

By Income

$25,000 and over	5.2%	7.6%	12.8%
Under $25,000 ...	5.5	8.0	13.5

By Politics

Republicans	4.8%	7.2%	12.0%
Democrats	6.0	8.4	14.4
Independents	5.4	7.8	13.2

Misery Index Trend

		Median Averages		
	Year-end forecasts	Inflation rate	Unemploy-ment rate	Total
December 1983	1984	6.1%	7.6%	13.7%
November 1982	1983	7.3	10.7	18.0
June 1982	1982	7.9	10.6	18.5
January 1982	1982	10.2	9.4	19.6
March 1981	1981	13.5	8.2	21.7
November 1980	1981	13.6	7.1	20.7

Note: Americans' ongoing optimism about the nation's economy is reflected in their current forecast of what the "misery index" will be at this time next year. The index—a combination of the public's estimates of the inflation and unemployment rates—now stands at 13.2%, the lowest level recorded since Gallup began this economic barometer soon after the 1980 presidential election.

In the latest Gallup Poll, the public's average estimate of the inflation rate one year from now is 5.4%. Their estimate of the unemployment rate in mid-1986 is 7.8%. The public's forecasts are slightly higher than the current government estimates of about 4% inflation and 7.3% unemployment (where it has remained for the last four months).

The misery index was created in 1976 by presidential candidate Jimmy Carter to dramatize the failure of the Ford administration to improve the economy. Candidate Ronald Reagan, in turn, found the index an effective political weapon to use against President Carter during the 1980 campaign. Reagan's landslide reelection last November was heavily dependent on the strength of the national economy.

JUNE 16

CONFIDENCE IN AMERICA TO DEAL WITH WORLD PROBLEMS

Interviewing Date: 5/17–20/85
Survey #253-G

How much confidence do you have in the ability of the United States to deal wisely with present world problems—very great, considerable, or very little confidence?

Very great	19%
Considerable	49
Little	19
Very little	11
None (volunteered)	1
No opinion	1

By Sex
Male

Very great	20%
Considerable	44
Little	21
Very little	13
None (volunteered)	1
No opinion	1

Female

Very great	18%
Considerable	54
Little	16
Very little	9
None (volunteered)	1
No opinion	2

By Ethnic Background
White

Very great	19%
Considerable	50
Little	19

Very little 11
None (volunteered) . . . . *
No opinion 1

Nonwhite

Very great 17%
Considerable 41
Little 17
Very little 19
None (volunteered) 4
No opinion 2

Black

Very great 19%
Considerable 40
Little 18
Very little 16
None (volunteered) 5
No opinion 2

By Education
College Graduate

Very great 14%
Considerable 54
Little 22
Very little 8
None (volunteered) 1
No opinion 1

College Incomplete

Very great 18%
Considerable 55
Little 18
Very little 7
None (volunteered) 1
No opinion 1

High-School Graduate

Very great 17%
Considerable 51
Little 16
Very little 14
None (volunteered) 1
No opinion 1

Less Than High-School Graduate

Very great 24%
Considerable 38
Little 20
Very little 16
None (volunteered) . . . . *
No opinion 2

By Age
18–29 Years

Very great 15%
Considerable 52
Little 20
Very little 11
None (volunteered) 1
No opinion 1

30–49 Years

Very great 17%
Considerable 52
Little 18
Very little 11
None (volunteered) 1
No opinion 1

50 Years and Over

Very great 23%
Considerable 44
Little 18
Very little 12
None (volunteered) 1
No opinion 2

By Politics
Republicans

Very great 24%
Considerable 56
Little 15
Very little 5
None (volunteered) . . . . *
No opinion . . . . *

Democrats

Very great	16%
Considerable	45
Little	20
Very little	16
None (volunteered)	1
No opinion	2

Independents

Very great	16%
Considerable	47
Little	22
Very little	12
None (volunteered)	1
No opinion	2

Those Who Approve of Reagan's Handling of Foreign Policy (43%)

Very great	25%
Considerable	56
Little	11
Very little	7
None (volunteered)	*
No opinion	1

Those Who Disapprove of Reagan's Handling of Foreign Policy (45%)

Very great	13%
Considerable	43
Little	26
Very little	16
None (volunteered)	1
No opinion	1

*Less than 1%

Has your confidence in the ability of America to deal with world problems tended to go up lately, go down, or remain about the same?

Go up	16%
Go down	22
Remain the same	60
No opinion	2

By Sex
Male

Go up	18%
Go down	21
Remain the same	60
No opinion	1

Female

Go up	14%
Go down	23
Remain the same	61
No opinion	2

By Ethnic Background
White

Go up	17%
Go down	21
Remain the same	61
No opinion	1

Nonwhite

Go up	11%
Go down	32
Remain the same	55
No opinion	2

Black

Go up	10%
Go down	32
Remain the same	56
No opinion	2

By Education
College Graduate

Go up	15%
Go down	24
Remain the same	59
No opinion	2

College Incomplete

Go up	20%
Go down	24
Remain the same	55
No opinion	1

High-School Graduate

Go up 15%
Go down 21
Remain the same 63
No opinion 1

Less Than High-School Graduate

Go up 13%
Go down 21
Remain the same 63
No opinion 3

By Age
18–29 Years

Go up 18%
Go down 21
Remain the same 60
No opinion 1

30–49 Years

Go up 17%
Go down 23
Remain the same 59
No opinion 1

50 Years and Over

Go up 14%
Go down 21
Remain the same 63
No opinion 2

By Politics
Republicans

Go up 24%
Go down 12
Remain the same 64
No opinion .... *

Democrats

Go up 11%
Go down 30
Remain the same 57
No opinion 2

Independents

Go up 14%
Go down 24
Remain the same 60
No opinion 2

Those Who Approve of Reagan's Handling of Foreign Policy (43%)

Go up 25%
Go down 8
Remain the same 66
No opinion 1

Those Who Disapprove of Reagan's Handling of Foreign Policy (45%)

Go up 8%
Go down 37
Remain the same 54
No opinion 1

*Less than 1%

Note: A two-thirds' majority of Americans expresses at least considerable confidence in this nation's ability to deal wisely with present world problems, according to a recently completed Gallup Poll. The survey also shows evidence that recent events in the international arena have shaken some respondents' faith in our conduct of foreign policy.

In the latest Gallup survey, 68% express either very great (19%) or considerable (49%) confidence in U.S. competency in foreign affairs. Far fewer say they have little (19%), very little (11%), or no confidence at all (1%). In the same survey, 60% report their confidence in America's ability to cope with world problems has not changed recently, while 16% say it has gone up and 22%, gone down.

When the same questions were asked five years ago during the Carter administration, only 53% expressed considerable or more confidence in U.S. ability to deal with world problems, compared to the 68% who now do so. In the 1980 survey, a 45% plurality also said their confidence in our ability had gone down recently, while 10% said it had gone up and 41% that it was unchanged.

Those findings were recorded after a period of confrontations and diplomatic setbacks for the United States in international affairs, including the failure to secure the release of American hostages in Iran, the Soviet invasion of Afghanistan, and the breakdown of the SALT II ratification.

Perhaps surprisingly, the current national majority expressing at least considerable confidence in America's ability in world affairs, in addition to receiving heavy backing in Republican-oriented population groups, also includes majorities of Democrats (61%), blacks (59%), persons whose formal education ended before graduation from high school (62%), and those from other groups that tend to be hostile toward the Reagan administration's policies. In fact, a 56% majority of survey respondents who specifically disapprove of President Ronald Reagan's handling of foreign policy nonetheless say they have very great or considerable confidence in America's ability to deal wisely with world affairs.

JUNE 20
MARIJUANA

Interviewing Date: 5/17–20/85
Survey #253-G

Do you think the use of marijuana should be made legal, or not?

Should 23%
Should not 73
No opinion 4

By Sex
Male

Should 29%
Should not 68
No opinion 3

Female

Should 18%
Should not 78
No opinion 4

By Ethnic Background
White

Should 22%
Should not 74
No opinion 4

Nonwhite

Should 30%
Should not 66
No opinion 4

Black

Should 31%
Should not 64
No opinion 5

By Education
College Graduate

Should 29%
Should not 67
No opinion 4

College Incomplete

Should 29%
Should not 68
No opinion 3

High-School Graduate

Should 20%
Should not 77
No opinion 3

Less Than High-School Graduate

Should 18%
Should not 78
No opinion 4

By Region
East

Should 28%
Should not 69
No opinion 3

Midwest

Should	20%
Should not	76
No opinion	4

South

Should	20%
Should not	76
No opinion	4

West

Should	26%
Should not	71
No opinion	3

By Age
18–24 Years

Should	28%
Should not	69
No opinion	3

25–29 Years

Should	30%
Should not	62
No opinion	8

30–49 Years

Should	27%
Should not	70
No opinion	3

50–64 Years

Should	16%
Should not	82
No opinion	2

65 Years and Over

Should	13%
Should not	83
No opinion	4

By Income
$50,000 and Over

Should	23%
Should not	74
No opinion	3

$35,000–$49,999

Should	26%
Should not	69
No opinion	5

$25,000–$34,999

Should	22%
Should not	75
No opinion	3

$15,000–$24,999

Should	23%
Should not	73
No opinion	4

$10,000–$14,999

Should	25%
Should not	73
No opinion	2

Under $10,000

Should	19%
Should not	76
No opinion	5

By Politics
Republicans

Should	17%
Should not	79
No opinion	4

Democrats

Should	24%
Should not	72
No opinion	4

Independents

Should 30%
Should not 68
No opinion 2

By Religion
Protestants

Should 18%
Should not 79
No opinion 3

Catholics

Should 22%
Should not 73
No opinion 5

By Occupation
Professional and Business

Should 26%
Should not 70
No opinion 4

Clerical and Sales

Should 23%
Should not 76
No opinion 1

Manual Workers

Should 25%
Should not 72
No opinion 3

Nonlabor Force

Should 15%
Should not 82
No opinion 3

Selected National Trend

	Favor	Oppose	No opinion
1980	25%	70%	5%
1979	25	70	5
1977	28	66	6

1973	16	78	6
1972	15	81	4
1969	12	84	4

Do you think the possession of small amounts of marijuana should or should not be treated as a criminal offense?

Should 50%
Should not 46
No opinion 4

By Sex
Male

Should 45%
Should not 52
No opinion 3

Female

Should 55%
Should not 40
No opinion 5

By Ethnic Background
White

Should 50%
Should not 46
No opinion 4

Nonwhite

Should 48%
Should not 46
No opinion 6

Black

Should 46%
Should not 46
No opinion 8

By Education
College Graduate

Should 41%
Should not 56
No opinion 3

College Incomplete

Should 47%
Should not 48
No opinion 5

High-School Graduate

Should 52%
Should not 45
No opinion 3

Less Than High-School Graduate

Should 56%
Should not 39
No opinion 5

By Region
East

Should 40%
Should not 56
No opinion 4

Midwest

Should 54%
Should not 44
No opinion 2

South

Should 57%
Should not 39
No opinion 4

West

Should 47%
Should not 48
No opinion 5

By Age
18–24 Years

Should 47%
Should not 49
No opinion 4

25–29 Years

Should 40%
Should not 56
No opinion 4

30–49 Years

Should 46%
Should not 50
No opinion 4

50–64 Years

Should 59%
Should not 39
No opinion 2

65 Years and Over

Should 60%
Should not 35
No opinion 5

By Income
$50,000 and Over

Should 48%
Should not 49
No opinion 3

$35,000–$49,999

Should 48%
Should not 49
No opinion 3

$25,000–$34,999

Should 49%
Should not 48
No opinion 3

$15,000–$24,999

Should 50%
Should not 44
No opinion 6

$10,000–$14,999

Should 51%
Should not 47
No opinion 2

Under $10,000

Should 56%
Should not 39
No opinion 5

By Politics
Republicans

Should 57%
Should not 38
No opinion 5

Democrats

Should 51%
Should not 46
No opinion 3

Independents

Should 39%
Should not 57
No opinion 4

By Religion
Protestants

Should 57%
Should not 39
No opinion 4

Catholics

Should 44%
Should not 52
No opinion 4

By Occupation
Professional and Business

Should 46%
Should not 51
No opinion 3

Clerical and Sales

Should 45%
Should not 54
No opinion 1

Manual Workers

Should 50%
Should not 46
No opinion 4

Nonlabor Force

Should 57%
Should not 37
No opinion 6

Selected National Trend

	Favor	Oppose	No opinion
1980	43%	52%	5%
1977	41	53	6

Note: The ground swell of public opinion in the mid-1970s toward more liberal marijuana laws appears to have run its course. Fewer respondents today than at any time since 1977 favor either legalizing the use of marijuana or removing the criminal sanctions on its possession. The latest Gallup Poll finds 23% voting in favor of, and 73% opposed to, legalization, not significantly different from the 25% to 70% division of opinion in both 1980 and 1979, but well below the 28% to 66% recorded in 1977. Earlier surveys found little public support for legalizing the use of marijuana.

Similarly, 50% currently say that the possession of small amounts of marijuana should be treated as a criminal offense, while 46% disagree. In 1980 and 1977, small majorities backed the removal of criminal penalties for possession.

Young adults (18 to 29 years) and persons who attended college—groups in which the highest incidence of marijuana use is found—continue to evince somewhat more liberal attitudes toward pot than do their counterparts. However, the greatest shifts toward mainstream viewpoints have occurred among these groups:

Legalization of Use of Marijuana

(Percent Opposing)

	1985	1977	Point change
18–29 years	66%	46%	+20
30–49 years	70	68	+ 2
50 years and over	82	80	+ 2
College education	68%	51%	+17
High school	77	69	+ 8
Grade school	78	81	− 3

Possession of Marijuana Treated as Criminal Offense

(Percent Favoring)

	1985	1977	Point change
18–29 years	44%	29%	+15
30–49 years	46	45	+ 1
50 years and over	59	48	+11
College education	45%	25%	+20
High school	53	46	+ 7
Grade school	58	55	+ 3

JUNE 23
MOST IMPORTANT PROBLEM

Interviewing Date: 5/17–20/85
Survey #253-G

What do you think is the most important problem facing this country today?

	May 17–20, 1985	Jan. 1985	Aug. 1984
Threat of war; international tensions	23%	27%	2%
Unemployment	21	20	23
High cost of living; taxes	11	12	18
Excessive government spending; budget deficit	10	18	16
Economy (general)	8	6	8
Poverty; hunger	6	6	3

Moral, religious decline in society	6	2	3
Drug abuse	6	2	1
Crime	4	4	4
All others	21	16	13
No opinion	3	3	3
	119%*	116%*	114%*

*Total adds to more than 100% due to multiple responses.

All persons who named a problem were then asked: Which political party do you think can do a better job of handling the problem you have just mentioned—the Republican party or the Democratic party?

	May 17–20, 1985	Jan. 1985	Aug. 1984
Republican party	37%	39%	28%
Democratic party	31	29	35
No difference (volunteered)	23	24	24
No opinion	9	8	13

Note: International tensions and unemployment are the dominant concerns of the American people. Named next most often is the high cost of living, followed by government spending and the federal budget deficit.

In the latest Gallup Poll, threat of war and international unrest are cited by 23% as the most important problem facing the nation, with unemployment named by 21%, the high cost of living by 11%, and government spending by 10%. Concern over excessive government spending has declined from 18% in January; then it increased sharply from the year before, when 12% named it the nation's top problem. The economy in general, named by 8%, continues to trouble many Americans, with others citing poverty and hunger (6%), a perceived moral and religious decline (6%), drug abuse (6%), and crime (4%).

Unemployment, while still a serious problem, has declined slowly in the public's view as the nation's top concern. The current figure of 21% closely matches the 20% recorded in January, the lowest since the 1981–82 recession. In sharp contrast, in October 1982, 62% named unemployment as the major problem facing the nation. International tensions were mentioned in that survey by merely 6%, only one-fourth the current level.

A higher proportion of the public now believes the Republican party (37%), rather than the Democratic party (31%), can better handle the problem they consider most important. Throughout 1984, the public was evenly divided between the two parties, with the GOP reaching ascendancy last January. For each of the two preceding years, the Democratic party was the public's consistent preference. The Democrats' strongest recent showing occurred in April 1983, when they were the 2-to-1 choice over the GOP as better able to handle the most important problems facing the country, 41% to 20%. In May 1981, the Republicans led the Democrats on this key measurement, 36% to 21%.

JUNE 27
BIGGIST THREAT TO NATION

Interviewing Date: 6/7–10/85
Survey #255-G

In your opinion, which of the following will be the biggest threat to the country in the future—big business, big labor, or big government?

Business 22%
Labor 19
Government 50
No opinion 9

By Region
East

Business 25%
Labor 18
Government 46
No opinion 11

Midwest

Business 22%
Labor 19
Government 52
No opinion 7

South

Business 20%
Labor 22
Government 48
No opinion 10

West

Business 22%
Labor 17
Government 54
No opinion 7

By Politics
Republicans

Business 12%
Labor 29
Government 53
No opinion 6

Democrats

Business 28%
Labor 12
Government 49
No opinion 11

Independents

Business 25%
Labor 19
Government 48
No opinion 8

By Occupation
Professional and Business

Business 18%
Labor 24
Government 53
No opinion 5

Clerical and Sales

Business	24%
Labor	15
Government	46
No opinion	15

Blue Collar Workers

Business	26%
Labor	15
Government	51
No opinion	8

Labor Union Households

Business	26%
Labor	12
Government	54
No opinion	8

Nonlabor Union Households

Business	21%
Labor	21
Government	49
No opinion	9

Selected National Trend

	Business	Labor	Government	No opinion
1983	19%	18%	51%	12%
1981	22	22	46	10
1979	28	17	43	12
1977	23	26	39	12
1968	12	26	46	16
1967	14	21	49	16
1959	15	41	14	30

Note: Far more Americans say that big government poses a greater threat to the nation than does either big business or big labor, a recurrent theme of the Reagan administration. In the latest Gallup Poll, 50% cite government, 22% business, and 19% labor as the greatest cause for future concern. These figures, though not significantly changed from 1983, represent a dramatic reversal in the public's views since 1959, when the question was first asked. At that time, merely 14% considered big government the greatest threat, while 41% named big labor and 15% big business.

Roughly equal proportions of Republicans (53%), Democrats (49%), and independents (48%) currently cite big government. However, Republicans and Democrats are sharply divided on whether big labor or big business represents the second greatest threat. Among Republicans, 29% single out labor and 12% business; among Democrats, these figures are virtually reversed, with 12% citing labor and 28% business.

JUNE 30
REAGAN'S TAX PROPOSALS

Interviewing Date: 6/7–10/85
Survey #254-G

President Ronald Reagan recently announced his plan for overhauling the federal tax system. From everything you've heard or read about it, do you think the amount of taxes you now pay would go down a lot, go down a little, go up a little, go up a lot, or stay about the same if the Reagan tax plan were put into effect?

Go down a lot	2%
Go down a little	24
Go up a little	19
Go up a lot	11
Stay same	30
No opinion	14

By Sex
Male

Go down	29%
Go up	28
Stay same	32
No opinion	11

Female

Go down	23%
Go up	34
Stay same	27
No opinion	16

By Ethnic Background
White

Go down 27%
Go up 31
Stay same 30
No opinion 12

Black

Go down 18%
Go up 33
Stay same 24
No opinion 25

By Education
College Graduate

Go down 25%
Go up 38
Stay same 30
No opinion 7

College Incomplete

Go down 29%
Go up 32
Stay same 30
No opinion 9

High-School Graduate

Go down 27%
Go up 31
Stay same 28
No opinion 14

Less Than High-School Graduate

Go down 20%
Go up 25
Stay same 33
No opinion 22

By Politics
Republicans

Go down 31%
Go up 25
Stay same 34
No opinion 10

Democrats

Go down 22%
Go up 34
Stay same 29
No opinion 15

Independents

Go down 24%
Go up 34
Stay same 28
No opinion 14

By Income
$35,000 and Over

Go down 25%
Go up 39
Stay same 29
No opinion 7

$15,000–$34,999

Go down 29%
Go up 30
Stay same 28
No opinion 13

Under $15,000

Go down 23%
Go up 25
Stay same 33
No opinion 19

Next, I'd like your opinion about how some other groups would be affected. For each group I name, please tell me whether you think their taxes would go up, go down, or stay about the same under the new plan:

Wealthy families?

Go up 31%
Go down 34
Stay same 23
No opinion 12

Middle income families?

Go up 40%
Go down 21
Stay same 29
No opinion 10

Poor families?

Go up 17%
Go down 48
Stay same 24
No opinion 11

Large companies?

Go up 45%
Go down 23
Stay same 19
No opinion 13

Small companies?

Go up 36%
Go down 18
Stay same 29
No opinion 17

Do you think the new plan would make for a fairer distribution of the tax load among all taxpayers, one that's less fair, or wouldn't it be much different from the present system?

Fairer tax load 31%
Less fair 21
Not much different 34
No opinion 14

By Sex
Male

Fairer tax load 33%
Less fair 21
Not much different 35
No opinion 11

Female

Fairer tax load 28%
Less fair 22
Not much different 35
No opinion 18

By Ethnic Background
White

Fairer tax load 33%
Less fair 20
Not much different 34
No opinion 13

Black

Fairer tax load 14%
Less fair 29
Not much different 30
No opinion 27

By Education
College Graduate

Fairer tax load 44%
Less fair 19
Not much different 30
No opinion 7

College Incomplete

Fairer tax load 33%
Less fair 22
Not much different 33
No opinion 12

High-School Graduate

Fairer tax load 29%
Less fair 22
Not much different 34
No opinion 15

Less Than High-School Graduate

Fairer tax load 18%
Less fair 22
Not much different 38
No opinion 22

By Politics

Republicans

Fairer tax load 47%
Less fair 13
Not much different 30
No opinion 10

Democrats

Fairer tax load 19%
Less fair 28
Not much different 36
No opinion 17

Independents

Fairer tax load 28%
Less fair 21
Not much different 35
No opinion 16

By Income

$35,000 and Over

Fairer tax load 38%
Less fair 22
Not much different 33
No opinion 7

$15,000–$34,999

Fairer tax load 34%
Less fair 20
Not much different 35
No opinion 11

Under $15,000

Fairer tax load 23%
Less fair 22
Not much different 33
No opinion 22

Note: President Ronald Reagan's communications skills may be put to a severe test as he seeks to sell the American people on his proposed tax reform program. At present, many are undecided about its merits, while others are negatively disposed.

A majority of the public currently favors the president's overall tax program, with three in ten believing it would provide a fairer distribution of the tax load than the present system does, one in two saying it would provide tax relief for poor families, and one in four hoping that their own taxes would be reduced. Nevertheless, many disapprove of key features of the new plan, fear their taxes would increase, and believe the new tax forms would be just as difficult to fill out as the present ones.

If President Reagan's tax plan were put into effect, a 30% plurality thinks their taxes would stay about the same as they are now, while 24% think their taxes would go down a little, and 19% that theirs would go up a little. Comparatively few believe their taxes would either go up a lot (11%) or down a lot (2%). The survey reveals a fairly even division of opinion among major population groups on the probable effect of the Reagan program.

Paradoxically, Republicans as a group hold somewhat more sanguine attitudes—31% say their taxes would go down, while 25% say theirs would go up—despite the fact that upper-income and college-educated groups, key Republican constituencies, are chief among those who think their taxes would increase. Democrats and independents are slightly more inclined to the view that their taxes would go up rather than down, with this opinion more prevalent among blacks and women. Public opinion on the fairness issue also tends to follow party lines, with Republicans and Republican-oriented population groups more inclined to view the Reagan program as fairer, rather than less fair, and with Democrats holding the opposite opinion.

In a just completed face-to-face Gallup Poll that explored the Reagan tax proposals in depth, a 50% majority favors the president's overall program, while 28% are opposed and an unusually large 22% are undecided. This general assessment was made after respondents were questioned in detail about many specific facets of the tax reform plan, and thus may be said to represent their informed and considered present judgments. That as many as one in five are unable or unwilling to express an opinion undoubtedly reflects the complexity of the plan.

JULY 1
REAGAN'S TAX PROPOSALS—
CHANGE IN TAX SYSTEM

Interviewing Date: 6/7–10/85
Survey #254-G

Please tell me whether you approve or disapprove of each of these proposed changes in the tax system:

Raising more tax revenues from corporations and less from individuals?

Approve 77%
Disapprove 11
No opinion 12

By Education
College Graduate

Approve 76%
Disapprove 13
No opinion 11

College Incomplete

Approve 82%
Disapprove 12
No opinion 6

High-School Graduate

Approve 79%
Disapprove 9
No opinion 12

Less Than High-School Graduate

Approve 72%
Disapprove 10
No opinion 18

By Region
East

Approve 75%
Disapprove 12
No opinion 13

Midwest

Approve 81%
Disapprove 9
No opinion 10

South

Approve 72%
Disapprove 14
No opinion 14

West

Approve 84%
Disapprove 7
No opinion 9

By Age
18–29 Years

Approve 77%
Disapprove 11
No opinion 12

30–49 Years

Approve 77%
Disapprove 12
No opinion 11

50 Years and Over

Approve 77%
Disapprove 11
No opinion 12

By Income
$50,000 and Over

Approve 73%
Disapprove 18
No opinion 9

$35,000–$49,999

Approve 84%
Disapprove 9
No opinion 7

$25,000–$34,999

Approve 78%
Disapprove 13
No opinion 9

$15,000–$24,999

Approve 76%
Disapprove 12
No opinion 12

$10,000–$14,999

Approve 77%
Disapprove 11
No opinion 12

Under $10,000

Approve 75%
Disapprove 7
No opinion 18

By Politics
Republicans

Approve 77%
Disapprove 12
No opinion 11

Democrats

Approve 78%
Disapprove 11
No opinion 11

Independents

Approve 77%
Disapprove 10
No opinion 13

By Occupation
Professional and Business

Approve 75%
Disapprove 14
No opinion 11

Clerical and Sales

Approve 80%
Disapprove 10
No opinion 10

Manual Workers

Approve 77%
Disapprove 9
No opinion 14

Nonlabor Force

Approve 78%
Disapprove 10
No opinion 12

Labor Union Households

Approve 86%
Disapprove 7
No opinion 7

Nonlabor Union Households

Approve 75%
Disapprove 12
No opinion 13

Lowering the top tax bracket for individuals from 50% to 35%?

Approve 50%
Disapprove 35
No opinion 15

By Education
College Graduate

Approve 61%
Disapprove 31
No opinion 8

College Incomplete

Approve	52%
Disapprove	38
No opinion	10

High-School Graduate

Approve	46%
Disapprove	36
No opinion	18

Less Than High-School Graduate

Approve	44%
Disapprove	33
No opinion	23

By Region
East

Approve	48%
Disapprove	38
No opinion	14

Midwest

Approve	47%
Disapprove	37
No opinion	16

South

Approve	53%
Disapprove	28
No opinion	19

West

Approve	50%
Disapprove	39
No opinion	11

By Age
18–29 Years

Approve	50%
Disapprove	34
No opinion	16

30–49 Years

Approve	52%
Disapprove	34
No opinion	14

50 Years and Over

Approve	47%
Disapprove	37
No opinion	16

By Income
$50,000 and Over

Approve	56%
Disapprove	35
No opinion	9

$35,000–$49,999

Approve	52%
Disapprove	39
No opinion	9

$25,000–$34,999

Approve	49%
Disapprove	38
No opinion	13

$15,000–$24,999

Approve	47%
Disapprove	37
No opinion	16

$10,000–$14,999

Approve	52%
Disapprove	32
No opinion	16

Under $10,000

Approve	44%
Disapprove	31
No opinion	25

By Politics
Republicans
Approve 56%
Disapprove 32
No opinion 12

Democrats
Approve 47%
Disapprove 37
No opinion 16

Independents
Approve 47%
Disapprove 35
No opinion 18

By Occupation
Professional and Business
Approve 58%
Disapprove 33
No opinion 9

Clerical and Sales
Approve 51%
Disapprove 36
No opinion 13

Manual Workers
Approve 44%
Disapprove 35
No opinion 21

Nonlabor Force
Approve 46%
Disapprove 36
No opinion 18

Labor Union Households
Approve 48%
Disapprove 40
No opinion 12

Nonlabor Union Households
Approve 50%
Disapprove 34
No opinion 16

Allowing charitable deductions only for people who itemize their deductions?
Approve 44%
Disapprove 44
No opinion 12

By Education
College Graduate
Approve 48%
Disapprove 48
No opinion 4

College Incomplete
Approve 48%
Disapprove 46
No opinion 6

High-School Graduate
Approve 45%
Disapprove 44
No opinion 11

Less Than High-School Graduate
Approve 36%
Disapprove 39
No opinion 25

By Region
East
Approve 39%
Disapprove 46
No opinion 15

Midwest
Approve 47%
Disapprove 44
No opinion 9

South

Approve 43%
Disapprove 43
No opinion 14

West

Approve 47%
Disapprove 45
No opinion 8

By Age
18–29 Years

Approve 39%
Disapprove 48
No opinion 13

30–49 Years

Approve 44%
Disapprove 46
No opinion 10

50 Years and Over

Approve 47%
Disapprove 40
No opinion 13

By Income
$50,000 and Over

Approve 57%
Disapprove 37
No opinion 6

$35,000–$49,999

Approve 49%
Disapprove 45
No opinion 6

$25,000–$34,999

Approve 46%
Disapprove 48
No opinion 6

$15,000–$24,999

Approve 41%
Disapprove 47
No opinion 12

$10,000–$14,999

Approve 33%
Disapprove 53
No opinion 14

Under $10,000

Approve 38%
Disapprove 38
No opinion 24

By Politics
Republicans

Approve 48%
Disapprove 43
No opinion 9

Democrats

Approve 42%
Disapprove 45
No opinion 13

Independents

Approve 42%
Disapprove 45
No opinion 13

By Occupation
Professional and Business

Approve 48%
Disapprove 45
No opinion 7

Clerical and Sales

Approve 48%
Disapprove 42
No opinion 10

Manual Workers

Approve 40%
Disapprove 45
No opinion 15

Nonlabor Force

Approve 43%
Disapprove 40
No opinion 17

Labor Union Households

Approve 46%
Disapprove 48
No opinion 6

Nonlabor Union Households

Approve 43%
Disapprove 43
No opinion 14

Eliminating the present tax deduction for state and local taxes?

Approve 26%
Disapprove 58
No opinion 16

By Education
College Graduate

Approve 25%
Disapprove 67
No opinion 8

College Incomplete

Approve 31%
Disapprove 58
No opinion 11

High-School Graduate

Approve 27%
Disapprove 56
No opinion 17

Less Than High-School Graduate

Approve 20%
Disapprove 56
No opinion 24

By Region
East

Approve 24%
Disapprove 61
No opinion 15

Midwest

Approve 27%
Disapprove 60
No opinion 13

South

Approve 26%
Disapprove 52
No opinion 22

West

Approve 27%
Disapprove 63
No opinion 10

By Age
18–29 Years

Approve 32%
Disapprove 50
No opinion 18

30–49 Years

Approve 27%
Disapprove 59
No opinion 14

50 Years and Over

Approve 21%
Disapprove 64
No opinion 15

By Income

$50,000 and Over

Approve 27%
Disapprove 65
No opinion 8

$35,000–$49,999

Approve 22%
Disapprove 70
No opinion 8

$25,000–$34,999

Approve 23%
Disapprove 68
No opinion 9

$15,000–$24,999

Approve 28%
Disapprove 56
No opinion 16

$10,000–$14,999

Approve 25%
Disapprove 55
No opinion 20

Under $10,000

Approve 28%
Disapprove 42
No opinion 30

By Politics

Republicans

Approve 33%
Disapprove 55
No opinion 12

Democrats

Approve 24%
Disapprove 60
No opinion 16

Independents

Approve 21%
Disapprove 61
No opinion 18

By Occupation

Professional and Business

Approve 29%
Disapprove 61
No opinion 10

Clerical and Sales

Approve 33%
Disapprove 54
No opinion 13

Manual Workers

Approve 26%
Disapprove 56
No opinion 18

Nonlabor Force

Approve 19%
Disapprove 61
No opinion 20

Labor Union Households

Approve 17%
Disapprove 73
No opinion 10

Nonlabor Union Households

Approve 28%
Disapprove 55
No opinion 17

Taxing employer-provided health insurance up to the first $10 per month for individuals, and $25 per month for families?

Approve 23%
Disapprove 61
No opinion 16

By Education

College Graduate

Approve 21%
Disapprove 68
No opinion 11

College Incomplete

Approve 26%
Disapprove 66
No opinion 8

High-School Graduate

Approve 22%
Disapprove 60
No opinion 18

Less Than High-School Graduate

Approve 23%
Disapprove 54
No opinion 23

By Region

East

Approve 23%
Disapprove 60
No opinion 17

Midwest

Approve 25%
Disapprove 64
No opinion 11

South

Approve 22%
Disapprove 58
No opinion 20

West

Approve 23%
Disapprove 65
No opinion 12

By Age

18–29 Years

Approve 22%
Disapprove 63
No opinion 15

30–49 Years

Approve 22%
Disapprove 64
No opinion 14

50 Years and Over

Approve 25%
Disapprove 57
No opinion 18

By Income

$50,000 and Over

Approve 30%
Disapprove 61
No opinion 9

$35,000–$49,999

Approve 18%
Disapprove 74
No opinion 8

$25,000–$34,999

Approve 21%
Disapprove 68
No opinion 11

$15,000–$24,999

Approve 23%
Disapprove 62
No opinion 15

$10,000–$14,999

Approve 21%
Disapprove 60
No opinion 19

Under $10,000

Approve 27%
Disapprove 45
No opinion 28

By Politics
Republicans

Approve 28%
Disapprove 58
No opinion 14

Democrats

Approve 23%
Disapprove 60
No opinion 17

Independents

Approve 17%
Disapprove 67
No opinion 16

By Occupation
Professional and Business

Approve 24%
Disapprove 66
No opinion 10

Clerical and Sales

Approve 23%
Disapprove 63
No opinion 14

Manual Workers

Approve 21%
Disapprove 63
No opinion 16

Nonlabor Force

Approve 24%
Disapprove 50
No opinion 26

Labor Union Households

Approve 21%
Disapprove 69
No opinion 10

Nonlabor Union Households

Approve 23%
Disapprove 60
No opinion 17

All things considered, would you say you are mostly in favor of, or mostly opposed to, the new tax proposal?

Favor 49%
Oppose 29
No opinion 22

By Education
College Graduate

Favor 61%
Oppose 27
No opinion 12

College Incomplete

Favor 54%
Oppose 30
No opinion 16

High-School Graduate

Favor 47%
Oppose 30
No opinion 23

Less Than High-School Graduate

Favor 40%
Oppose 27
No opinion 33

By Region
East

Favor 41%
Oppose 36
No opinion 23

Midwest

Favor 53%
Oppose 28
No opinion 19

South

Favor 50%
Oppose 23
No opinion 27

West

Favor 55%
Oppose 29
No opinion 16

By Age
18–29 Years

Favor 48%
Oppose 32
No opinion 20

30–49 Years

Favor 51%
Oppose 28
No opinion 21

50 Years and Over

Favor 50%
Oppose 27
No opinion 23

By Income
$50,000 and Over

Favor 59%
Oppose 30
No opinion 11

$35,000–$49,999

Favor 56%
Oppose 31
No opinion 13

$25,000–$34,999

Favor 55%
Oppose 26
No opinion 19

$15,000–$24,999

Favor 51%
Oppose 29
No opinion 20

$10,000–$14,999

Favor 43%
Oppose 29
No opinion 28

Under $10,000

Favor 38%
Oppose 28
No opinion 34

By Politics
Republicans

Favor 66%
Oppose 17
No opinion 17

Democrats

Favor 39%
Oppose 37
No opinion 24

Independents

Favor 47%
Oppose 29
No opinion 24

By Occupation
Professional and Business

Favor 57%
Oppose 32
No opinion 11

Clerical and Sales

Favor 40%
Oppose 32
No opinion 28

Manual Workers

Favor 45%
Oppose 29
No opinion 26

Nonlabor Force

Favor 46%
Oppose 26
No opinion 28

Labor Union Households

Favor 46%
Oppose 33
No opinion 21

Nonlabor Union Households

Favor 50%
Oppose 28
No opinion 22

Those Who Perceive New Tax Program As Fairer Than Old

Favor 89%
Oppose 5
No opinion 6

Those Who Perceive New Tax Program As Less Fair Than Old

Favor 17%
Oppose 70
No opinion 13

Those Who Perceive New Tax Program As Not Much Different From Old

Favor 47%
Oppose 30
No opinion 23

Those Whose Taxes Would Go Down Under New Program

Favor 78%
Oppose 12
No opinion 10

Those Whose Taxes Would Stay the Same Under New Program

Favor 59%
Oppose 23
No opinion 18

Those Whose Taxes Would Go Up Under New Program

Favor 30%
Oppose 52
No opinion 18

Those Who Think Most Taxpayers Could Fill Out New Tax Forms

Favor 66%
Oppose 21
No opinion 13

Those Who Think Most Taxpayers Could Not Fill Out New Tax Forms

Favor 38%
Oppose 46
No opinion 16

In filing your federal income tax this year, did you or another family member fill out the forms yourselves, or did you pay a professional tax preparer to do them for you?

Did them ourselves 39%
Paid professional 52
Didn't have to file (volunteered) 7
Not sure 2

By Education

College Graduate

Did them ourselves 54%
Paid professional 44
Didn't have to file (volunteered) 1
Not sure 1

College Incomplete

Did them ourselves 43%
Paid professional 52
Didn't have to file (volunteered) 4
Not sure 1

High-School Graduate

Did them ourselves 38%
Paid professional 54
Didn't have to file (volunteered) 5
Not sure 3

Less Than High-School Graduate

Did them ourselves 27%
Paid professional 54
Didn't have to file (volunteered) 17
Not sure 2

By Region
East

Did them ourselves 42%
Paid professional 47
Didn't have to file (volunteered) 7
Not sure 4

Midwest

Did them ourselves 42%
Paid professional 50
Didn't have to file (volunteered) 6
Not sure 2

South

Did them ourselves 39%
Paid professional 52
Didn't have to file (volunteered) 8
Not sure 1

West

Did them ourselves 33%
Paid professional 60
Didn't have to file (volunteered) 6
Not sure 1

By Age
18–29 Years

Did them ourselves 51%
Paid professional 40
Didn't have to file (volunteered) 7
Not sure 2

30–49 Years

Did them ourselves 40%
Paid professional 56
Didn't have to file (volunteered) 3
Not sure 1

50 Years and Over

Did them ourselves 31%
Paid professional 56
Didn't have to file (volunteered) 11
Not sure 2

By Income
$50,000 and Over

Did them ourselves 41%
Paid professional 58
Didn't have to file (volunteered) 1
Not sure .... *

$35,000–$49,999

Did them ourselves 51%
Paid professional 47
Didn't have to file (volunteered) .... *
Not sure 2

$25,000–$34,999

Did them ourselves 41%
Paid professional 58
Didn't have to file (volunteered) .... *
Not sure 1

$15,000–$24,999

Did them ourselves 42%
Paid professional 52
Didn't have to file (volunteered) 4
Not sure 2

$10,000–$14,999

Did them ourselves 37%
Paid professional 53
Didn't have to file (volunteered) 8
Not sure 2

Under $10,000

Did them ourselves 28%
Paid professional 44
Didn't have to file (volunteered) 26
Not sure 2

By Politics
Republicans

Did them ourselves 41%
Paid professional 53
Didn't have to file (volunteered) 5
Not sure 1

Democrats

Did them ourselves 35%
Paid professional 54
Didn't have to file (volunteered) 9
Not sure 2

Independents

Did them ourselves 44%
Paid professional 49
Didn't have to file (volunteered) 5
Not sure 2

By Occupation
Professional and Business

Did them ourselves 49%
Paid professional 48
Didn't have to file (volunteered) 2
Not sure 1

Clerical and Sales

Did them ourselves 40%
Paid professional 49
Didn't have to file (volunteered) 8
Not sure 3

Manual Workers

Did them ourselves 40%
Paid professional 52
Didn't have to file (volunteered) 6
Not sure 2

Nonlabor Force

Did them ourselves 28%
Paid professional 54
Didn't have to file (volunteered) 17
Not sure 1

*Less than 1%

From what you've heard or read about it, do you think the new tax system would be simple enough so that most taxpayers could fill out the forms themselves?

Yes 47%
No 35
No opinion 18

By Education
College Graduate

Yes 58%
No 34
No opinion 8

College Incomplete

Yes 49%
No 37
No opinion 14

High-School Graduate

Yes 47%
No 34
No opinion 19

Less Than High-School Graduate

Yes 35%
No 36
No opinion 29

By Region

East

Yes 49%
No 34
No opinion 17

Midwest

Yes 46%
No 36
No opinion 18

South

Yes 46%
No 30
No opinion 24

West

Yes 47%
No 42
No opinion 11

By Age

18–29 Years

Yes 52%
No 29
No opinion 19

30–49 Years

Yes 52%
No 34
No opinion 14

50 Years and Over

Yes 37%
No 41
No opinion 22

By Income

$35,000 and Over

Yes 53%
No 36
No opinion 11

$15,000–$34,999

Yes 49%
No 35
No opinion 16

Under $15,000

Yes 38%
No 35
No opinion 27

By Politics

Republicans

Yes 53%
No 34
No opinion 13

Democrats

Yes 40%
No 39
No opinion 21

Independents

Yes 48%
No 32
No opinion 20

By Occupation

Professional and Business

Yes 55%
No 34
No opinion 11

Clerical and Sales

Yes 45%
No 38
No opinion 17

Manual Workers

Yes 46%
No 33
No opinion 21

Nonlabor Force

Yes 37%
No 38
No opinion 25

Those Who Had Their 1984 Tax Returns Prepared by a Professional

Yes 38%
No 45
No opinion 17

Those Who Prepared Their Own 1984 Tax Returns

Yes 60%
No 24
No opinion 16

Note: Proponents of Ronald Reagan's tax reforms now outnumber detractors by a 5-to-3 ratio. A 49% majority favors the president's overall program, while 29% are opposed and an unusually large 22% are undecided. This general assessment was made after the other questions were asked, and thus may be said to represent Americans' informed and considered present judgments.

Of five specific features explored in the survey, only one—shifting more of the tax burden from individuals to corporations—has overwhelming public support, with 77% approving and 11% disapproving. Lowering the top tax bracket for individuals from 50% to 35% is also favored, but by a narrower (and coincidental) 50% to 35% margin. An even division of opinion is found for another provision of the Reagan plan, which permits charitable deductions only for people who itemize their deductions, with 44% approving and 44% disapproving.

Two proposed features are heavily opposed. Eliminating the present deduction for state and local taxes is approved by 26% and disapproved by 58%, while taxing employer-provided health insurance benefits up to certain limits is favored by only 23% and opposed by 61%.

With few exceptions, a plurality in every population group claims their 1984 federal income taxes were prepared by professional tax services. The exceptions are 18 to 29 year olds, college graduates, persons from households in which the chief wage earner is employed in business or the professions, and those whose family income is between $35,000 and $50,000 per year.

Considering these survey findings, it is understandable that only 47% of respondents think Reagan's new tax system would be simple enough for most taxpayers to fill out their own tax returns, while 35% doubt this would be possible. About one person in five is undecided on this question, an indication that many believe they do not know enough about the president's plan to form opinions.

Persons in the survey who are accustomed to preparing their own taxes are far more confident that most taxpayers could cope with any new tax forms that the Reagan program might issue. On the other hand, those who have employed tax services to compute their taxes are skeptical that self-preparation could become the norm.

JULY 7
REPUBLICAN PRESIDENTIAL CANDIDATES

Interviewing Date: 6/7–10/85
Survey #254-G

Asked of Republicans: Would you please look over this list and tell me which of these persons, if any, you have heard of? Now will you please tell me which of these persons you know something about?

	Heard of	Know something about
George Bush	95%	82%
Robert Dole	70	51
Howard Baker	69	50
Jeane Kirkpatrick	62	42
Jesse Helms	61	39
Elizabeth Dole	59	41
James Baker	52	30
Jack Kemp	40	27
William Brock	33	18
Paul Laxalt	28	16
Pete Domenici	19	12
Richard Thornburgh	18	9

James Thompson	18	12
Richard Lugar	17	9
Robert Packwood	16	9
Thomas Kean	15	9
Lewis Lehrman	12	9
Newt Gingrich	7	4
Trent Lott	6	4

Asked of Republicans and independents: Which one of these persons would you like to see nominated as the Republican party's candidate for president in 1988? And who would be your second choice?

	Republicans*	Independents*
Bush	53%	35%
Baker, H.	22	22
Dole, R.	18	21
Kemp	10	8
Kirkpatrick	9	9
Baker, J.	5	5
Dole, E.	5	4
Helms	4	4
Thornburgh	3	3
Thompson	3	1
Kean	2	3
Domenici	2	2
Laxalt	2	1
Lehrman	2	1
Brock	2	**
Lugar	1	2
Packwood	1	2
Gingrich	**	1
Lott	**	**

*First and second choices combined
**Less than 1%

Asked of Republicans and independents: Suppose the choice for president in the Republican convention in 1988 narrows down to Howard Baker, George Bush, and Robert Dole. Which one would you prefer to have the Republican convention select? [Those who were undecided were asked: As of today, do you lean more toward Baker, Bush, or Dole for the Republican presidential nomination in 1988?]

	Republicans	Independents
Bush	58%	40%
Baker	19	25
Dole	15	19
Undecided	8	16

Note: Vice-president George Bush is the Republicans' early choice to be their party's standard-bearer in the 1988 presidential election. In the latest (mid-June) Gallup Poll, Bush receives 53% of GOP nomination votes to 22% for former Senate Majority Leader Howard Baker and 18% for present Majority Leader Robert Dole. Farther down the list of possible nominees are Representative Jack Kemp, the choice of 10%, and former UN Ambassador Jeane Kirkpatrick, with 9% of Republicans' votes.

None of the fourteen other persons on a list of nineteen possible successors to President Ronald Reagan receives more than 5% of Republicans' combined first and second choices for the GOP nomination. These include Treasury Secretary James Baker and Transportation Secretary Elizabeth Dole, each with 5%; Senator Jesse Helms of North Carolina, 4%; Illinois Governor James Thompson and Pennsylvania Governor Richard Thornburgh, each with 3%. Rounding out the list are New Jersey Governor Thomas Kean, New Mexico Senator Pete Domenici, Nevada Senator Paul Laxalt, New York businessman Lewis Lehrman, and Labor Secretary William Brock, each with 2%; Senators Richard Lugar (Indiana) and Robert Packwood (Oregon), 1% each; and Representatives Newt Gingrich (Georgia) and Trent Lott (Mississippi), each with less than 1% of the vote.

In a nomination contest pitting the three leaders—Bush, Howard Baker, and Robert Dole—against each other, Bush, with 58% of Republicans' votes, is the 3-to-1 choice over either runner-up Baker (19%) or Dole (15%), with 8% undecided. The 4% difference between the Baker and Dole vote is not statistically meaningful.

The race is somewhat closer among independents, who may vote in some state Republican primaries, but Bush nonetheless emerges as the clear winner over both his potential rivals. The vice-president is the choice of 40% of independents, Baker of 25%, and Dole of 19%, with 16% undecided. Again, the margin between Baker and Dole is a statistical standoff.

JULY 11
DEMOCRATIC PRESIDENTIAL CANDIDATES

Interviewing Date: 6/7–10/85
Survey #254-G

Asked of Democrats: Would you please look over this list and tell me which of these persons, if any, you have heard of? Now will you please tell me which of these persons you know something about?

	Heard of	Know something about
Edward Kennedy	91%	75%
Jesse Jackson	91	70
Geraldine Ferraro	86	70
Gary Hart	82	59
Lee Iacocca	57	44
Tom Bradley	50	30
Jay Rockefeller	49	22
Mario Cuomo	44	30
Dianne Feinstein	38	24
Charles Robb	30	17
Bill Bradley	28	16
Sam Nunn	20	9
Mark White	16	6
Patricia Schroeder	15	4
Dale Bumpers	14	7
Bruce Babbitt	9	4
Joseph Biden	6	3
Tony Coelho	6	2

Asked of Democrats and independents: Which one of these persons would you like to see nominated as the Democratic party's candidate for president in 1988? And who would be your second choice?

	Democrats*	Independents*
Kennedy	46%	26%
Hart	31	28
Cuomo	15	17
Jackson	14	8
Ferraro	12	7
Iacocca	11	20
Bradley, T.	5	3
Bradley, B.	4	5
Rockefeller	3	3
Robb	3	1
Feinstein	2	3
Bumpers	2	1
Nunn	1	2
Biden	1	1
White	1	1
Babbitt	1	**
Schroeder	**	**
Coelho	**	**

*First and second choices combined
**Less than 1%

Asked of Democrats and independents: Suppose the choice for president in the Democratic convention in 1988 narrows down to Gary Hart and Edward Kennedy. Which one would you prefer to have the Democratic convention select?

	Democrats	Independents
Kennedy	59%	37%
Hart	34	47
Undecided	7	16

Note: Senator Edward Kennedy of Massachusetts and Senator Gary Hart of Colorado are the top early choices of Democrats to be their party's standard-bearer in the 1988 presidential election. In the latest (mid-June) Gallup Poll, Kennedy receives 46% of combined first and second choices, while Hart receives 31%.

Four people are in the next group: New York Governor Mario Cuomo with 15%; the Reverend Jesse Jackson with 14%; 1984 Democratic vice-presidential candidate Geraldine Ferraro with 12%; and the chairman of the Chrysler Corporation, Lee Iacocca, with 11%. Following are Los Angeles

Mayor Tom Bradley (5%), and Senator Bill Bradley of New Jersey (4%). None of the ten other persons on a list of eighteen tested receives more than 3% of Democrats' combined first- and second-choice votes for the nomination.

Among independents, who may vote in some state Democratic primaries, four men are in close contention: Hart with 28%; Kennedy, 26%; Iacocca, 20%; and Cuomo, 17%. Independents' votes also influence the major contenders. In a nomination contest pitting only the two current leaders, Kennedy and Hart, against each other, Kennedy, with 59% of Democrats' votes, is the clear choice over Hart, who receives 34% of the vote. The race, however, shifts in favor of Hart, 47% to 37%, among independents.

With more than three years remaining before the party actually selects its presidential nominee, name recognition plays an important role in the possible candidates' current standings with the Democratic rank and file. At present, only six out of eighteen names on the list are familiar to at least half of Democrats. And only four are sufficiently well known to the extent that half or more claim to know something about each person.

JULY 14
CONFIDENCE IN INSTITUTIONS

Interviewing Date: 5/17–20/85
Survey #253-G

I am going to read you a list of institutions in American society. Would you please tell me how much confidence you, yourself, have in each one—a great deal, quite a lot, some, or very little:

Church or organized religion?

	Great deal or quite a lot
National	66%

By Sex

Male	64%
Female	69

By Ethnic Background

White	65%
Nonwhite	72
Black	72

By Education

College graduate	61%
College incomplete	60
High-school graduate	70
Less than high-school graduate	71

By Region

East	57%
Midwest	70
South	75
West	59

By Age

18–29 years	65%
30–49 years	63
50 years and over	71

By Politics

Republicans	75%
Democrats	67
Independents	57

By Religion

Protestants	73%
Catholics	69

Selected National Trend

1984*	64%
1983	62
1981	64
1979	65
1977	64
1975	68
1973	66

Newsweek Poll conducted by the Gallup Organization Inc. This refers as well to the 1984 percentage in every Selected National Trend in this section.

The military?

	Great deal or quite a lot
National	61%

By Sex

Male	60%
Female	63

By Ethnic Background

White	62%
Nonwhite	55
Black	57

By Education

College graduate	50%
College incomplete	64
High-school graduate	64
Less than high-school graduate	64

By Region

East	55%
Midwest	63
South	64
West	63

By Age

18–29 years	59%
30–49 years	59
50 years and over	66

By Income

$25,000 and over	61%
Under $25,000	63

By Politics

Republicans	71%
Democrats	57
Independents	56

Selected National Trend

1984	58%
1983	53
1981	50

1979	54
1977	57
1975	58

U.S. Supreme Court?

	Great deal or quite a lot
National	55%

By Sex

Male	56%
Female	54

By Ethnic Background

White	55%
Nonwhite	57
Black	56

By Education

College graduate	62%
College incomplete	60
High-school graduate	52
Less than high-school graduate	50

By Region

East	57%
Midwest	57
South	53
West	53

By Age

18–29 years	58%
30–49 years	56
50 years and over	53

By Income

$25,000 and over	62%
Under $25,000	51

By Politics

Republicans	58%
Democrats	55
Independents	54

Selected National Trend

1984	51%
1983	42
1981	46
1979	45
1977	46
1975	49
1973	44

*Banks and banking?**

	Great deal or quite a lot
National	51%

By Sex

Male	48%
Female	54

By Ethnic Background

White	51%
Nonwhite	47
Black	45

By Education

College graduate	54%
College incomplete	53
High-school graduate	50
Less than high-school graduate	49

By Region

East	48%
Midwest	53
South	54
West	46

By Age

18–29 years	49%
30–49 years	46
50 years and over	57

By Income

$50,000 and over	48%
$35,000–$49,999	54
$25,000–$34,999	54
$15,000–$24,999	51
$10,000–$14,999	48
Under $10,000	50

By Politics

Republicans	55%
Democrats	54
Independents	44

Selected National Trend

1984	51%
1983	51
1981	46
1979	60

*When respondents were asked about their confidence in savings & loan and savings banks, 36% replied "a great deal" or "quite a lot."

Public schools?

	Great deal or quite a lot
National	48%

By Sex

Male	46%
Female	50

By Ethnic Background

White	48%
Nonwhite	48
Black	47

By Education

College graduate	47%
College incomplete	49
High-school graduate	49
Less than high-school graduate	49

By Region

East	38%
Midwest	54
South	51
West	51

By Age

18–24 years	51%
25–29 years	43
30–49 years	49
50 years and over	48

By Politics

Republicans	51%
Democrats	52
Independents	41

Selected National Trend

1984	47%
1983	39
1981	42
1979	53
1977	54
1973	58

Congress?

	Great deal or quite a lot
National	39%

By Sex

Male	37%
Female	43

By Ethnic Background

White	40%
Nonwhite	32
Black	33

By Education

College graduate	40%
College incomplete	32
High-school graduate	33
Less than high-school graduate	38

By Region

East	43%
Midwest	39
South	35
West	38

By Age

18–29 years	40%
30–49 years	34
50 years and over	43

By Politics

Republicans	43%
Democrats	39
Independents	34

Selected National Trend

1984	29%
1983	28
1981	29
1979	34
1977	40
1975	40
1973	42

Newspapers?

	Great deal or quite a lot
National	35%

By Sex

Male	35%
Female	35

By Ethnic Background

White	34%
Nonwhite	40
Black	36

By Education

College graduate	29%
College incomplete	35
High-school graduate	37
Less than high-school graduate	37

By Region

East	36%
Midwest	37
South	31
West	37

By Age

18–29 years	35%
30–49 years	35
50 years and over	36

By Politics

Republicans	30%
Democrats	41
Independents	33

Selected National Trend

1984	34%
1983	38
1981	35
1979	51
1973	39

Big business?

	Great deal or quite a lot
National	31%

By Sex

Male	32%
Female	31

By Ethnic Background

White	32%
Nonwhite	30
Black	29

By Education

College graduate	33%
College incomplete	34
High-school graduate	32
Less than high-school graduate	28

By Region

East	30%
Midwest	31
South	30
West	37

By Age

18–29 years	33%
30–49 years	30
50 years and over	31

By Politics

Republicans	38%
Democrats	28
Independents	28

Selected National Trend

1984	29%
1983	28
1981	20
1979	32
1977	33
1975	34
1973	26

Television?

	Great deal or quite a lot
National	29%

By Sex

Male	27%
Female	31

By Ethnic Background

White	28%
Nonwhite	38
Black	36

By Education

College graduate	17%
College incomplete	29
High-school graduate	32
Less than high-school graduate	35

By Region

East	28%
Midwest	27
South	31
West	32

By Age

18–24 years	33%
25–29 years	26
30–49 years	28
50–64 years	25
65 years and over	35

By Politics

Republicans	27%
Democrats	33
Independents	26

Selected National Trend

1984	25%
1983	25
1981	25
1979	38
1973	37

Organized labor?

	Great deal or quite a lot
National	28%

By Sex

Male	29%
Female	27

By Ethnic Background

White	27%
Nonwhite	34
Black	33

By Education

College graduate	13%
College incomplete	29
High-school graduate	29
Less than high-school graduate	37

By Region

East	32%
Midwest	27
South	26
West	28

By Age

18–29 years	37%
30–49 years	23
50 years and over	27

By Occupation

Professional and business	18%
Clerical and sales	30
Manual workers	35
Nonlabor force	29
Labor union households	39
Nonlabor union households	26

Selected National Trend

1984	30%
1983	26
1981	28
1979	36
1977	39
1975	38
1973	30

Note: Public confidence in the U.S. Supreme Court, Congress, public schools, and the military has increased sharply since 1983. The percentage of survey respondents expressing a great deal or quite a lot of confidence in the Supreme Court has risen 13 percentage points in two years, from 42% to 55%. The increase has been 11 points in the case of Congress over the same period of time, 9 points for public schools, and 8 points for the military.

However, little change, statistically speaking, has occurred since 1983 in respondents' confidence in the six other institutions tested. These are organized religion, banks and banking, newspapers, big business, television, and organized labor. Nevertheless, the current level of confidence in at least half of these institutions either exceeds or statistically ties previous highs recorded in surveys since 1983.

Today, as in each of the earlier surveys on confidence in institutions, the church or organized religion is the highest rated, with 66% saying they have a great deal or quite a lot of confidence in it. Next is the military, with 61% saying they have a high degree of confidence, followed by the

Supreme Court (55%), banks and banking (51%), the public schools (48%), Congress (39%), newspapers (35%), and big business (31%). The last two institutions on this year's list are television (29%) and organized labor (28%).

JULY 18
AMERICA'S GREATEST PRESIDENTS

Interviewing Date: 6/7–10/85
Survey #254-G

Which three U.S. presidents do you regard as the greatest?

The following is the list of choices with the first, second, and third choices combined:

John Kennedy 56%
Abraham Lincoln 48
Franklin Roosevelt 41
Harry Truman 26
George Washington 25
Ronald Reagan 21
Dwight Eisenhower 16
Richard Nixon 11
Jimmy Carter 9
Thomas Jefferson 7
Theodore Roosevelt 7
Lyndon Johnson 5
Woodrow Wilson 1
Herbert Hoover 1
All others 3
Don't know 2

The following are the top ten choices of Republicans and Democrats:

Choices of Republicans

Abraham Lincoln 54%
John Kennedy 44
Ronald Reagan 42
Theodore Roosevelt 29
George Washington 27
Dwight Eisenhower 22
Harry Truman 22
Richard Nixon 17

Thomas Jefferson 9
Jimmy Carter 3

Choices of Democrats

John Kennedy 71%
Franklin Roosevelt 51
Abraham Lincoln 42
Harry Truman 27
George Washington 20
Jimmy Carter 15
Dwight Eisenhower 13
Ronald Reagan 10
Richard Nixon 7
Thomas Jefferson 4

Greatest Presidents, 1975

(First, Second, and Third Choices Combined)

John Kennedy 52%
Abraham Lincoln 49
Franklin Roosevelt 45
Harry Truman 37
George Washington 25
Dwight Eisenhower 24
Theodore Roosevelt 9
Lyndon Johnson 9
Thomas Jefferson 8
Woodrow Wilson 5
Richard Nixon 5
All others 9
Don't know 3

Note: John Kennedy, Abraham Lincoln, Franklin Roosevelt, Harry Truman, and George Washington are voted by the public as the five greatest presidents in U.S. history, exactly the same positions they held a decade ago in 1975. President Ronald Reagan is the sixth highest vote-getter with 21%, putting him in a virtual tie with Washington.

Over the last decade Dwight Eisenhower, seventh in the voting, has lost some luster with the public, with his level of support dropping from 24% to 16%. Richard Nixon, on the other hand, now in eighth place, has registered a gain in public esteem since 1975. Rounding out the current top ten are Jimmy Carter (9%) and Thomas Jefferson (7%).

Predictably, there are wide differences between the current views of Republicans and Democrats on the greatest presidents. Lincoln, Kennedy, and Reagan are the top three choices of Republicans, while Kennedy, Roosevelt, and Lincoln are preferred by Democrats. Interesting differences in choices are also recorded by age groups. Survey respondents 18 to 29 years old put Kennedy in first place, while persons age 50 and older give their votes to Roosevelt.

JULY 21
PARTY BETTER FOR PEACE AND PROSPERITY

Interviewing Date: 6/7–10/85
Survey #254-G

Looking ahead for the next few years, which political party do you think would be more likely to keep the United States out of World War III—the Republican party or the Democratic party?

Republican 35%
Democratic 37
No difference (volunteered) 19
No opinion 9

By Sex
Male

Republican 39%
Democratic 32
No difference (volunteered) 21
No opinion 8

Female

Republican 31%
Democratic 42
No difference (volunteered) 17
No opinion 10

By Ethnic Background
White

Republican 37%
Democratic 35
No difference (volunteered) 20
No opinion 8

Nonwhite

Republican 21%
Democratic 53
No difference (volunteered) 14
No opinion 12

Black

Republican 18%
Democratic 58
No difference (volunteered) 12
No opinion 12

By Education
College Graduate

Republican 40%
Democratic 36
No difference (volunteered) 19
No opinion 5

College Incomplete

Republican 37%
Democratic 38
No difference (volunteered) 18
No opinion 7

High-School Graduate

Republican 36%
Democratic 33
No difference (volunteered) 20
No opinion 11

Less Than High-School Graduate

Republican 27%
Democratic 42
No difference (volunteered) 18
No opinion 13

By Region

East

Republican	32%
Democratic	37
No difference (volunteered)	21
No opinion	10

Midwest

Republican	35%
Democratic	34
No difference (volunteered)	19
No opinion	12

South

Republican	37%
Democratic	38
No difference (volunteered)	17
No opinion	8

West

Republican	35%
Democratic	40
No difference (volunteered)	19
No opinion	6

By Age

18–29 Years

Republican	36%
Democratic	41
No difference (volunteered)	16
No opinion	7

30–49 Years

Republican	36%
Democratic	40
No difference (volunteered)	16
No opinion	8

50 Years and Over

Republican	33%
Democratic	32
No difference (volunteered)	24
No opinion	11

By Politics

Republicans

Republican	66%
Democratic	13
No difference (volunteered)	15
No opinion	6

Democrats

Republican	16%
Democratic	63
No difference (volunteered)	13
No opinion	8

Independents

Republican	29%
Democratic	31
No difference (volunteered)	29
No opinion	11

Selected National Trend

	Republican party	Democratic party	No differ- ence; no opinion
March 1985	39%	33%	28%
September 1984	38	38	24
August 1984	36	40	24
April 1984	30	42	28
September 1983	26	39	35
October 1982	29	38	33
April 1981	29	34	37
September 1980	25	42	33
August 1976	29	32	39
September 1972	32	28	40
October 1968	37	24	39
October 1964	22	45	33
October 1960	40	25	35
October 1956	46	16	38
January 1952	36	15	49
September 1951	28	21	51

Which political party—the Republican party or the Democratic party—do you think will do a better job of keeping the country prosperous?

Republican 44%
Democratic 35
No difference (volunteered) 13
No opinion 8

By Sex
Male

Republican 49%
Democratic 32
No difference (volunteered) 12
No opinion 7

Female

Republican 40%
Democratic 37
No difference (volunteered) 13
No opinion 10

By Ethnic Background
White

Republican 48%
Democratic 31
No difference (volunteered) 13
No opinion 8

Nonwhite

Republican 18%
Democratic 60
No difference (volunteered) 9
No opinion 13

Black

Republican 15%
Democratic 67
No difference (volunteered) 6
No opinion 12

By Education
College Graduate

Republican 61%
Democratic 23
No difference (volunteered) 12
No opinion 4

College Incomplete

Republican 50%
Democratic 30
No difference (volunteered) 12
No opinion 8

High-School Graduate

Republican 44%
Democratic 33
No difference (volunteered) 14
No opinion 9

Less Than High-School Graduate

Republican 26%
Democratic 51
No difference (volunteered) 11
No opinion 12

By Region
East

Republican 43%
Democratic 32
No difference (volunteered) 12
No opinion 13

Midwest

Republican 44%
Democratic 31
No difference (volunteered) 16
No opinion 9

South

Republican 44%
Democratic 37
No difference (volunteered) 12
No opinion 7

West

Republican 47%
Democratic 38
No difference (volunteered) 10
No opinion 5

By Age

18-29 Years

Republican 48%
Democratic 32
No difference (volunteered) 12
No opinion 8

30-49 Years

Republican 46%
Democratic 35
No difference (volunteered) 11
No opinion 8

50 Years and Over

Republican 39%
Democratic 36
No difference (volunteered) 15
No opinion 10

By Politics

Republicans

Republican 81%
Democratic 6
No difference (volunteered) 8
No opinion 5

Democrats

Republican 19%
Democratic 65
No difference (volunteered) 9
No opinion 7

Independents

Republican 42%
Democratic 25
No difference (volunteered) 20
No opinion 13

Selected National Trend

	Republican party	Democratic party	No difference; no opinion
March 1985	48%	32%	20%
September 1984	49	33	18
August 1984	48	36	16
April 1984	44	36	20
September 1983	33	40	27
October 1982	34	43	23
April 1981	40	31	29
September 1980	35	36	29
August 1976	23	47	30
September 1972	38	35	27
October 1968	34	37	29
October 1964	21	53	26
October 1960	31	46	23
October 1956	39	39	22
January 1952	31	35	34
September 1951	29	37	34

Note: After steady losses over the last two years to the Republicans on the key issues of peace and prosperity, the Democratic party has held its ground in the latest (June) survey. Both parties are now in a statistical tie (GOP: 35%, Democrats: 37%) as the one voters perceive as better able to keep peace. In March the GOP held the lead. On prosperity, the Republican party still outdistances the Democrats, 44% to 35%, but the gap has narrowed.

The March survey represented the first time the Republicans have held a substantial lead on both these crucial issues since Gallup began these measurements in 1951. In the 1950s and early 1960s, the GOP was perceived by voters as the "party of peace." The Republicans relinquished this lead, however, during the 1964 presidential campaign, in which GOP contender Barry Goldwater was labeled by some voters as "trigger happy." But two years later the Republicans were back on top. In the 1970s both parties were given equal credit as better able to keep the nation out of a world war. The Democrats, however, moved clearly ahead in 1980 and retained the lead until last September, when the GOP drew even.

On the issue of prosperity, the Republicans have had a significant advantage over the Democrats in only three years since 1951: in 1981 (during the first year of Ronald Reagan's presidency), 1984, and 1985.

JULY 25
JOGGING

Interviewing Date: 6/7–10/85
Survey #254-G

Do you happen to jog, or not?

	Yes
National	15%

By Sex

Male	20%
Female	11

By Ethnic Background

White	15%
Nonwhite	17
Black	16

By Education

College graduate	23%
College incomplete	21
High-school graduate	13
Less than high-school graduate	8

By Region

East	16%
Midwest	15
South	14
West	17

By Age

18–24 years	32%
25–29 years	19
30–49 years	17
50–64 years	8
65 years and over	4

By Occupation

Professional and business	22%
Clerical and sales	13
Manual workers	16
Nonlabor force	4

Selected National Trend

	Yes
1984	18%
1982	14
1980	12
1977	11
1961	6

Asked of those who jog: About how often do you jog?

	1985	1984
Less than once a week	18%	5%
Once or twice a week	31	25
Three or four times a week	28	35
Every day or almost every day	21	34
Not sure	2	1

Also asked of those who jog: On the average, how far do you usually jog, in terms of miles or fractions of miles?

Less than two miles	44%
Two to three miles	24
Three miles or more	30
Not sure	2

Selected National Trend

	1984	1982	1977
Less than two miles	32%	48%	60%
Two to three miles	29	25	23
Three miles or more	39	24	14
Not sure	*	3	3

*Less than 1%

Note: Although jogging continues to be one of the nation's most popular recreational activities, with 15% in the latest survey saying they jog, the quarter-century uptrend has leveled out in 1985. In 1961, when the measurement was started, the figure was only 6%.

Not only has the number of joggers leveled out in 1985, but a decrease is found as well in the frequency of jogging and the average distance covered. The percentage of joggers who jog every day or almost every day is 21%; last year the figure was 34%. Those who run three miles or more are at 30%, compared to 39% in 1984.

Sex, education, and age play important roles in the popularity of this exercise. Twice the proportion of men (20%) as women (11%) are joggers, and persons who attended college (23%) also are twice as likely to be joggers as those with less formal education (11%). But the most important factor is age. From a peak of 32% among 18 to 24 year olds, participation falls off to merely 4% among those age 65 and older. Among those 30 to 49 years old, 17%, close to the national average, are joggers.

JULY 28
RELOCATION OF URBAN POOR

Interviewing Date: 6/7–10/85
Survey #254-G

A plan has been proposed to invite unemployed people now living in large cities to move to areas of the nation where job opportunities are better. Under the plan, the federal government would provide housing vouchers to help pay the family rent anywhere in the United States. Would you favor or oppose such a plan?

Favor 51%
Oppose 40
No opinion 9

By Sex
Male

Favor 47%
Oppose 44
No opinion 9

Female

Favor 55%
Oppose 36
No opinion 9

By Ethnic Background
White

Favor 47%
Oppose 44
No opinion 9

Nonwhite

Favor 76%
Oppose 17
No opinion 7

Black

Favor 74%
Oppose 18
No opinion 8

By Education
College Graduate

Favor 41%
Oppose 52
No opinion 7

College Incomplete

Favor 53%
Oppose 40
No opinion 7

High-School Graduate

Favor 50%
Oppose 41
No opinion 9

Less Than High-School Graduate

Favor 59%
Oppose 30
No opinion 11

By Region
East
Favor 55%
Oppose 34
No opinion 11

Midwest
Favor 47%
Oppose 46
No opinion 7

South
Favor 51%
Oppose 42
No opinion 7

West
Favor 51%
Oppose 39
No opinion 10

By Age
18–29 Years
Favor 64%
Oppose 29
No opinion 7

30–49 Years
Favor 46%
Oppose 46
No opinion 8

50 Years and Over
Favor 47%
Oppose 42
No opinion 11

By Community Location
Central Cities
Favor 56%
Oppose 35
No opinion 9

Suburbs
Favor 50%
Oppose 40
No opinion 10

Rural Areas
Favor 49%
Oppose 44
No opinion 7

Note: By a 5-to-4 vote, the American people favor a proposal for unemployed people now living in large cities to move to areas where job opportunities are better. Under the plan, the federal government would provide housing vouchers to help pay the family rent anywhere in the United States.

Among nonwhites in the latest survey, support is nearly 5 to 1 in favor. Heavy backing for the plan is found also among younger adults, residents of the most urbanized areas of the nation, and persons in low income groups.

For more than a decade the Gallup Poll, on the basis of a similar question, has found substantial public support for voluntarily relocating poor families from the big cities to areas of the nation where living conditions and job opportunities are better. Urban specialists point out that many large cities cannot cope with their large dependent populations and that the poor do not have much hope of improving their lot so long as they are concentrated in financially distressed cities. They also contend that the much publicized "urban renaissance"—the back-to-the-city movement of middle- and upper-income families—is largely an illusion, since the concentration of minorities and poverty-level families in the central cities continues to increase.

A crucial factor behind the voluntary relocation plan is recognition of the fact that labor force mobility is essential to the health of the American economy. While one solution to the problem of ghettos is to bring new businesses into center city areas, many planners have reached the conclusion that it is better to move people to jobs, rather than jobs to people.

As reported recently in the *New York Times*, the Reagan administration has sharply reduced federal aid intended to restore the cities, has nearly halted construction of federally subsidized housing, and is now instituting the first subsidy that could be used by the chronically unemployed to move to where the jobs are. This subsidy would be a housing voucher to help pay the household rent anywhere in the United States. Nobody can predict how many people actually would move or find jobs.

A five-year, $1 billion program to demonstrate the use of vouchers began in San Antonio this spring and is expected to be operating by August 1 in twenty cities and states, including New York City, New Haven, and New Jersey. Administration officials say it is their plan and hope that by the 1990s vouchers will replace virtually all federally assisted housing programs, which now cost about $10 billion each year. They believe this will help make the poor far more mobile than they have been since the 1930s and, in the process, help blacks break away from the isolation of the inner cities.

AUGUST 1
PRESIDENT REAGAN

Interviewing Date: 7/12–15/85
Survey #255-G

Do you approve or disapprove of the way Ronald Reagan is handling his job as president?

Approve 63%
Disapprove 28
No opinion 9

By Sex
Male

Approve 65%
Disapprove 27
No opinion 8

Female

Approve 60%
Disapprove 30
No opinion 10

By Ethnic Background
White

Approve 66%
Disapprove 25
No opinion 9

Nonwhite

Approve 36%
Disapprove 53
No opinion 11

Black

Approve 28%
Disapprove 62
No opinion 10

By Education
College Graduate

Approve 65%
Disapprove 29
No opinion 6

College Incomplete

Approve 72%
Disapprove 21
No opinion 7

High-School Graduate

Approve 66%
Disapprove 26
No opinion 8

Less Than High-School Graduate

Approve 47%
Disapprove 39
No opinion 14

By Region
East

Approve 63%
Disapprove 27
No opinion 10

Midwest

Approve 62%
Disapprove 30
No opinion 8

South

Approve 64%
Disapprove 26
No opinion 10

West

Approve 62%
Disapprove 31
No opinion 7

By Age
18–29 Years

Approve 63%
Disapprove 25
No opinion 12

30–49 Years

Approve 65%
Disapprove 27
No opinion 8

50 Years and Over

Approve 60%
Disapprove 33
No opinion 7

By Income
$50,000 and Over

Approve 74%
Disapprove 20
No opinion 6

$35,000–$49,999

Approve 71%
Disapprove 25
No opinion 4

$25,000–$34,999

Approve 67%
Disapprove 26
No opinion 7

$15,000–$24,999

Approve 67%
Disapprove 25
No opinion 8

$10,000–$14,999

Approve 59%
Disapprove 30
No opinion 11

Under $10,000

Approve 43%
Disapprove 42
No opinion 15

By Politics
Republicans

Approve 87%
Disapprove 9
No opinion 4

Democrats

Approve 39%
Disapprove 50
No opinion 11

Independents

Approve 64%
Disapprove 25
No opinion 11

Selected National Trend

	Approve	Dis-approve	No opinion
1985			
June 7–10	58%	32%	10%
May 17–20	55	37	8
April 12–15	52	37	11
March 8–11	56	37	7

February 15–18	60	31	9
January 25–28	64	28	8
January 11–14	62	29	9

Now let me ask you about some specific problems. As I read off each problem, would you tell me whether you approve or disapprove of the way President Reagan is handling that problem:

Economic conditions in this country?

Approve 53%
Disapprove 39
No opinion 8

By Sex
Male

Approve 56%
Disapprove 38
No opinion 6

Female

Approve 50%
Disapprove 40
No opinion 10

By Ethnic Background
White

Approve 55%
Disapprove 36
No opinion 9

Nonwhite

Approve 32%
Disapprove 61
No opinion 7

Black

Approve 24%
Disapprove 69
No opinion 7

By Education
College Graduate

Approve 56%
Disapprove 38
No opinion 6

College Incomplete

Approve 62%
Disapprove 32
No opinion 6

High-School Graduate

Approve 53%
Disapprove 39
No opinion 8

Less Than High-School Graduate

Approve 40%
Disapprove 47
No opinion 13

By Region
East

Approve 51%
Disapprove 40
No opinion 9

Midwest

Approve 51%
Disapprove 41
No opinion 8

South

Approve 57%
Disapprove 35
No opinion 8

West

Approve 51%
Disapprove 42
No opinion 7

By Age

18–29 Years

Approve 55%
Disapprove 36
No opinion 9

30–49 Years

Approve 53%
Disapprove 41
No opinion 6

50 Years and Over

Approve 50%
Disapprove 40
No opinion 10

By Politics

Republicans

Approve 77%
Disapprove 17
No opinion 6

Democrats

Approve 31%
Disapprove 60
No opinion 9

Independents

Approve 51%
Disapprove 40
No opinion 9

Selected National Trend

	Approve
1985	
May 17–20	47%
March 8–11	51
January 11–14	51
1984	
November–December	57
June–July	48
May	49
January	48

Foreign policy?

Approve 50%
Disapprove 37
No opinion 13

By Sex

Male

Approve 53%
Disapprove 37
No opinion 10

Female

Approve 47%
Disapprove 36
No opinion 17

By Ethnic Background

White

Approve 52%
Disapprove 35
No opinion 13

Nonwhite

Approve 36%
Disapprove 48
No opinion 16

Black

Approve 32%
Disapprove 51
No opinion 17

By Education

College Graduate

Approve 53%
Disapprove 39
No opinion 18

College Incomplete

Approve 58%
Disapprove 33
No opinion 9

High-School Graduate

Approve 51%
Disapprove 35
No opinion 14

Less Than High-School Graduate

Approve 36%
Disapprove 43
No opinion 21

By Region
East

Approve 50%
Disapprove 38
No opinion 12

Midwest

Approve 47%
Disapprove 35
No opinion 18

South

Approve 51%
Disapprove 36
No opinion 13

West

Approve 50%
Disapprove 38
No opinion 12

By Age
18–29 Years

Approve 51%
Disapprove 37
No opinion 12

30–49 Years

Approve 50%
Disapprove 37
No opinion 13

50 Years and Over

Approve 48%
Disapprove 36
No opinion 16

By Politics
Republicans

Approve 68%
Disapprove 20
No opinion 12

Democrats

Approve 35%
Disapprove 51
No opinion 14

Independents

Approve 48%
Disapprove 38
No opinion 14

Selected National Trend

	Approve
1985	
May 17–20	43%
March 8–11	45
January 11–14	52
1984	
November–December	50
June–July	39
May	37
January	38

Relations with the Soviet Union?

Approve 52%
Disapprove 31
No opinion 7

By Sex
Male

Approve 55%
Disapprove 32
No opinion 13

Female

Approve 49%
Disapprove 30
No opinion 21

By Ethnic Background
White

Approve 54%
Disapprove 29
No opinion 17

Nonwhite

Approve 39%
Disapprove 46
No opinion 15

Black

Approve 38%
Disapprove 46
No opinion 16

By Education
College Graduate

Approve 57%
Disapprove 31
No opinion 12

College Incomplete

Approve 61%
Disapprove 25
No opinion 14

High-School Graduate

Approve 56%
Disapprove 29
No opinion 15

Less Than High-School Graduate

Approve 33%
Disapprove 39
No opinion 28

By Region
East

Approve 51%
Disapprove 32
No opinion 17

Midwest

Approve 57%
Disapprove 28
No opinion 15

South

Approve 50%
Disapprove 30
No opinion 20

West

Approve 51%
Disapprove 34
No opinion 15

By Age
18–29 Years

Approve 53%
Disapprove 30
No opinion 17

30–49 Years

Approve 53%
Disapprove 30
No opinion 17

50 Years and Over

Approve 51%
Disapprove 32
No opinion 17

By Politics
Republicans

Approve 66%
Disapprove 20
No opinion 14

Democrats

Approve 40%
Disapprove 42
No opinion 18

Independents

Approve 53%
Disapprove 30
No opinion 17

Selected National Trend

                                    Approve
1985
May 17–20 ....51%
March 8–11 53
January 11–14 54
1984
November–December 52
May 46
February 43

Situation in Nicaragua?

Approve 29%
Disapprove 45
No opinion 26

By Sex
Male

Approve 33%
Disapprove 47
No opinion 20

Female

Approve 25%
Disapprove 44
No opinion 31

By Ethnic Background
White

Approve 29%
Disapprove 44
No opinion 27

Nonwhite

Approve 21%
Disapprove 56
No opinion 23

Black

Approve 18%
Disapprove 59
No opinion 23

By Education
College Graduate

Approve 31%
Disapprove 49
No opinion 20

College Incomplete

Approve 33%
Disapprove 45
No opinion 22

High-School Graduate

Approve 28%
Disapprove 45
No opinion 27

Less Than High-School Graduate

Approve 22%
Disapprove 45
No opinion 33

By Region
East

Approve 28%
Disapprove 45
No opinion 27

Midwest

Approve 27%
Disapprove 49
No opinion 24

South

Approve 33%
Disapprove 37
No opinion 30

West

Approve 25%
Disapprove 53
No opinion 22

By Age
18–29 Years

Approve 23%
Disapprove 50
No opinion 27

30–49 Years

Approve 30%
Disapprove 48
No opinion 22

50 Years and Over

Approve 31%
Disapprove 39
No opinion 30

By Politics
Republicans

Approve 41%
Disapprove 30
No opinion 29

Democrats

Approve 19%
Disapprove 58
No opinion 23

Independents

Approve 27%
Disapprove 50
No opinion 23

Selected National Trend

Approve

1985
May 17–20 ....29%
January 11–14 26
1984
November–December 34
May 28
February 29
January 28

Nuclear disarmament negotiations with the Soviet Union?

Approve 49%
Disapprove 33
No opinion 18

By Sex
Male

Approve 54%
Disapprove 33
No opinion 13

Female

Approve 44%
Disapprove 33
No opinion 23

By Ethnic Background
White

Approve 51%
Disapprove 31
No opinion 18

Nonwhite

Approve 34%
Disapprove 48
No opinion 18

Black

Approve 31%
Disapprove 51
No opinion 18

By Education

College Graduate

Approve 47%
Disapprove 36
No opinion 17

College Incomplete

Approve 52%
Disapprove 34
No opinion 14

High-School Graduate

Approve 56%
Disapprove 30
No opinion 14

Less Than High-School Graduate

Approve 37%
Disapprove 35
No opinion 28

By Region

East

Approve 45%
Disapprove 36
No opinion 19

Midwest

Approve 53%
Disapprove 31
No opinion 16

South

Approve 52%
Disapprove 29
No opinion 19

West

Approve 45%
Disapprove 37
No opinion 18

By Age

18–29 Years

Approve 50%
Disapprove 34
No opinion 16

30–49 Years

Approve 48%
Disapprove 37
No opinion 15

50 Years and Over

Approve 49%
Disapprove 28
No opinion 23

By Politics

Republicans

Approve 64%
Disapprove 22
No opinion 14

Democrats

Approve 37%
Disapprove 45
No opinion 18

Independents

Approve 47%
Disapprove 33
No opinion 20

Selected National Trend

	Approve
1985	
May 17–20	49%
March 8–11	49
January 11–14	52
1984	
November–December	47

Note: The American people responded to news of President Ronald Reagan's impending operation in mid-July by boosting his overall job performance rating to 63% approval, a 5-point improvement over the 58% recorded a month earlier. The public's assessment of his handling of the economy and foreign policy also rose commensurately, but little credit accrued to him for his handling of relations with the Soviet Union, the nuclear disarmament negotiations, or the situation in Nicaragua.

President Reagan's current overall job appraisal of 63% approval statistically matches the high ratings he garnered after his landslide reelection victory last November and at the start of his second term this year. Following a pattern that has occurred to every postwar president at a similar point in his tenure, Reagan's popularity then declined moderately, from an average of 60% approval during the first three months of 1985 to 55% during the second quarter. His low for the year to date was recorded in April, when 52% approved of his performance in office. Since then, his ratings have gradually trended upward.

In the case of Reagan's recent cancer surgery, there is evidence that the public's sympathy vote became even stronger than that found in the pre-operation Gallup Poll. A *Newsweek* poll, conducted by the Gallup Organization immediately after the July 15 operation, found 68% approving of the president's job performance.

AUGUST 4
ALCOHOLIC BEVERAGES

Interviewing Date: 2/15–18/85 (U.S. only)*
Survey #250-G

> Asked in twenty-three nations: Has drinking (the use of alcohol) ever been a cause of trouble in your family?

	Yes
Iceland	32%
Brazil	25
Philippines	25
United States	21

*International findings are based on in-person surveys conducted during June and July 1985.

South Korea	20
Australia	18
Canada	17
Switzerland	15
Colombia	4
Republic of Ireland	14
Japan	14
Norway	14
Argentina	13
Finland	13
Mexico	12
Belgium	11
Greece	11
Great Britain	10
Sweden	10
Netherlands	9
Uruguay	9
West Germany	9
Israel	2
Average:	15%

> Asked in twenty-three nations: Do you have occasion to use alcoholic beverages such as liquor, wine, or beer, or are you a total abstainer?

	Those who drink
Greece	89%
Sweden	86
Netherlands	84
Great Britain	83
Norway	82
Iceland	82
Switzerland	80
Mexico	78
Colombia	77
Canada	77
Australia	76
South Korea	76
Finland	74
Argentina	72
West Germany	71
Belgium	69
Japan	69
Republic of Ireland	68
United States	67
Uruguay	67

Brazil			60
Philippines			56
Israel			44
Average:			73%

Denmark	61	32	5
West Germany	56	33	10
Netherlands	54	34	6
Canada	52	38	9
Belgium	45	39	9
Great Britain	44	44	10
Japan	17	40	32

Asked in twenty-two nations* of those who drink: Do you sometimes drink more than you think you should?

	Yes
Republic of Ireland	51%
South Korea	51
Japan	49
Iceland	43
Australia	38
Great Britain	36
Finland	35
Greece	34
Canada	33
Norway	33
United States	32
West Germany	30
Brazil	23
Colombia	22
Belgium	20
Mexico	20
Philippines	20
Sweden	19
Israel	14
Netherlands	14
Uruguay	13
Argentina	8
Average:	29%

*Not asked in Switzerland

Asked in thirteen nations: In your country, today, how serious a problem do you think alcoholism is?

	Very serious	Quite serious	Not very/not at all
France	74%	22%	2%
Italy	74	21	5
United States	71	26	2
Republic of Ireland	71	23	4
Spain	66	23	10
Northern Ireland	61	33	4

Note: Alcohol abuse is a problem of global dimensions, with one person in seven (15%) in a recent twenty-three-nation survey, on average, reporting that drinking has been a cause of trouble in his or her family. In the United States, 21% report alcohol-related family problems, putting this country toward the top of the list of participating nations. Only in Iceland (32%), Brazil (25%), and the Philippines (25%) are higher incidences reported. South Korea (20%), Australia (18%), and Canada (17%) also are slightly above the international norm.

Toward the low end of the scale, with 10% or fewer citing family problems relating to alcohol abuse, are Great Britain (10%), Sweden (10%), the Netherlands (9%), Uruguay (9%), and West Germany (9%). The lowest incidence is found in Israel, cited by only 2% of survey respondents there.

As for consumption, nine in ten Greek adults (89%) drink alcoholic beverages, twice the proportion recorded in Israel (44%). High proportions of drinkers also are reported in Sweden (86%), the Netherlands (84%), Great Britain (83%), Norway (82%), Iceland (82%), and Switzerland (80%). Mexico, where 78% are drinkers, and Colombia (77%) are slightly above the twenty-three-nation average of 73%. The United States (67%) and Ireland (68%) rate below the international average.

Among drinkers, those most likely to say they sometimes drink more than they think they should are the Irish, South Koreans, and Japanese, with about half in each nation giving this response. Next are the Icelanders (43%). Also above the 29% international average for this category are residents of Australia, Great Britain, Finland, Greece, Canada, Norway, the United States, and West Germany. The lowest level of overindulgence is found in Argentina, where only 8% admit to occasionally drinking too much.

Large majorities in virtually all of the thirteen nations polled say that alcoholism is a very serious problem in their countries. Most likely to describe alcoholism in these terms are the French (74% say alcoholism is very serious), Italians (74%), Americans (71%), and citizens of the Republic of Ireland (also 71%). Next are the Spanish (66%), Northern Irish (61%), Danes (61%), followed by West Germans (56%), Dutch (54%), and Canadians (52%). Less than a majority but still a sizable proportion of Belgians (45%) consider alcoholism to be a very serious problem in their nation, followed by the British (44%) and Japanese (17%).

AUGUST 8
PERSONAL FINANCES

Interviewing Date: 6/10–23/85
Special Telephone Survey

We are interested in how people's financial situation may have changed. Would you say that you are financially better off now than you were a year ago, or are you financially worse off now?

Better	43%
Worse	29
Same (volunteered)	26
No opinion	2

Selected National Trend

	Better	Worse	Same	No opinion
1985				
March	48%	25%	26%	1%
1984				
November–December	43	24	32	1
September	39	26	34	1
July	40	25	34	1
March	36	26	37	1
1983				
June	28	39	32	1
March	25	46	28	1
1982				
November	28	37	34	1
July–August	25	46	26	3
February	28	47	24	1
1981				
October	28	43	28	1
June	33	35	30	2

Now looking ahead, do you expect that at this time next year you will be financially better off than now, or worse off than now?

Better	52%
Worse	19
Same (volunteered)	19
No opinion	10

Selected National Trend

	Better	Worse	Same	No opinion
1985				
March	57%	12%	26%	5%
1984				
November–December	50	17	28	5
September	53	9	28	10
July	52	12	28	8
March	54	11	28	7
1983				
June	43	19	28	10
March	45	22	24	9
1982				
November	41	22	27	10
July–August	37	29	24	10
February	42	31	21	6
1981				
October	40	31	21	8
June	44	25	23	8

Here is the trend of the two questions combined:

Overall Financial Outlook

	Optimists	Pessimists	Neutral	No opinion
1985				
June 10–23	45%	20%	24%	11%
March	52	14	29	5

1984				
November–				
December	48	18	29	5
September	47	11	32	10
July	47	15	30	8
March	46	14	33	7
1983				
June	34	24	32	10
March	32	28	30	10
1982				
November	32	25	33	10
July–August	28	34	27	11
February	31	33	29	7
1981				
October	NA	NA	NA	NA
June	36	27	28	9

Note: Amid signs of sluggish growth in the nation's economy, Americans have lowered their sights somewhat for their personal financial well-being. Still, optimists continue to outnumber pessimists by a wide margin.

In the latest Gallup audit of financial expectations, 52% say they expect to be better off one year from now, 19% think their situation will be about the same, and 19% foresee a downturn. By comparison, in March 57% were optimistic, 26% neutral, and 12% pessimistic about the year ahead. Although the current level of financial pessimism is statistically no higher than that recorded last December, one must go back to surveys conducted during the 1981–82 recession to find significantly higher levels of pessimism.

Asked to rate their current financial status vis-à-vis one year ago, 43% of respondents see an improvement, 26% perceive no change, and 29% claim to be worse off. When both questions— looking ahead and looking back—are combined into an overall index, optimists are found to outnumber pessimists by about a 2-to-1 ratio, 45% to 20%. In the March survey, this ratio was a more robust 4 to 1, with 52% classified as optimists and 14% as pessimists.

Not surprisingly, there is a strong political cast to the public's economic forecasts, with Republicans far more likely than Democrats to have an optimistic outlook. In the current survey, for example, 66% of Republicans, but only 37% of

Democrats, say they expect to be better off next year than they are now.

The Reagan administration recently lowered its forecast for economic growth in 1985, from almost 4% to 3%. Many private economists, however, say even this revised target will be difficult to attain, since it will require growth of 5% during the second half, after the first six months' sluggish 1% gain.

AUGUST 8
ATOMIC BOMB—FORTY YEARS AGO

Special Report

By an overwhelming margin, the American public in 1945 approved of the use of the atomic bomb on Japanese cities. In a Gallup Poll taken shortly after U.S. planes dropped the bombs on Hiroshima and Nagasaki on August 6 and 9, 85% of American adults endorsed the use of these weapons, with 10% opposed. No significant differences of opinion were recorded by sex, age, or level of formal education.

In a similar poll conducted two weeks later, 69% said it was "a good thing" that the atomic bomb had been developed, while 17% thought it was "a bad thing"; 14% withheld judgment. It should be recalled that at the time President Harry Truman made his momentous decision to use the bomb, Allied invasion of the Japanese homeland was considered imminent, with heavy casualties expected on both sides.

AUGUST 11
PRESIDENTIAL TRIAL HEATS

Interviewing Date: 7/12–15/85
Survey #255-G

Asked of registered voters: Suppose the 1988 presidential election were being held today. If Vice-president George Bush were the Republican candidate and Senator Edward Kennedy were the Democratic candidate, which would you like to see win? [Those who named other candidates or were undecided

were then asked: As of today, do you lean more to Bush, the Republican, or to Kennedy, the Democrat?]

Bush 46%
Kennedy 46
Other; undecided 8

By Politics
Republicans

Bush 82%
Kennedy 13
Other; undecided 5

Democrats

Bush 16%
Kennedy 78
Other; undecided 6

Independents

Bush 44%
Kennedy 41
Other; undecided 15

Asked of registered voters: Suppose the 1988 presidential election were being held today. If Vice-president George Bush were the Republican candidate and the Reverend Jesse Jackson were the Democratic candidate, which would you like to see win? [Those who named other candidates or were undecided were then asked: As of today, do you lean more to Bush, the Republican, or to Jackson, the Democrat?]

Bush 68%
Jackson 22
Other; undecided 10

By Politics
Republicans

Bush 92%
Jackson 3
Other; undecided 5

Democrats

Bush 48%
Jackson 41
Other; undecided 11

Independents

Bush 68%
Jackson 18
Other; undecided 14

Asked of registered voters: Suppose the 1988 presidential election were being held today. If Vice-president George Bush were the Republican candidate and Lee Iacocca, chairman of the Chrysler Corporation, were the Democratic candidate, which would you like to see win? [Those who named other candidates or were undecided were then asked: As of today, do you lean more to Bush, the Republican, or to Iacocca, the Democrat?]

Bush 52%
Iacocca 35
Other; undecided 13

By Politics
Republicans

Bush 74%
Iacocca 18
Other; undecided 8

Democrats

Bush 35%
Iacocca 49
Other; undecided 16

Independents

Bush 49%
Iacocca 37
Other; undecided 14

Asked of registered voters: Suppose the 1988 presidential election were being held today. If Vice-president George Bush were the

Republican candidate and New York Governor Mario Cuomo were the Democratic candidate, which would you like to see win? [Those who named other candidates or were undecided were then asked: As of today, do you lean more to Bush, the Republican, or to Cuomo, the Democrat?]

Bush 55%
Cuomo 31
Other; undecided 14

By Politics
Republicans

Bush 86%
Cuomo 7
Other; undecided 7

Democrats

Bush 30%
Cuomo 55
Other; undecided 15

Independents

Bush 54%
Cuomo 26
Other; undecided 20

Asked of registered voters: Suppose the 1988 presidential election were being held today. If Vice-president George Bush were the Republican candidate and Senator Gary Hart were the Democratic candidate, which would you like to see win? [Those who named other candidates or were undecided were then asked: As of today, do you lean more to Bush, the Republican, or to Hart, the Democrat?]

Bush 50%
Hart 39
Other; undecided 11

By Politics
Republicans

Bush 81%
Hart 13
Other; undecided 6

Democrats

Bush 27%
Hart 62
Other; undecided 11

Independents

Bush 47%
Hart 39
Other; undecided 14

Note: GOP Vice-president George Bush and Democratic Senator Edward Kennedy would win the same share of the popular vote if the 1988 presidential election were held now, according to a test election conducted recently by the Gallup Poll. In the mid-July survey, Bush and Kennedy, the early favorites for their parties' 1988 presidential nominations, are each the choice of 46% of registered voters, with 8% naming other candidates or undecided. Kennedy held a narrow 47% to 41% lead over Bush in a trial heat held last February among a sample of the total adult population.

Other current popular candidates for the Democratic nomination fare less well in test elections against Bush. Colorado Senator Gary Hart, a frontrunner in the contest of the 1984 Democratic nomination, loses to Bush in a simulated 1988 race, 50% to 39%. Statistically similar results are recorded when Bush is pitted against Chrysler Corporation Chairman Lee Iacocca. The latter, while formally disavowing political ambitions, has been prominently in the news since he rescued financially ailing Chrysler and wrote a best-selling book about the experience. In the presidential trial heat, Bush leads Iacocca, 52% to 35%.

Bush also is the victor against New York Governor Mario Cuomo, keynote speaker at the 1984 Democratic convention, with Bush selected by 55% of registered voters nationwide to Cuomo's 31%. (In Cuomo's native East, he loses to Bush by a less decisive 49% to 41% edge.)

The vice-president receives 68% of the vote in a test election against the Reverend Jesse Jackson, another prominent figure in the 1984 election, who wins 22% of the current vote. It is interesting to note that the outcome of the current Bush-Jackson contest almost exactly matches the results of the final, preconvention Reagan-Jackson test election in 1984, which showed Ronald Reagan leading Jackson, 68% to 21%.

While Bush receives overwhelming support from his fellow Republicans in all five test elections, some interesting variations are noted in the trial heat choices of Democrats and independents. The top Democratic vote-getter, not surprisingly, is Kennedy, winning 78% of Democrats to Bush's 16%. Each of the other possible Democratic nominees, however, surrenders one-fourth or more of Democrats' votes to Republican Bush.

Hart, for instance, wins 62% of the Democratic vote to 27% for Bush. Cuomo beats Bush among Democrats by a 55% to 30% margin. Iacocca prevails over Bush among Democrats, 49% to 35%. Jackson actually loses to Bush among Democrats, 41% to 48%.

Among registered independents, who comprise about one-fourth of the nation's voters and who strongly supported Hart's 1984 bid for the Democratic nomination, the Colorado senator places second to Kennedy in the test races against Bush. The Bush-Kennedy contest among independents results in a 44% to 41% statistical draw, while the Bush-Hart race is a close 47% to 39%. Iacocca, too, exhibits considerable independent strength, losing to Bush by 37% to 49%. Cuomo and Jackson, at this early stage, lose heavily to Bush among independents, by 26% to 54% and 18% to 68%, respectively.

AUGUST 15
HONESTY AND ETHICAL STANDARDS

Interviewing Date: 7/12–15/85
Survey #255-G

How would you rate the honesty and ethical standards of people in these different fields—very high, high, average, low, or very low:

Clergymen?

Very high; high 67%
Average 26
Low; very low 4
No opinion 3

Druggists, pharmacists?

Very high; high 65%
Average 30
Low; very low 3
No opinion 2

Medical doctors?

Very high; high 58%
Average 33
Low; very low 8
No opinion 1

Dentists?

Very high; high 56%
Average 37
Low; very low 5
No opinion 2

College teachers?

Very high; high 54%
Average 35
Low; very low 5
No opinion 6

Engineers?

Very high; high 53%
Average 37
Low; very low 3
No opinion 7

Policemen?

Very high; high 47%
Average 41
Low; very low 10
No opinion 2

Bankers?

Very high; high 37%
Average 51
Low; very low 9
No opinion 3

Television reporters, commentators?

Very high; high 33%
Average 48
Low; very low 15
No opinion 4

Funeral directors?

Very high; high 31%
Average 45
Low; very low 15
No opinion 9

Journalists?

Very high; high 31%
Average 47
Low; very low 17
No opinion 5

Newspaper reporters?

Very high; high 29%
Average 52
Low; very low 16
No opinion 3

Lawyers?

Very high; high 27%
Average 40
Low; very low 30
No opinion 3

Business executives?

Very high; high 23%
Average 54
Low; very low 18
No opinion 5

Senators?

Very high; high 23%
Average 53
Low; very low 21
No opinion 3

Building contractors?

Very high; high 20%
Average 53
Low; very low 21
No opinion 6

Congressmen?

Very high; high 20%
Average 49
Low; very low 27
No opinion 4

Stockbrokers?

Very high; high 20%
Average 51
Low; very low 10
No opinion 19

Local political officeholders?

Very high; high 18%
Average 53
Low; very low 24
No opinion 5

State political officeholders?

Very high; high 15%
Average 55
Low; very low 24
No opinion 6

Realtors?

Very high; high 15%
Average 49
Low; very low 31
No opinion 5

Labor union leaders?

Very high; high 13%
Average 35
Low; very low 45
No opinion 7

Advertising practitioners?

Very high; high	.....................12%
Average	42
Low; very low	39
No opinion	 7

Insurance salesmen?

Very high; high	.....................10%
Average	49
Low; very low	38
No opinion	 3

Car salesmen?

Very high; high	.... 5%
Average	32
Low; very low	59
No opinion	 4

Note: Of twenty-five occupations cited, the public rates clergymen and pharmacists highest in terms of their perceived honesty and ethical standards. Clergymen, as in each of the earlier surveys, come out at the top of the scale, with 67% of respondents giving them a very high or high rating. Next are pharmacists or druggists, with a 65% positive rating. Following closely are medical doctors, dentists, college teachers, engineers, and policemen, with positive scores ranging from 58% to 47%. In the next tier are bankers, television reporters and commentators, funeral directors, journalists, newspaper reporters, and lawyers, with ratings from 37% to 29%.

Ten occupational groups are given very high or high ratings by only 23% to 12%. These are business executives, senators, building contractors, congressmen, stockbrokers, local and state political officeholders, realtors, labor union leaders, and advertising practitioners. Insurance and car salesmen occupy the last two positions, receiving positive ratings from 10% and 5% of survey respondents, respectively.

The current findings offer further evidence of the poor public image of politicians in the United States. And collectively, the occupations that receive the lowest scores for honesty and ethics are those that involve selling. Only about one person in ten rates the ethics of realtors, insurance salesmen, advertising practitioners, or auto salesmen in positive terms. In contrast, about three persons in ten rate each of these occupations as very low or low.

Although some occupations receive low ratings in these studies, it is important to bear in mind that the findings reflect the public's perceptions and are not necessarily indicative of the true ethical standards of the groups examined. At the same time, however, the results suggest a need for remedial efforts on the part of poorly rated professions and occupations.

AUGUST 18
AIDS

Interviewing Date: June 1985
Special Telephone Survey*

Have you heard or read about a disease called AIDS—Acquired Immune Deficiency Syndrome?

	June 1985 Yes	June 1983 Yes
National	95%	77%

By Region

East	95%	85%
Midwest	93	74
South	94	66
West	97	84

Asked of those who replied in the affirmative: To the best of your knowledge, who is most likely to get AIDS?

	National	New York City only
Homosexual males	71%	68%
Blood transfusion recipients	13	16
Haitians	7	18
Drug users	5	15

*The results are from special surveys commissioned by the City of New York's Department of Health in cooperation with the National Center for Disease Control.

Also asked of the aware group: To the best of your knowledge, in what way is AIDS spread; that is, how do people usually get it?

	National	New York City only
Sexual contacts	57%	62%
Infected blood	27	25
Shared drug needles	5	15

Also asked of the aware group: I am going to read you some statements about AIDS. For each, please tell me if you think the statement is probably true, or if you think it is probably false:

	National Probably true	New York City only Probably true
Some people can get AIDS when they receive blood transfusions	92%	90%
Drug users who share needles have a high risk of getting AIDS	84	86
Most people with AIDS are homosexual men	80	73
Some wives and girlfriends of drug users have gotten AIDS	68	71
There is a great danger that AIDS will soon spread to all kinds of people in our country	66	69
You can get AIDS by being in a crowded place with someone who has it	9	15

Note: Although the public correctly identifies homosexual or bisexual men as bearing the greatest current risk of contracting AIDS (Acquired Immune Deficiency Syndrome), more than six in ten adult Americans believe there is a serious danger the disease will soon spread to all kinds of people. A recent nationwide study conducted by the Gallup Organization for the City of New York's Department of Health also reveals growing public awareness of AIDS, with 95% saying they have heard or read of the disease. In June 1983, when Gallup first asked this question, 77% were aware of AIDS. Thus, high awareness of AIDS is now found throughout the nation.

In the survey, about seven in ten respondents nationwide (71%) correctly identify homosexual or bisexual men as being at risk. Far fewer cite blood transfusion recipients, including hemophiliacs (13%), Haitians (7%), or drug users (5%). The at-risk population almost exclusively comprises homosexual or bisexual men, intravenous drug users, people who receive blood transfusions from infected donors, and the sexual partners and children of AIDS victims. Public health officials note that although the spread of the disease is rampant among the at-risk groups, its incidence outside these groups remains stable, at only 1% of reported cases.

Questioned about the spread of the disease, two-thirds (66%) of those aware of AIDS—representing 62% of the general adult population—think that "there is a great danger that AIDS will soon spread to all kinds of people in our country." Also thought to be true, by 9% nationally, are the mistaken beliefs that AIDS can be transmitted by shaking hands with, or being in crowded places with, AIDS victims. Moreover, nine in ten nationally (92%) agree that "some people can get AIDS when they receive blood transfusions," and only slightly fewer (84%) think "drug users who share needles have a high risk of getting AIDS." Eight in ten respondents nationally (80%) believe that "most people with AIDS are homosexual men," while comparatively fewer, 68%, believe that "some wives and girlfriends of drug users have gotten AIDS."

Since 1981, when the disease was first identified, over 12,000 cases of AIDS have been recorded, with nearly half of these cases reported in New York City. The disease now is the leading cause of death in the city among men age 25 to 44; during June, a record of 226 new cases of AIDS was reported. The mortality rate is now about 50%.

AUGUST 22
RATING POLITICAL LEADERS

Interviewing Date: 7/12–15/85
Survey #255-G

You will note that the ten boxes on this card go from the highest position of +5 for someone you have a very favorable opinion of all the way down to the lowest position of −5 for someone you have a very unfavorable opinion of. How far up or down the scale would you rate the following?

	Highly favorable (+5, +4)	Highly unfavorable (−4, −5)
Ronald Reagan	40%	8%
Edward Kennedy ...	25	7
Lee Iacocca	25	3
George Bush	23	5
Gary Hart	14	3
Jesse Jackson	13	13
Mario Cuomo	13	3
Howard Baker	10	2
Robert Dole	8	3

Note: The closeness of the 1988 test race between Vice-president George Bush and Senator Edward Kennedy is reflected in a measurement of the personality factor, with each man winning about the same proportion of highly favorable votes from the electorate. One-fifth of survey respondents nationwide (23%) give Bush this rating on a 10-point attitudinal scale, while a similar percentage (25%) give Kennedy a highly favorable rating. Turning to the negative end, we again see closely comparable figures, with 5% holding highly unfavorable opinions of Bush and 7% of Kennedy. Interestingly, Chrysler Chairman Lee Iacocca scores at 25% as well as Bush and Kennedy on this scale, despite the fact that he has been in the national spotlight for a shorter length of time.

The latest Gallup survey sought to measure the personal appeal of popular candidates for the Republican and Democratic nominations in 1988. The personality factor, together with issues and party loyalty, has proved to be an important barometer of presidential election results, as determined by Gallup surveys over the last three decades.

Bush, Kennedy, and Iacocca, of the eight possible candidates tested, score highest. In weighing the scores of the other five, however, it should be borne in mind that these persons have lower name recognition scores. Following the top three in the rankings are Senator Gary Hart (14%), the Reverend Jesse Jackson (13%), New York Governor Mario Cuomo (13%), Senator Howard Baker (10%), and Senator Robert Dole (8%).

AUGUST 25
SOUTH AFRICA

Interviewing Date: 8/13–15/85
Special Telephone Survey

How closely would you say you've followed the recent events in South Africa—very closely, fairly closely, or not very closely?

Very closely 17%
Fairly closely 46
Not very closely 36
Not sure 1

By Sex
Male

Very closely 20%
Fairly closely 45
Not very closely 34
Not sure 1

Female

Very closely 14%
Fairly closely 47
Not very closely 38
Not sure 1

By Ethnic Background
White

Very closely 14%
Fairly closely 48
Not very closely 37
Not sure 1

Nonwhite

Very closely 36%
Fairly closely 32
Not very closely 30
Not sure 2

Black

Very closely 39%
Fairly closely 31
Not very closely 27
Not sure 3

By Education
College Graduate

Very closely 20%
Fairly closely 53
Not very closely 27
Not sure .... *

College Incomplete

Very closely 17%
Fairly closely 53
Not very closely 30
Not sure .... *

High-School Graduate

Very closely 16%
Fairly closely 40
Not very closely 44
Not sure .... *

Less Than High-School Graduate

Very closely 15%
Fairly closely 41
Not very closely 41
Not sure 3

By Region
East

Very closely 18%
Fairly closely 49
Not very closely 33
Not sure .... *

Midwest

Very closely 15%
Fairly closely 45
Not very closely 40
Not sure .... *

South

Very closely 19%
Fairly closely 43
Not very closely 36
Not sure 2

West

Very closely 17%
Fairly closely 48
Not very closely 34
Not sure 1

By Age
18–24 Years

Very closely 9%
Fairly closely 46
Not very closely 44
Not sure 1

25–29 Years

Very closely 17%
Fairly closely 39
Not very closely 41
Not sure 3

30–49 Years

Very closely 16%
Fairly closely 49
Not very closely 35
Not sure .... *

50 Years and Over

Very closely 21%
Fairly closely 46
Not very closely 32
Not sure 1

By Income
$25,000 and Over

Very closely 15%
Fairly closely 48
Not very closely 37
Not sure .... *

Under $25,000

Very closely 18%
Fairly closely 46
Not very closely 35
Not sure 1

By Politics
Republicans

Very closely 18%
Fairly closely 45
Not very closely 37
Not sure .... *

Democrats

Very closely 21%
Fairly closely 42
Not very closely 36
Not sure 1

Independents

Very closely 13%
Fairly closely 51
Not very closely 35
Not sure 1

*Less than 1%

Do you happen to know whether or not black South Africans have the right to vote?

No, do not (correct) 48%
Yes, do 20
Not sure 32

By Sex
Male

No, do not (correct) 47%
Yes, do 22
Not sure 31

Female

No, do not (correct) 49%
Yes, do 17
Not sure 34

By Ethnic Background
White

No, do not (correct) 49%
Yes, do 19
Not sure 32

Nonwhite

No, do not (correct) 40%
Yes, do 25
Not sure 35

Black

No, do not (correct) 39%
Yes, do 26
Not sure 35

By Education
College Graduate

No, do not (correct) 60%
Yes, do 17
Not sure 23

College Incomplete

No, do not (correct) 56%
Yes, do 15
Not sure 29

High-School Graduate

No, do not (correct) 44%
Yes, do 18
Not sure 38

Less Than High-School Graduate

No, do not (correct) 30%
Yes, do 32
Not sure 38

By Region
East

No, do not (correct) 52%
Yes, do 23
Not sure 25

Midwest

No, do not (correct) 48%
Yes, do 18
Not sure 34

South

No, do not (correct) 44%
Yes, do 21
Not sure 35

West

No, do not (correct) 49%
Yes, do 15
Not sure 36

By Age
18–24 Years

No, do not (correct) 46%
Yes, do 20
Not sure 34

25–29 Years

No, do not (correct) 42%
Yes, do 14
Not sure 44

30–49 Years

No, do not (correct) 54%
Yes, do 18
Not sure 28

50 Years and Over

No, do not (correct) 45%
Yes, do 23
Not sure 32

By Income
$25,000 and Over

No, do not (correct) 56%
Yes, do 16
Not sure 28

Under $25,000

No, do not (correct) 44%
Yes, do 22
Not sure 34

By Politics
Republicans

No, do not (correct) 48%
Yes, do 21
Not sure 31

Democrats

No, do not (correct) 46%
Yes, do 20
Not sure 34

Independents

No, do not (correct) 53%
Yes, do 17
Not sure 30

Do you happen to know what proportion of South Africans is black? Would you say three-fourths or more, somewhere between one-half and three-fourths, somewhere between one-fourth and one-half, or less than one-fourth are black?

Three-fourths or more (correct) 59%
Between one-half and three-fourths 24
Between one-fourth and one-half 3
Less than one-fourth 1
Not sure 13

Asked of the highly informed group (the 63% who say they have followed recent events in South Africa very or fairly closely) and the informed group (the 36% who have followed the South African situation at least fairly closely, and know that blacks there do not have the right to vote and that blacks comprise more than a majority of the total population): In the South African situation, are your sympathies more with the black population or more with the South African government?

	Highly informed group	Informed group
Black population	76%	67%
South African government	10	11
Both equally (volunteered)	4	4
Neither (volunteered)	3	3
White population (volunteered)	*	1
Don't know	7	14

By Sex
Male

Black population	80%	71%
South African government	8	11
Both equally (volunteered)	3	4
Neither (volunteered)	3	4
White population (volunteered)	1	1
Don't know	5	9

Female

Black population	71%	64%
South African government	12	11

Both equally (volunteered)	5	5
Neither (volunteered)	2	1
White population (volunteered)	*	*
Don't know	10	19

By Ethnic Background
White

Black population	75%	66%
South African government	11	11
Both equally (volunteered)	4	4
Neither (volunteered)	3	3
White population (volunteered)	*	1
Don't know	7	15

Nonwhite

Black population	85%	76%
South African government	5	7
Both equally (volunteered)	2	4
Neither (volunteered)	1	4
White population (volunteered)	*	*
Don't know	7	9

Black

Black population	88%	76%
South African government	6	9
Both equally (volunteered)	2	6
Neither (volunteered)	*	2
White population (volunteered)	*	*
Don't know	4	7

By Education
College Graduate

Black population	82%	77%
South African government	5	7

Both equally (volunteered)	3	3
Neither (volunteered)	4	4
White population (volunteered)	*	*
Don't know	6	9

College Incomplete

Black population	80%	76%
South African government	6	7
Both equally (volunteered)	3	4
Neither (volunteered)	3	4
White population (volunteered)	*	*
Don't know	8	9

High-School Graduate

Black population	68%	60%
South African government	16	15
Both equally (volunteered)	3	5
Neither (volunteered)	2	1
White population (volunteered)	1	1
Don't know	10	18

Less Than High-School Graduate

Black population	68%	50%
South African government	24	13
Both equally (volunteered)	8	5
Neither (volunteered)	*	3
White population (volunteered)	*	3
Don't know	*	26

By Region

East

Black population	79%	75%
South African government	14	13

Both equally (volunteered)	2	3
Neither (volunteered)	1	2
White population (volunteered)	*	1
Don't know	4	6

Midwest

Black population	73%	62%
South African government	7	11
Both equally (volunteered)	7	7
Neither (volunteered)	3	2
White population (volunteered)	*	*
Don't know	10	18

South

Black population	67%	60%
South African government	10	10
Both equally (volunteered)	4	5
Neither (volunteered)	5	4
White population (volunteered)	*	*
Don't know	14	21

West

Black population	87%	73%
South African government	6	10
Both equally (volunteered)	2	1
Neither (volunteered)	1	3
White population (volunteered)	2	3
Don't know	2	10

By Age

18–29 Years

Black population	86%	77%
South African government	5	11

Both equally (volunteered)	3	3
Neither (volunteered)	3	2
White population (volunteered)	*	*
Don't know	3	7

30–49 Years

Black population	80%	77%
South African government	10	10
Both equally (volunteered)	3	4
Neither (volunteered)	3	3
White population (volunteered)	*	1
Don't know	4	5

50 Years and Over

Black population	63%	50%
South African government	13	11
Both equally (volunteered)	6	5
Neither (volunteered)	2	3
White population (volunteered)	1	2
Don't know	15	29

By Politics
Republicans

Black population	72%	58%
South African government	13	16
Both equally .(volunteered)	3	4
Neither (volunteered)	4	4
White population (volunteered)	*	*
Don't know	8	18

Democrats

Black population	79%	71%
South African government	9	10

Both equally (volunteered)	4	6
Neither (volunteered)	1	2
White population (volunteered)	1	1
Don't know	6	10

Independents

Black population	78%	74%
South African government	8	7
Both equally (volunteered)	4	4
Neither (volunteered)	4	3
White population (volunteered)	*	*
Don't know	6	12

*Less than 1%

Do you approve or disapprove of the way the Reagan administration is dealing with the South African situation?

	Total sample	Highly informed group	Informed group
Approve	35%	41%	40%
Disapprove	32	40	44
No opinion	33	19	16

Those Who Approve of Reagan's Overall Job Performance (65%)

Approve	47%
Disapprove	19
No opinion	34

Those Who Disapprove of Reagan's Overall Job Performance (26%)

Approve	14%
Disapprove	60
No opinion	26

Those Who Have No Opinion of Reagan's Overall Job Performance (9%)

Approve 12%
Disapprove 42
No opinion 46

Asked of the entire sample: What, if anything, do you think the United States should do next?

Remain impartial; don't get involved 44%
Impose economic sanctions (general) 8
Institute trade embargo 5
Support black population (general) 4
Withdraw U.S. investments 3
Apply diplomatic, political pressure 2
Miscellaneous 10
Don't know; no answer 29
_____
105%*

*Multiple responses were given.

Note: The overwhelming weight of American public opinion is supportive of the black majority in South Africa, but comparatively few advocate that the United States pursue more aggressive policies to deal with Pretoria's apartheid racial system. In a special Gallup Poll completed in August, 59% say they sympathize more with the black South African population, 11% take the part of the government, while 7% are sympathetic toward both factions. Almost one in four (23%) does not express an opinion on the issue.

Respondents with an active interest in the situation—the 63% who say they have followed recent events in South Africa very or fairly closely—express greater sympathy for the black majority than for the government by a 67% to 11% margin. And, when the views of informed Americans (the 36% who have followed the South African situation at least fairly closely and know that blacks there do not have the right to vote, although they comprise a majority of the total population) are examined, this group is found to side with the black population by 76% to 10%.

The dominant response, cited by 44% of respondents, is that the United States should continue to maintain its impartial stance and, at least

for the present, not become more actively involved. Other responses include: impose economic sanctions (8%), institute a trade embargo (5%), give general support to the blacks (4%), withdraw U.S. investments (3%), and continue to apply political and diplomatic pressure to end apartheid (2%). Three in ten (29%) are unable to offer suggestions.

Gallup surveys that have queried the public about U.S. assistance in other areas of the world almost invariably have found a strong penchant for noninvolvement. In a 1983 poll, for example, 55% opined that the United States should not get involved in the internal affairs of friendly Central American governments, while 35% thought we should give military assistance to these nations.

AUGUST 29
PRESIDENT REAGAN

Interviewing Date: 8/13–15/85
Special Telephone Survey

Do you approve or disapprove of the way Ronald Reagan is handling his job as president?

Approve 65%
Disapprove 26
No opinion 9

As shown in the comparison table, President Reagan's current performance rating is matched only by that accorded Lyndon Johnson at a similar period in his incumbency, at roughly the midpoint of the first year of his elected term. Reagan's latest approval score tops those received by Presidents Richard Nixon, Dwight Eisenhower, and Harry Truman at this point in their tenures:

	Survey period	Approve	Dis-approve	No opinion
Reagan	Aug. 1985	65%	26%	9%
Nixon	Aug. 1973	36	54	10
Johnson	Aug. 1965	64	25	11
Eisenhower	Aug. 1957	59	23	18
Truman	Sept. 1949	51	31	18

Do you feel that President Reagan has been a more effective president in his second term than in his first term, less effective, or do you feel there hasn't been much difference?

More effective 14%
Less effective 20
No difference 61
No opinion 5

By Politics
Republicans

More effective 19%
Less effective 16
No difference 59
No opinion 6

Democrats

More effective 9%
Less effective 26
No difference 26
No opinion 3

Independents

More effective 13%
Less effective 19
No difference 65
No opinion 3

Note: In mid-August, as Ronald Reagan rests and recuperates at his Santa Barbara ranch, he continues to receive a strong vote of confidence from the American people for his handling of his presidential duties. In the latest Gallup Poll, 65% approve of his job performance, while 26% disapprove and 9% are undecided. Not since the honeymoon period following his 1981 inauguration has a significantly larger proportion approved of the president's performance in office.

In July the public responded to news of Reagan's cancer operation by boosting his approval rating 5 percentage points. His current strong job rating marks a continuation of an upward trend that began last May.

Some political observers have faulted the president's job performance so far this year, citing his "lame duck" status, among other factors. However, while 20% of the public think Reagan has been less effective this year than he was during his first term, this is largely offset by the 14% who say he has been a more effective president this term than last. A 61% majority expresses the belief that there has not been much difference between his first and second terms.

As expected, political partisanship plays a major role in determining the public's attitudes in this regard. Republicans, for example, are quite evenly divided between those who say Reagan has been more effective this term (19%) rather than less effective (16%). Democrats, on the other hand, come down heavily on the side that he has been less (26%) rather than more (9%) effective this term. The slight weight of independent opinion is on the negative side, 19% to 13%. Overriding these differences is the fact that substantial majorities of all political stripes perceive no difference in Reagan's first and second term effectiveness.

SEPTEMBER 1
REAGAN'S TAX PROPOSALS

Interviewing Date: 8/13–15/85
Special Telephone Survey

From everything that you have heard or read about it, do you think the amount of taxes you now pay would go up, go down, or stay about the same, if the administration's proposed overhaul of the federal tax system were put into effect?

Go up 46%
Go down 11
Stay the same 30
Don't know 13

By Sex
Male

Go up 47%
Go down 13
Stay the same 30
Don't know 10

Female

Go up	46%
Go down	9
Stay the same	29
Don't know	16

By Ethnic Background
White

Go up	44%
Go down	11
Stay the same	32
Don't know	13

Nonwhite

Go up	61%
Go down	6
Stay the same	17
Don't know	16

Black

Go up	60%
Go down	7
Stay the same	16
Don't know	17

By Education
College Graduate

Go up	42%
Go down	12
Stay the same	37
Don't know	9

College Incomplete

Go up	47%
Go down	10
Stay the same	30
Don't know	13

High-School Graduate

Go up	50%
Go down	13
Stay the same	25
Don't know	12

Less Than High-School Graduate

Go up	42%
Go down	6
Stay the same	31
Don't know	21

By Region
East

Go up	47%
Go down	9
Stay the same	30
Don't know	14

Midwest

Go up	40%
Go down	12
Stay the same	34
Don't know	14

South

Go up	48%
Go down	10
Stay the same	30
Don't know	12

West

Go up	51%
Go down	14
Stay the same	23
Don't know	12

By Age
18–29 Years

Go up	44%
Go down	15
Stay the same	26
Don't know	15

30–49 Years

Go up	50%
Go down	12
Stay the same	30
Don't know	8

50 Years and Over

Go up	45%
Go down	6
Stay the same	32
Don't know	17

By Income
$50,000 and Over

Go up	49%
Go down	9
Stay the same	35
Don't know	7

$35,000–$49,999

Go up	49%
Go down	8
Stay the same	33
Don't know	10

$25,000–$34,999

Go up	41%
Go down	14
Stay the same	34
Don't know	11

Under $25,000

Go up	45%
Go down	11
Stay the same	34
Don't know	10

By Politics
Republicans

Go up	39%
Go down	12
Stay the same	35
Don't know	14

Democrats

Go up	51%
Go down	8
Stay the same	29
Don't know	12

Independents

Go up	47%
Go down	15
Stay the same	26
Don't know	12

Do you think the new plan would make for a fairer distribution of the tax load among all taxpayers, one that is less fair, or wouldn't it be much different from the present system?

Fairer than old	25%
Less fair than old	20
Not much different	40
No opinion	15

Note: The public's confidence in some of the key elements of President Ronald Reagan's proposed overhaul of the federal tax system is showing signs of erosion. First, public opinion has shifted quite sharply toward the view that their taxes would go up if the Reagan tax plan were put into effect, with a corresponding decline in those who say their taxes would go down. Second, there has been some slippage in the proportion saying the Reagan program would more equitably distribute the tax load among all taxpayers than the present system does.

In the latest (mid-August) Gallup Poll, a 46% plurality believes their taxes would go up under the proposed tax program, while 30% think theirs would stay about the same as they are now, and 11% believe theirs would go down. In June, when Gallup first measured public opinion on this issue, 32% thought their taxes would go up, 29% said they would stay the same, and 25% thought they would go down if the Reagan plan were enacted. Comparing the findings of the two surveys, the greatest shift in opinion has occurred among Republicans, of whom 45% said in June (compared to 32% at present) that the Reagan proposal would be fairer than the present tax system.

SEPTEMBER 5
CIGARETTE SMOKING

Interviewing Date: 6/7–10/85
Survey #254-G

Have you, yourself, smoked any cigarettes in the past week?

	Yes
National	35%

By Sex

Male	37%
Female	39

By Ethnic Background

White	34%
Black	39

By Education

College graduate	23%
College incomplete	31
High-school graduate	40
Less than high-school graduate	39

By Region

East	36%
Midwest	38
South	31
West	34

By Age

18–29 years	38%
30–49 years	40
50–64 years	37
65 years and over	16

By Income

$25,000 and over	32%
Under $25,000	38

By Occupation

Professional and business	34%
Clerical and sales	38
Skilled workers	36
Unskilled workers	42

Labor union households	42
Nonlabor union households	33

Selected National Trend

	Yes
1983	38%
1981	35
1978	36
1977	38
1974	40
1972	43
1971	42
1969	40
1958	45
1957	42
1954	45
1949	44
1944	41

Note: Despite strong health warnings and stiff taxes that bring the retail cost in most states to over $1 per pack, at least one American adult in three is a cigarette smoker. In the latest Gallup Smoking Audit, 35% report having smoked cigarettes during the week prior to being interviewed. Although this is statistically unchanged from the 38% recorded in the previous (1983) audit, it matches the figure reported in 1981 and represents the lowest proportion of smokers since Gallup began conducting these audits in 1944. The proportion of smokers in the adult population has declined gradually since the U.S. surgeon general's historic 1964 report linking cigarette smoking to serious illnesses such as cancer and heart disease.

As in Gallup audits since 1977, slightly more men (37%) than women (32%) now are smokers. (In earlier surveys, there were far more men than women smokers: in 1954, for example, 57% of men, but only 32% of women, said they smoked cigarettes.) Also, education is closely related to whether or not people smoke. In the current audit, only 23% of college graduates are cigarette smokers, with the proportion rising to 31% among those who attended college but did not receive a degree, and to 40% among those with no college exposure.

Occupation is another related factor, with members of labor union (blue collar) households reporting a significantly higher incidence of smoking (42%) than those from nonunion homes (33%). As for age, smoking drops off sharply among persons 65 and over—only 16% are smokers—but similar levels are reported in other age groups.

SEPTEMBER 8
FEDERAL BUDGET DEFICIT

Interviewing Date: 8/13–15/85
Special Telephone Survey

In your opinion, is the current federal budget deficit a very serious problem for the country, a fairly serious problem, not a serious problem, or is this something you haven't thought much about?

Very serious 57%
Fairly serious 21
Not serious 2
Not thought much about;
   no opinion 20

By Education
College Graduate

Very serious 62%
Fairly serious 27
Not serious 3
Not thought much about;
   no opinion 8

College Incomplete

Very serious 65%
Fairly serious 22
Not serious 1
Not thought much about;
   no opinion 12

High-School Graduate

Very serious 51%
Fairly serious 20
Not serious 2
Not thought much about;
   no opinion 27

Less Than High-School Graduate

Very serious 50%
Fairly serious 15
Not serious 1
Not thought much about;
   no opinion 34

By Region
East

Very serious 54%
Fairly serious 21
Not serious 2
Not thought much about;
   no opinion 23

Midwest

Very serious 59%
Fairly serious 21
Not serious 4
Not thought much about;
   no opinion 16

South

Very serious 59%
Fairly serious 20
Not serious 2
Not thought much about;
   no opinion 19

West

Very serious 53%
Fairly serious 25
Not serious .... *
Not thought much about;
   no opinion 22

By Age

18–29 Years

Very serious 40%
Fairly serious 27
Not serious 4
Not thought much about;
  no opinion 29

30–49 Years

Very serious 59%
Fairly serious 24
Not serious 2
Not thought much about;
  no opinion 15

50 Years and Over

Very serious 67%
Fairly serious 14
Not serious 1
Not thought much about;
  no opinion 18

By Politics

Republicans

Very serious 54%
Fairly serious 25
Not serious 5
Not thought much about;
  no opinion 16

Democrats

Very serious 59%
Fairly serious 18
Not serious 1
Not thought much about;
  no opinion 22

Independents

Very serious 57%
Fairly serious 20
Not serious 2
Not thought much about;
  no opinion 21

*Less than 1%

As you may know, Congress recently approved a budget for fiscal 1986, which starts October 1. Do you expect the federal deficit a year from now will be larger or smaller than it is now, or don't you expect the deficit to change much during the coming year?

Larger next year 47%
Smaller next year 8
Not much change .38
No opinion 7

By Education

College Graduate

Larger next year 55%
Smaller next year 8
Not much change .34
No opinion 3

College Incomplete

Larger next year 49%
Smaller next year 7
Not much change .36
No opinion 8

High-School Graduate

Larger next year 45%
Smaller next year .10
Not much change .38
No opinion 7

Less Than High-School Graduate

Larger next year 38%
Smaller next year 5
Not much change .45
No opinion 12

By Region

East

Larger next year 48%
Smaller next year .10
Not much change .37
No opinion 5

Midwest

Larger next year .46%
Smaller next year 6
Not much change 39
No opinion 9

South

Larger next year .43%
Smaller next year 8
Not much change 40
No opinion 9

West

Larger next year .52%
Smaller next year 8
Not much change 34
No opinion 6

By Age
18–29 Years

Larger next year .38%
Smaller next year 12
Not much change 43
No opinion 7

30–49 Years

Larger next year .55%
Smaller next year 5
Not much change 33
No opinion 7

50 Years and Over

Larger next year .46%
Smaller next year 7
Not much change 39
No opinion 8

By Politics
Republicans

Larger next year .42%
Smaller next year 10
Not much change 42
No opinion 6

Democrats

Larger next year .54%
Smaller next year 4
Not much change 35
No opinion 7

Independents

Larger next year .45%
Smaller next year 9
Not much change 38
No opinion 8

Would you approve or disapprove of raising personal income taxes to reduce the federal deficit?

Approve 25%
Disapprove 68
No opinion 7

By Education
College Graduate

Approve 33%
Disapprove 62
No opinion 5

College Incomplete

Approve 26%
Disapprove 68
No opinion 6

High-School Graduate

Approve 22%
Disapprove 73
No opinion 5

Less Than High-School Graduate

Approve 23%
Disapprove 65
No opinion 12

By Region

East

Approve 23%
Disapprove 72
No opinion 5

Midwest

Approve 25%
Disapprove 70
No opinion 5

South

Approve 28%
Disapprove 65
No opinion 7

West

Approve 26%
Disapprove 63
No opinion 11

By Age

18–29 Years

Approve 22%
Disapprove 71
No opinion 7

30–49 Years

Approve 27%
Disapprove 69
No opinion 4

50 Years and Over

Approve 26%
Disapprove 64
No opinion 10

By Income

$35,000 and Over

Approve 34%
Disapprove 62
No opinion 4

$15,000–$34,999

Approve 25%
Disapprove 70
No opinion 5

Under $15,000

Approve 22%
Disapprove 69
No opinion 9

By Politics

Republicans

Approve 27%
Disapprove 67
No opinion 6

Democrats

Approve 25%
Disapprove 69
No opinion 6

Independents

Approve 26%
Disapprove 66
No opinion 8

Note: The American people do not see eye to eye with the Reagan administration on the prospects for a lower federal budget deficit in fiscal 1986, with nearly half (47%) predicting a larger deficit and another four in ten (38%) seeing little change. The White House Office of Management and the Budget recently projected that the deficit for the fiscal year starting October 1 would be $178 billion. The office said the 1985 deficit would be $211 billion.

In view of the public's grim forecast, it is not surprising to learn that six in ten (57%) survey respondents label the current deficit "a very serious problem," consistent with earlier findings. The extent of the public's concern is reflected by the fact that fully one-fourth (25%) would approve of raising personal income taxes to reduce the deficit, with that proportion rising to one-third among college graduates.

Surprisingly little political coloration is found in the survey findings, with Republicans and independents nearly as pessimistic as Democrats about the prospects for a smaller deficit next year. They all are about as likely to consider it a very serious problem, and about as apt to favor an increase in personal taxes to reduce the deficit.

SEPTEMBER 9
BALANCED BUDGET AMENDMENT

Interviewing Date: 8/13–15/85
Special Telephone Survey

Have you heard or read about the proposal for a constitutional amendment that would require the federal government to balance the national budget each year?

	Yes
National	57%

Asked of the entire sample: Under the proposed amendment, any federal budget passed by Congress would have projected tax revenues that are equal to projected government spending, unless a three-fifths' majority of Congress voted not to do so. Would you favor or oppose this amendment to the Constitution?

Favor	49%
Oppose	27
No opinion	24

By Sex
Male

Favor	55%
Oppose	28
No opinion	17

Female

Favor	44%
Oppose	25
No opinion	31

By Education
College Graduate

Favor	59%
Oppose	27
No opinion	14

College Incomplete

Favor	49%
Oppose	26
No opinion	25

High-School Graduate

Favor	47%
Oppose	28
No opinion	25

Less Than High-School Graduate

Favor	39%
Oppose	28
No opinion	33

By Region
East

Favor	48%
Oppose	32
No opinion	20

Midwest

Favor	49%
Oppose	24
No opinion	27

South

Favor	49%
Oppose	23
No opinion	28

West

Favor	49%
Oppose	30
No opinion	21

By Age

18–29 Years

Favor 49%
Oppose 28
No opinion 23

30–49 Years

Favor 54%
Oppose 29
No opinion 17

50 Years and Over

Favor 43%
Oppose 24
No opinion 33

By Politics

Republicans

Favor 55%
Oppose 22
No opinion 23

Democrats

Favor 44%
Oppose 36
No opinion 20

Independents

Favor 51%
Oppose 25
No opinion 24

Those Who Have Heard or Read About the Proposed Constitutional Amendment

Favor 54%
Oppose 28
No opinion 18

Note: With the White House projecting a $178 billion budget deficit for fiscal 1986, which starts October 1, strong popular support is found for a constitutional amendment that would require the federal government to balance the budget each year. In the latest Gallup survey, a 49% plurality favors, while 27% oppose, an amendment mandating that any budget passed by the Congress would project tax revenues equal to projected government spending, unless a three-fifths' majority of Congress voted otherwise. About one-fourth of survey respondents (24%) do not express an opinion. At least a plurality in all major population groups supports the proposal, with majorities of men (55%), Republicans (55%), and college-educated persons of both sexes (59%) expressing approval. Earlier Gallup Polls, employing slightly different question wording, also found heavy public backing for a balanced budget amendment.

The debate over an amendment has assumed new urgency, since thirty-two of the thirty-four required states already have petitioned Congress for a convention to propose such an amendment. Thus, proponents are only two states short of their goal. Recently, a new dimension was added to the debate, challenging the validity of some of the state petitions on the grounds that most were approved more than seven years ago and thus do not represent an expression of the current popular will.

The last constitutional convention was held in 1787, two years before George Washington was elected president. Since 1787 all proposed amendments to the Constitution have been suggested by Congress after being approved by a two-thirds' vote of both houses. But there is another legal method of proposing constitutional change, according to Article V of the Constitution: "On the application of the legislatures of two-thirds of the several states, [Congress] shall call a convention for proposing amendments."

SEPTEMBER 15
ECONOMIC SITUATION

Interviewing Date: 8/13–15/85
Special Telephone Survey

The economy is now in the third year of recovery from the recession of 1981–82. Of course, no one knows for sure, but what is your best guess as to how long this recovery will last before the economy turns down again? Will the recovery end this year, early next year, later next year, or later than that?

This year	5%
Early next year	12
Later next year	15
Later than that	51
Never end (volunteered)	3
No opinion	14

By Sex
Male

This year	6%
Early next year	14
Later next year	15
Later than that	52
Never end (volunteered)	2
No opinion	11

Female

This year	5%
Early next year	10
Later next year	14
Later than that	50
Never end (volunteered)	3
No opinion	18

By Education
College Graduate

This year	4%
Early next year	18
Later next year	17
Later than that	46
Never end (volunteered)	2
No opinion	13

College Incomplete

This year	6%
Early next year	6
Later next year	19
Later than that	49
Never end (volunteered)	2
No opinion	18

High-School Graduate

This year	5%
Early next year	12
Later next year	14
Later than that	58
Never end (volunteered)	3
No opinion	8

Less Than High-School Graduate

This year	7%
Early next year	13
Later next year	7
Later than that	45
Never end (volunteered)	3
No opinion	25

By Region
East

This year	8%
Early next year	11
Later next year	16
Later than that	49
Never end (volunteered)	3
No opinion	13

Midwest

This year	6%
Early next year	13
Later next year	14
Later than that	51
Never end (volunteered)	2
No opinion	14

South

This year	3%
Early next year	9
Later next year	16
Later than that	55
Never end (volunteered)	1
No opinion	16

West

This year	5%
Early next year	17
Later next year	14

Later than that 45
Never end (volunteered) 4
No opinion 15

By Age
18–29 Years

This year 4%
Early next year 9
Later next year 17
Later than that 61
Never end (volunteered) 1
No opinion 8

30–49 Years

This year 6%
Early next year 13
Later next year 16
Later than that 53
Never end (volunteered) 2
No opinion 10

50–64 Years

This year 6%
Early next year 12
Later next year 14
Later than that 43
Never end (volunteered) 3
No opinion 22

65 Years and Over

This year 6%
Early next year 14
Later next year 10
Later than that 37
Never end (volunteered) 5
No opinion 28

By Income
$35,000 and Over

This year 6%
Early next year 13
Later next year 20
Later than that 48
Never end (volunteered) 2
No opinion 11

$15,000–$34,999

This year 6%
Early next year 13
Later next year 16
Later than that 52
Never end (volunteered) 2
No opinion 11

Under $15,000

This year 3%
Early next year 10
Later next year 12
Later than that 54
Never end (volunteered) 4
No opinion 17

By Politics
Republicans

This year 4%
Early next year 8
Later next year 15
Later than that 57
Never end (volunteered) 1
No opinion 15

Democrats

This year 7%
Early next year 15
Later next year 15
Later than that 47
Never end (volunteered) 3
No opinion 13

Independents

This year 7%
Early next year 12
Later next year 16
Later than that 49
Never end (volunteered) 3
No opinion 13

Selected National Trend

	May 1984*	September 1983*
This year	11%	6%
Early next year	15	12
Later next year	21	20
Later than that	34	38
Never end (volunteered) . . .	3	5
No opinion	16	19

*In these surveys, the introductory part of the question read: *As you know, the economy has begun to recover from recession this year, with increased production, employment, and profits.*

Note: Although economists are divided about the direction of the nation's economy, the public is now more bullish than ever that the recovery will continue. In the latest Gallup Poll, eight persons in ten (83%) say they expect the recovery to last at least until the end of this year, with 54% predicting economic good times will prevail into 1987 or beyond.

Perhaps conditioned by the duration of the recovery, which began almost three years ago after the severe 1981–82 recession, the public is now more optimistic than in surveys conducted in 1983 and 1984. In September 1983, for example, only 43% thought the recovery would last beyond the end of 1984. In May 1984, the proportion saying the recovery would extend beyond the end of 1985 had dropped to 37%. Now, as noted above, 54% are comparatively bullish.

Conversely, in the 1983 survey, 38% thought the recovery would start to fade out by the end of 1984. In 1984, 47% thought it would last only until the end of 1985. In the current survey, only 32% say it will run out of steam by the end of next year.

Republicans are only slightly more bullish than Democrats about the recovery's duration, with 58% of the former and 50% of the latter saying it will last at least into 1987. Similarly, 12% of Republicans and 22% of Democrats believe a downturn will occur by early next year.

Optimism declines steadily as age increases, with 18 to 29 year olds considerably more likely to think the recovery will last beyond next year (62%) than those 30 to 49 (55%), 50 to 64 (46%), or 65 and older (42%). Large proportions in the two older age groups are undecided.

SEPTEMBER 19
SPORTS PARTICIPATION

Interviewing Date: 5/17–20/85
Survey #253-G

Which of these sports and activities have you, yourself, participated in within the last twelve months? [Respondents were handed a card listing fifty sports and activities.]

	National*
Swimming	41%
Fishing	34
Bicycling	33
Bowling	25
Jogging	23
Softball	22
Camping	21
Pool, billiards	19
Weight training	19
Aerobics, dancercize	18
Hiking	18
Motorboating	16
Volleyball	16
Basketball	15
Calisthenics	15
Hunting	14
Baseball	13
Golf	13
Tennis	13
Table tennis	12
Canoeing, rowing	9
Frisbee	9
Horseback riding	9
Roller skating	9
Target shooting	9
Racquetball	8
Skiing	8
Waterskiing	7

Touch football 6
Ice skating 5
Sailing 5

*Participation in one or more of the listed activities was reported by 86% of men and 73% of women.

Men's Top Activities

Fishing 44%
Swimming 42
Bicycling 32
Pool, billiards 28
Softball 28
Weight training 26
Bowling 25
Jogging 25
Basketball 24
Hunting 23

Women's Top Activities

Swimming 41%
Bicycling 33
Aerobics, dancercize 28
Bowling 25
Fishing 24
Jogging 21
Camping 20
Hiking 17
Softball 16
Volleyball 15

Following are highlights of the trends for selected sports and activities that have been tracked regularly since the early Gallup audits:

Selected National Trend

	1984	1980	1972	1966	1959
Swimming	41%	37%	42%	33%	33%
Fishing	30	24	24	*	32
Bowling	21	24	28	27	18
Softball	18	16	13	15	*
Volleyball	14	13	12	12	4
Motorboating	14	12	20	16	*
Golf	12	8	14	11	8
Tennis	11	14	12	9	4

*Not asked

Note: Swimming, fishing, and bicycling were American adults' favorite sports and recreational activities in 1985, as they have been for many years. For the 1985 Gallup Leisure Activities Audit, a representative national cross section of 1,528 adults, age 18 and older, was asked which of fifty activities they had participated in during a recent twelve-month period. Eight persons in ten (79%) say they were involved in one or more of the activities studied; last year the figure was 82%, a statistically insignificant difference.

Swimming was the most popular recreational activity in 1985, engaged in by 41%, identical to the figure recorded in last year's audit. Swimming has been the public's favorite participatory sport since these measurements began in 1959.

Runners-up this year are fishing (34%) and bicycling (33%), followed by bowling (25%), jogging (23%), softball (22%), and camping (21%). Rounding out the top ten are pool and billiards, reported by 19%; weight training and other body-building activities (19%); aerobics and dancercize (18%); and hiking (18%).

In this year's survey, the following sports and activities were each named by fewer than 5% of adults: archery, badminton, distance running, handball, hang gliding, martial arts, platform and paddle tennis, scuba diving, skateboarding, skeet and trap shooting, snorkeling, soccer, squash, surfing, sky diving, windsurfing, and yoga.

SEPTEMBER 22
ITEM VETO POWER

Interviewing Date: 8/13–15/85
Special Telephone Survey

At the present time, when Congress passes a bill, the president cannot veto parts of that bill, but must accept it in full or veto it. Do you think this should be changed so that the president can veto some items in a bill without vetoing the entire bill?

Favor 71%
Oppose 22
No opinion 7

By Education

College Graduate

Favor 69%
Oppose 26
No opinion 5

College Incomplete

Favor 68%
Oppose 27
No opinion 5

High-School Graduate

Favor 75%
Oppose 19
No opinion 6

Less Than High-School Graduate

Favor 68%
Oppose 18
No opinion 14

By Politics

Republicans

Favor 78%
Oppose 18
No opinion 4

Democrats

Favor 63%
Oppose 29
No opinion 8

Independents

Favor 73%
Oppose 20
No opinion 7

Selected National Trend

	Favor	Oppose	No opinion
1983	67%	25%	8%
1978	70	19	11
1975	69	20	11
1945	57	14	29

Note: Reflecting perhaps their concern over the federal budget deficit, the public strongly supports giving presidents the line-item veto, the right to kill certain items in a bill passed by Congress without having to veto the whole bill. In the latest Gallup Poll, 71% of the public favor giving presidents this power, while 22% are opposed and 7% undecided. Heavy backing comes from all political persuasions, with support expressed by 78% of Republicans, 63% of Democrats, and 73% of independents.

Large majorities in Gallup surveys spanning four decades have favored changing the present rule. When the issue was first presented to the public in 1945, 57% voted in favor of the item veto. Proponents argue that giving presidents the authority to veto individual items in appropriations bills would stop "pork-barrel" legislation—the inclusion in the budget of items that primarily serve the narrow political interests of some members of Congress without regard to the wisdom of the measures on their own merits. Others contend that eliminating the expensive riders that are frequently tacked on to proposed bills would save millions of dollars. Although their remarks were later interpreted as simply reflecting a desire for greater power for the executive branch, President Ronald Reagan and Senator Edward Kennedy, in a rare example of bipartisan accord, both recently called for giving presidents line-item veto power.

The main argument of those who favor the present system is that it gives the legislative branch more power. A president is forced to accept items (especially in appropriations bills) that he might not otherwise accept.

SEPTEMBER 26
DEFAULTED COLLEGE LOANS

Interviewing Date: 8/13–15/85
Special Telephone Survey

> At present, people who receive low cost, federally guaranteed student loans to attend college have not repaid more than $4 billion of these loans. The government recently announced it would give these people sixty

days to work out a repayment schedule. If that doesn't work, the Internal Revenue Service will start withholding any income tax refunds these people may have coming, up to the amounts they still owe on their student loans. Does this sound to you like a good idea, or a poor idea?

Good idea 82%
Poor idea 15
No opinion 3

By Sex
Male

Good idea 82%
Poor idea 16
No opinion 2

Female

Good idea 82%
Poor idea 15
No opinion 3

By Ethnic Background
White

Good idea 84%
Poor idea 13
No opinion 3

Nonwhite

Good idea 66%
Poor idea 31
No opinion 3

Black

Good idea 66%
Poor idea 30
No opinion 4

By Education
College Graduate

Good idea 89%
Poor idea 9
No opinion 2

College Incomplete

Good idea 82%
Poor idea 15
No opinion 3

High-School Graduate

Good idea 82%
Poor idea 15
No opinion 3

Less Than High-School Graduate

Good idea 71%
Poor idea 25
No opinion 4

By Region
East

Good idea 81%
Poor idea 18
No opinion 1

Midwest

Good idea 85%
Poor idea 12
No opinion 3

South

Good idea 81%
Poor idea 14
No opinion 5

West

Good idea 79%
Poor idea 20
No opinion 1

By Age
18–24 Years

Good idea 71%
Poor idea 27
No opinion 2

25–29 Years

Good idea 86%
Poor idea 14
No opinion .... *

30–49 Years

Good idea 83%
Poor idea 14
No opinion 3

50 Years and Over

Good idea 83%
Poor idea 13
No opinion 4

By Politics
Republicans

Good idea 85%
Poor idea 12
No opinion 3

Democrats

Good idea 77%
Poor idea 21
No opinion 2

Independents

Good idea 84%
Poor idea 14
No opinion 2

*Less than 1%

Note: A government plan to withhold federal tax refunds from persons who have defaulted on their college loans receives overwhelming support from the public. In the latest Gallup Poll, 82% favor such a plan, while 15% are opposed and 3% undecided. Somewhat less support is found among 18 to 24 year olds, those who would be most affected by implementation of the loan repayment program. Nevertheless, they too give heavy backing (71% to 27%). College graduates are among the plan's staunchest supporters, with 89% in favor and only 9% opposed. Strong support also is found among those of all political persuasions and in every region of the nation.

Under the college loan program, begun in 1965, the federal government insures low-interest loans made by private banks and other institutions. If these loans are not repaid on time, the banks are reimbursed by the federal government. Last year the U.S. Education Department was forced to repay about $750 million in defaulted student loans; this year the figure is expected to top $1 billion. All told, some $4 billion in student loans is reported to be in default.

Many defaulters are thought to be among those who attended trade schools and community colleges for only one or two years and graduated or dropped out without sufficient training to ensure them of employment. However, the Reagan administration believes that too many loans were made to upper-income families that did not need financial assistance to pay for college costs.

Education Secretary William Bennett recently announced tough new measures to stem the rising tide of college loan defaults, requesting the Internal Revenue Service to invoke a law passed last year to start withholding federal tax refunds from student loan defaulters. His department also has referred the names of some 16,000 defaulters to the Justice Department for prosecution. Under the law, federal employees who are in default may have their wages attached.

SEPTEMBER 29
AID TO PAROCHIAL SCHOOLS*

Interviewing Date: 5/17–20/85
Special Telephone Survey

Would you favor or oppose an amendment to the Constitution that would permit government financial aid to parochial schools?

Favor 45%
Oppose 47
No opinion 8

*This poll was sponsored by Phi Delta Kappa, the professional educational fraternity.

Selected National Trend

	Favor	Oppose	No opinion
1980	40%	49%	11%
1974	52	35	13

In some nations, the government allots a certain amount of money for each child for his education. The parents can then send the child to any public, parochial, or private school they choose. This is called the "voucher system." Would you like to see such an idea adopted in this country?

Favor 45%
Oppose 40
No opinion 15

By Sex
Male

Favor 46%
Oppose 40
No opinion 14

Female

Favor 43%
Oppose 40
No opinion 17

By Ethnic Background
White

Favor 43%
Oppose 42
No opinion 15

Nonwhite

Favor 59%
Oppose 26
No opinion 15

By Education
College Graduate

Favor 35%
Oppose 54
No opinion 11

College Incomplete

Favor 49%
Oppose 40
No opinion 11

High-School Graduate

Favor 47%
Oppose 36
No opinion 17

Less Than High-School Graduate

Favor 46%
Oppose 37
No opinion 17

Grade School

Favor 43%
Oppose 34
No opinion 23

By Region
East

Favor 53%
Oppose 31
No opinion 16

Midwest

Favor 35%
Oppose 51
No opinion 14

South

Favor 46%
Oppose 40
No opinion 14

West

Favor 44%
Oppose 39
No opinion 17

By Age

18–29 Years

Favor	55%
Oppose	31
No opinion	14

30–49 Years

Favor	46%
Oppose	42
No opinion	12

50 Years and Over

Favor	36%
Oppose	45
No opinion	19

By Religion

Protestants

Favor	42%
Oppose	43
No opinion	15

Catholics

Favor	51%
Oppose	33
No opinion	16

Public-School Parents Only

Favor	49%
Oppose	41
No opinion	10

Nonpublic-School Parents

Favor	63%
Oppose	32
No opinion	5

Selected National Trend

	Favor	Oppose	No opinion
1983	51%	38%	11%
1981	43	41	16
1971	38	44	18
1970	43	46	11

Note: Proponents of government aid to parochial schools—whether through a constitutional amendment or by means of the "voucher system"—are having a tough time winning public opinion to their side. The latest Gallup Poll finds 45% in favor and 47% opposed to a proposed amendment to the U.S. Constitution that would permit the government to provide financial aid to parochial schools, a marginal increase in approval since 1980 but a decidedly lower level of support than in 1974.

Another recent Gallup survey shows support for the voucher system to have slipped somewhat since 1983. Currently 45% favor such a system, while 40% are opposed. In the earlier survey, 51% said they liked the idea and 38% did not. Under the voucher system the government would provide a certain amount of money for the education of each child, regardless of whether that child attended a public, parochial, or other private secondary school.

As might be expected, Protestants and Catholics are far apart in their views on these two vital issues. Two-thirds of Catholics (67%), but only 38% of Protestants, favor the proposed amendment. The vote is closer in the case of the voucher system, with 51% of Catholics and 42% of Protestants expressing support for such a measure.

OCTOBER 3
PRESIDENT REAGAN

Interviewing Date: 9/13–16/85
Survey #257-G

Do you approve or disapprove of the way Ronald Reagan is handling his job as president?

Approve	60%
Disapprove	30
No opinion	10

By Sex

Male

Approve	65%
Disapprove	28
No opinion	7

Female

Approve 56%
Disapprove 32
No opinion 12

By Ethnic Background
White

Approve 64%
Disapprove 27
No opinion 9

Nonwhite

Approve 34%
Disapprove 55
No opinion 11

Black

Approve 28%
Disapprove 61
No opinion 11

By Education
College Graduate

Approve 61%
Disapprove 35
No opinion 4

College Incomplete

Approve 67%
Disapprove 25
No opinion 8

High-School Graduate

Approve 64%
Disapprove 27
No opinion 9

Less Than High-School Graduate

Approve 49%
Disapprove 36
No opinion 15

By Region
East

Approve 62%
Disapprove 27
No opinion 11

Midwest

Approve 54%
Disapprove 36
No opinion 10

South

Approve 60%
Disapprove 30
No opinion 10

West

Approve 66%
Disapprove 27
No opinion 7

By Age
18–29 Years

Approve 65%
Disapprove 24
No opinion 11

30–49 Years

Approve 61%
Disapprove 32
No opinion 7

50 Years and Over

Approve 57%
Disapprove 32
No opinion 11

By Politics
Republicans

Approve 85%
Disapprove 10
No opinion 5

Democrats

Approve 41%
Disapprove 48
No opinion 11

Independents

Approve 60%
Disapprove 30
No opinion 10

The following table compares Reagan's current standing with those of his predecessors in September of the first year of their second or elective term:

Presidential Performance Ratings

	Year	Approve	Dis-approve	No opinion
Reagan	1985	60%	30%	10%
Nixon	1973	34	56	10
Johnson	1965	63	24	13
Eisenhower	1957	59	26	15
Truman	1949	51	31	18

Note: The strong upward trend in President Ronald Reagan's popularity that saw his performance rating climb from 52% approval in April to 65% in August appears to have halted, at least for the time being. Still, Reagan's current rating ranks favorably with those received by Presidents Lyndon Johnson and Dwight Eisenhower and tops those of Richard Nixon and Harry Truman, at comparable points in their tenure.

In the latest (mid-September) Gallup Poll, 60% approve of Reagan's performance in office, while 30% disapprove and 10% are undecided. One month earlier, as the president recuperated at his California ranch from his cancer operation, 65% gave him a positive job rating and 26% a negative one.

The current slight decline in Reagan's standing with the American people may reflect, at least in part, a lessening of the "sympathy vote" associated with his operation in mid-July. Then, too, he has recently met opposition from Congress on such key policy issues as South Africa, the budget deficit, tax reform, the farm crisis, the trade imbalance, and demands for protectionist measures.

OCTOBER 6
SPECTATOR SPORTS

Interviewing Date: 7/12–15/85
Survey #255-G

What is your favorite sport to watch?

Football 26%
Baseball 21
Basketball 10
Tennis 4
Golf 3
Wrestling 3
Hockey 3
Boxing 2
Gymnastics 2
Auto racing 2
Ice skating 2
Touch football 2
Other 10
None 10

By Sex
Male

Football 34%
Baseball 22
Basketball 8

Female

Football 20%
Baseball 20
Basketball 12

By Ethnic Background
White

Football 27%
Baseball 21
Basketball 9

Black

Football 23%
Baseball 23
Basketball 20

By Education
Attended College
Football 30%
Baseball 19
Basketball 11

High School or Less
Football 24%
Baseball 22
Basketball 10

By Region
East
Football 18%
Baseball 25
Basketball 9

Midwest
Football 24%
Baseball 25
Basketball 9

South
Football 33%
Baseball 16
Basketball 12

West
Football 31%
Baseball 16
Basketball 11

By Age
18–29 Years
Football 31%
Baseball 20
Basketball 12

30–49 Years
Football 27%
Baseball 19
Basketball 11

50 Years and Over
Football 22%
Baseball 24
Basketball 7

By Income
$25,000 and Over
Football 31%
Baseball 17
Basketball 11

Under $25,000
Football 22%
Baseball 24
Basketball 10

Selected National Trend

	Football	Baseball	Basketball
1981	38%	16%	9%
1972	36	21	8
1960	21	34	9
1948	17	39	10
1937	26	36	11

Note: Football is still Americans' favorite spectator sport, but the dominance it enjoyed over second-ranked baseball as recently as 1981 has dropped sharply. Basketball remains in third place.

In the latest Gallup Sports Audit, 26% say football is the sport they most like to watch, while 21% name baseball and 10%, basketball. By comparison, in the 1981 audit football led baseball by better than a 2-to-1 margin, 38% to 16%, with basketball cited by 9%.

From Gallup's first audit in 1937 until 1960, baseball was the favorite of adult Americans. In 1972 football took over the number-one slot and has remained there ever since. Football has a disproportionate appeal to men, 34% of whom name it as their favorite, compared to 20% of women, among whom it is tied in appeal with baseball. It also enjoys somewhat greater popularity among younger adults, persons who attended college, the more affluent, and southerners and westerners. In the Midwest, football and baseball are statistically tied for the lead, while in the East baseball holds a modest edge. Among blacks, football, baseball, and basketball have about the same number of partisans, with the latter far more popular with blacks (20% name it their favorite) than with whites (9%).

It should be borne in mind that the figures do not distinguish between television viewing and watching sports in person. In addition, both amateur and professional sports may be included.

OCTOBER 10
MOVIE ATTENDANCE

Interviewing Date: 7/12–15/85
Survey #255-G

When was the last time you, yourself, went out to the movies?

	Attended within last month	Attended within last year
National	34%	59%

By Sex

Male	38%	61%
Female	31	57

By Education

College graduate	43%	75%
College incomplete	45	70
High-school graduate	32	59
Less than high-school graduate	21	34

By Region

East	31%	55%
Midwest	38	60
South	33	56
West	38	65

By Age

18–24 years	71%	88%
25–29 years	43	77
30–49 years	37	67
50–64 years	15	38
65 years and over	6	19

By Income

$25,000 and over	41%	69%
Under $25,000	30	51

By Occupation

Professional and business	44%	75%
Other white collar	41	62
Blue collar	37	61

The following table compares the monthly attendance figures reported in the 1985 and 1982 audits:

Movie Attendance Within Last Month

	1985	1982	Point change
National	34%	42%	− 8

By Sex

Male	38%	42%	− 4
Female	31	41	− 10

By Education

College	44%	57%	− 13
High school	31	40	− 9
Grade school	9	12	− 3

By Region

East	31%	39%	− 8
Midwest	38	45	− 7
South	33	35	− 2
West	38	45	− 7

By Age

18–24 years	71%	69%	+ 2
25–29 years	43	51	− 8
30–49 years	37	48	− 11
50–64 years	15	25	− 10
65 years and over	6	13	− 7

By Income

$25,000 and over	41%	55%	− 14
Under $25,000	30	35	− 5

Note: Although monthly moviegoing among all

adult Americans has declined quite sharply since 1982, adults under age 25 not only remain stalwart fans, but they also appear not to have cut back on their attendance in this period. Their interest is nearly twice that of the national average. In the latest Gallup audit, 34% of adults report having gone to one or more movies during the previous month, an 8-percentage point drop from the 42% attendance figure recorded in 1982, when the previous audit was conducted.

As in Gallup surveys dating back to the 1930s, moviegoing is far more popular with younger adults, with 71% of 18 to 24 year olds in the latest survey, compared to only 11% of those age 50 and older, citing attendance within the past month. (Teen-agers are even more devoted movegoers: 77% in the latest Gallup Youth Survey report attending monthly.)

In addition to age, education and income play important roles in determining patterns of moviegoing, with better educated and more affluent adults more likely than their counterparts to report monthly attendance. However, greater declines since 1982 are recorded among these adults, thus narrowing the differences in attendance between upscale and downscale groups. No consistent patterns are found by gender or geographic region.

Factors that may influence movie attendance among upscale adults are the increase since 1982 in the number of cable television subscribers, the steady proliferation of video cassette recorders, and the availability of recently released movies or rented or purchased video tapes. For many, especially the affluent, these aspects of the video revolution undoubtedly provide acceptable entertainment alternatives to attendance at movie theaters.

OCTOBER 13
CAREERS FOR YOUNG PEOPLE

Interviewing Date: 5/17–20/85
Survey #253-G

Supposing a young man (woman) came to you for advice on choosing a line of work or career. What kind of work or career would you recommend? And what would be your second choice?

	For young men*
Computers	39%
Medicine	17
Business	13
Engineering	12
Skilled work (crafts)	12
Electronics	11
Law	9
Military	6
Teaching	5
Accounting	5
Sales	3
Sciences	3
Auto mechanics	2
Politics	2
Others**	20
No opinion	30

	For young women*
Computers	32%
Medicine	17
Nursing	16
Business	13
Secretarial	12
Teaching	11
Law	8
Electronics	5
Engineering	5
Housewife	5
Accounting	4
Sales	3
Military	3
Sciences	2
Social work	2
Politics	2
Merchandising	2
Civil service	2
Skilled work (crafts)	2
Others**	15
No opinion	30

*First and second choices combined
**Named by less than 1% each

If you were just starting out and could choose your life's work all over again, would you choose the same line of work you are doing now, or a different line of work?

Same 50%
Different 46
Don't know 4

By Sex
Male

Same 52%
Different 44
Don't know 4

Female

Same 49%
Different 48
Don't know 3

By Ethnic Background
White

Same 52%
Different 44
Don't know 4

Nonwhite

Same 39%
Different 56
Don't know 5

Black

Same 39%
Different 55
Don't know 6

By Education
College Graduate

Same 58%
Different 40
Don't know 2

College Incomplete

Same 54%
Different 43
Don't know 3

High-School Graduate

Same 47%
Different 49
Don't know 4

Less Than High-School Graduate

Same 45%
Different 49
Don't know 6

By Age
18–24 Years

Same 43%
Different 48
Don't know 9

25–29 Years

Same 50%
Different 49
Don't know 1

30–49 Years

Same 47%
Different 51
Don't know 2

50–64 Years

Same 55%
Different 43
Don't know 2

65 Years and Over

Same 58%
Different 37
Don't know 5

Asked of the 46% who responded that they would prefer a different career: What kind of work would you choose if you could start over again?

Their choices of different careers for themselves closely resemble those they would advise for young men and women just beginning their careers. Computer work is the top choice, followed by medicine, nursing, business, teaching, skilled work, law, electronics, and engineering.

Note: Dramatic evidence of America's involvement in the computer revolution is seen in the careers the public would recommend to young men and women. In a recent Gallup Poll, computer science and technology is by far the leading field advised for young persons just starting out, topping the runners-up by a wide margin.

The careers proposed for young men and women offer tangible evidence of the breakdown of sexual stereotypes in employment. With the exceptions of nursing, secretarial work, and homemaking, the top choices for women also appear among those recommended for men.

In 1950, when the public was asked for their career recommendations for young men and women, the results were far different from today. Nursing, teaching, secretarial work, social service work, and home economics were the top-ranking choices for women, followed by dressmaker, beautician, stewardess, actress, and journalist. For men, the top ten were: doctor, engineer, businessman, clergyman, lawyer, civil servant, professor/teacher, banker, dentist, and veterinarian.

OCTOBER 17
VALUE OF A COLLEGE EDUCATION*

Interviewing Date: 5/17–26/85
Special Survey

How important is a college education today— very important, fairly important, or not too important?

*These findings are from a study jointly conducted by the Gallup Poll and Phi Delta Kappa, the professional educational fraternity.

	Very Important		
	1985	1978	Point change
National	64%	36%	+28
By Sex			
Male	63%	33%	+30
Female	65	39	+26
By Ethnic Background			
White	63%	35%	+28
Nonwhite	73	46	+27
By Education			
College graduate	68%	34%	+34
College incomplete	66	34	+32
High-school graduate	63	34	+29
Less than high-school graduate	62	41	+21
By Region			
East	69%	38%	+31
Midwest	65	32	+33
South	66	40	+26
West	55	35	+20
By Age			
18–29 years	66%	32%	+34
30–49 years	63	36	+27
50 years and over	64	39	+25
By Income			
$20,000 and over	64%	33%	+31
Under $20,000	64	38	+26

What do you feel are the chief advantages of a college education, if any?

Better jobs, job opportunities	52%
Higher income	18
Enhances knowledge	14
Good preparation for life	13
Opens doors, provides opportunities	10

Specialized training 10
Helps people mature 6
Higher social status 6
Exposure to new experiences, ideas 6
Teaches people to think 3
None 4
All others 1
No opinion 4
                                    147%*

*Multiple responses were given.

Note: Americans' perceptions of the value of a college education have soared in recent years, with many now seeing one as an essential route to better job opportunities. In the 1985 Gallup/Phi Delta Kappa survey on education, 64% say a college education is very important and an additional 27%, fairly important. Merely 7% dismiss college as not too important, while 2% are undecided.

As recently as 1978, only 36% thought college was very important, while a 46% plurality said it was fairly important and 16%, not too important. In a similar survey conducted two years ago, the proportion saying a college education was very important had grown to 58%, and another 31% said it was fairly important.

In the current survey, at least six in ten in almost every major population segment express the view that a college education is very important. These respondents include college graduates, those who attended but did not graduate from college, high-school graduates, and those whose formal education ended before high-school graduation. This view is found in about equal measure among men and women, in all age and income groups, and among whites and nonwhites.

By far the principal reason given as the chief advantage of a college education is that it leads to better jobs and a greater diversity of employment opportunities, mentioned by 52%. A companion advantage, cited by 18%, is that the college educated can expect to earn higher incomes. Other advantages noted are that a college education enhances knowledge (14%), prepares a person for

life (13%), opens doors and provides opportunities (10%), and offers specialized training (10%).

OCTOBER 24
UNITED NATIONS

Interviewing Date: 8/13–15/85
Special Telephone Survey

In general, do you feel the United Nations is doing a good job or a poor job in trying to solve the problems it has had to face?

Good job 28%
Poor job 54
No opinion 18

By Education
College Graduate

Good job 26%
Poor job 59
No opinion 15

College Incomplete

Good job 24%
Poor job 62
No opinion 14

High-School Graduate

Good job 33%
Poor job 48
No opinion 19

Less Than High-School Graduate

Good job 28%
Poor job 44
No opinion 28

By Age
18–29 Years

Good job 39%
Poor job 46
No opinion 15

30–49 Years

Good job 28%
Poor job 57
No opinion 15

50 Years and Over

Good job 20%
Poor job 56
No opinion 24

By Politics
Republicans

Good job 31%
Poor job 49
No opinion 20

Democrats

Good job 29%
Poor job 57
No opinion 14

Independents

Good job 26%
Poor job 56
No opinion 18

Selected National Trend

	Good job	Poor job	No opinion
1983	36%	51%	13%
1982	36	49	15
1980	31	53	16
1975	33	51	16
1971	35	43	22
1970	44	40	16
1967	49	35	16
1956	51	37	12

Do you think the United States should give up its membership in the United Nations, or not?

Should 11%
Should not 81
No opinion 8

By Education
College Graduate

Should 7%
Should not 89
No opinion 4

College Incomplete

Should 11%
Should not 83
No opinion 6

High-School Graduate

Should 10%
Should not 84
No opinion 6

Less Than High-School Graduate

Should 16%
Should not 59
No opinion 25

By Age
18–29 Years

Should 4%
Should not 89
No opinion 7

30–49 Years

Should 9%
Should not 85
No opinion 6

50 Years and Over

Should 18%
Should not 69
No opinion 13

By Politics

Republicans

Should	11%
Should not	81
No opinion	8

Democrats

Should	9%
Should not	81
No opinion	10

Independents

Should	11%
Should not	82
No opinion	7

Selected National Trend

	Should	Should not	No opinion
1983	12%	79%	9%
1982	12	79	9
1975	16	74	10
1967	10	85	5
1963	8	79	13
1962	9	86	5
1951	12	75	13

Can you name any of the agencies that are part of the United Nations?

	Percent naming one or more*
National	20%

By Education

College graduate	40%
College incomplete	17
High-school graduate	13
Less than high-school graduate	9

By Age

18–29 years	14%
30–49 years	25
50 years and over	18

By Politics

Republicans	20%
Democrats	18
Independents	22

*Awareness levels undoubtedly would have been higher if respondents had been given a list of agencies to prompt them.

Note: Americans' evaluation of the performance of the United Nations has never been more negative than it is now, forty years to the day since the organization was created. But only a small proportion would like the United States to give up its membership in the world body.

In the latest Gallup survey, 28% say the United Nations is doing a good job in trying to solve the problems it has had to face, but twice as many (54%) say it is not. The current 28% positive rating is the lowest recorded since this measurement was begun in 1956, down 10 points from February of this year. Among the key reasons given by those who think the organization is doing a poor job are concern over the many unresolved conflicts in the world today, the increase in terrorism, and the South African situation.

At the same time, however, only 11% of Americans surveyed want the United States to resign from the United Nations. This figure is about the same as those recorded in past years, but below the 16% recorded in 1975.

The survey also shows a widespread lack of awareness of UN agencies and the many roles played by the United Nations in the world. Only 20% of Americans are able to name any agency, on an unaided basis. The figure is even worse among those 18 to 29 years old (14%). Perhaps even more shocking, only 40% of college graduates are able to name any UN agency.

Today (October 15) is the 40th anniversary of the day in 1945 when the UN Charter became effective, with fifty-one member states (there are now 159). Proposals to establish an organization of nations for maintenance of world peace had led to the United Nations Conference on International Organization at San Francisco, April–June, where the charter of the United Nations was drawn up. It was signed on June 26 by fifty nations, and by

Poland, one of the original fifty-one, on October 15. The charter came into effect on October 24, 1945, upon ratification by the permanent members of the Security Council and a majority of other signers.

OCTOBER 27
SEX EDUCATION IN PUBLIC SCHOOLS*

Interviewing Date: 5/17–26/85
Special Survey

Do you feel the public elementary schools should or should not include sex education in grades 4 through 8?

	Favor
National	52%

By Sex

Male	46%
Female	57

By Education

College	63%
High school	47
Grade school	30

By Region

East	56%
Midwest	52
South	41
West	62

By Age

18–29 years	56%
30–49 years	59
50 years and over	41

Selected National Trend

1985	52%
1981	45

*These findings are from a study jointly conducted by the Gallup Poll and Phi Delta Kappa, the professional educational fraternity.

Asked of those who favor sex education in public elementary schools: Which topics should be covered?

	1985	1981
Birth control	48%	45%
Venereal disease	49	52
Biology of reproduction	89	83
Premarital sex	34	40
Nature of sexual intercourse	45	36
Abortion	28	26
Homosexuality	28	33

Do you feel the public high schools should or should not include sex education in their instructional program?

	Favor
National	75%

By Sex

Male	74%
Female	76

By Education

College	82%
High school	72
Grade school	58

By Region

East	80%
Midwest	72
South	69
West	83

By Age

18–29 years	83%
30–49 years	81
50 years and over	62

Selected National Trend

1985	75%
1981	70

Asked of those who favor sex education in public high schools: Which topics should be covered?

	1985	1981
Birth control	85%	79%
Venereal disease	84	84
Biology of reproduction	82	77
Premarital sex	62	60
Nature of sexual intercourse	61	53
Abortion	60	54
Homosexuality	48	45

Note: Greater public acceptance of sex education in the schools comes at a time of an alarming increase in teen-age pregnancies and the proliferation of sex-related diseases such as herpes and AIDS. The 1985 Gallup/Phi Delta Kappa survey on education shows three adults in four (75%) approving of sex education in the public high schools and 52% favoring such instruction in public elementary schools, in grades 4 through 8. Both figures represent significant increases since 1981, when 70% and 45% favored sex education in the high schools and elementary schools, respectively. In addition, a recent survey of teachers in which the same questions were asked showed overwhelming acceptance of sex education at both the high-school (86%) and grade-school (75%) levels.

Greater acceptance of sex education in the schools today, as in 1981, is found among younger people, the college educated, business and professional people, those in the highest income categories, residents of the largest cities, and westerners. Least approving are older people, those with less than a high-school diploma, and southerners.

When respondents who support the idea of sex education are asked to indicate which topics should be covered, differences emerge in terms of which are acceptable in high school, but not in elementary school. The one exception is the biology of reproduction, which more than eight in ten say should be covered in the elementary schools as well as in the high schools. In the case of venereal disease and birth control, eight out of ten think these subjects should be taught in the high schools, but only half say they should be taken up in the elementary schools.

The current survey of adults also reveals more liberal attitudes toward the subjects that should be covered in sex education classes than were reported in the 1981 survey. Significant increases are found in the proportions favoring the teaching of birth control, the biology of reproduction, the nature of sexual intercourse, and abortion.

OCTOBER 31
PRESIDENT REAGAN

Interviewing Date: 10/11–14/85
Survey #258-G

Do you approve or disapprove of the way Ronald Reagan is handling his job as president?

Approve	63%
Disapprove	29
No opinion	8

By Politics
Republicans

Approve	90%
Disapprove	6
No opinion	4

Democrats

Approve	39%
Disapprove	50
No opinion	11

Independents

Approve	63%
Disapprove	28
No opinion	9

1985 National Trend

	Approve	Dis- approve	No opinion
September 13–16	60%	30%	10%
August 13–15	65	26	9
July 12–15	63	28	9

June 7–10	58	32	10
May 17–20	55	37	8
April 12–15	52	37	11
March 8–11	56	37	7
February 15–18	60	31	9
January 25–28	64	28	8
January 11–14	62	29	9

Now let me ask you about some specific foreign and domestic problems. As I read off each problem, would you tell me whether you approve or disapprove of the way President Reagan is handling that problem:

Economic conditions in this country?

Approve 48%
Disapprove 44
No opinion 8

By Sex
Male

Approve 53%
Disapprove 41
No opinion 6

Female

Approve 44%
Disapprove 45
No opinion 11

By Ethnic Background
White

Approve 51%
Disapprove 41
No opinion 8

Nonwhite

Approve 27%
Disapprove 65
No opinion 8

Black

Approve 21%
Disapprove 71
No opinion 8

By Education
College Graduate

Approve 61%
Disapprove 36
No opinion 3

College Incomplete

Approve 51%
Disapprove 40
No opinion 9

High-School Graduate

Approve 45%
Disapprove 47
No opinion 8

Less Than High-School Graduate

Approve 41%
Disapprove 47
No opinion 12

By Region
East

Approve 53%
Disapprove 39
No opinion 8

Midwest

Approve 42%
Disapprove 49
No opinion 9

South

Approve 48%
Disapprove 43
No opinion 9

West

Approve 50%
Disapprove 44
No opinion 6

By Age

18–24 Years

Approve 47%
Disapprove 41
No opinion 12

25–29 Years

Approve 43%
Disapprove 48
No opinion 9

30–49 Years

Approve 53%
Disapprove 41
No opinion 6

50 Years and Over

Approve 45%
Disapprove 45
No opinion 10

By Politics

Republicans

Approve 73%
Disapprove 21
No opinion 6

Democrats

Approve 26%
Disapprove 64
No opinion 10

Independents

Approve 53%
Disapprove 40
No opinion 7

Unemployment?

Approve 44%
Disapprove 44
No opinion 12

By Sex

Male

Approve 51%
Disapprove 39
No opinion 10

Female

Approve 38%
Disapprove 48
No opinion 14

By Ethnic Background

White

Approve 47%
Disapprove 40
No opinion 13

Nonwhite

Approve 24%
Disapprove 71
No opinion 5

Black

Approve 17%
Disapprove 78
No opinion 5

By Education

College Graduate

Approve 61%
Disapprove 30
No opinion 9

College Incomplete

Approve 49%
Disapprove 40
No opinion 11

High-School Graduate

Approve 40%
Disapprove 47
No opinion 13

Less Than High-School Graduate

Approve 34%
Disapprove 53
No opinion 13

By Region
East

Approve 48%
Disapprove 39
No opinion 13

Midwest

Approve 43%
Disapprove 46
No opinion 11

South

Approve 44%
Disapprove 46
No opinion 10

West

Approve 42%
Disapprove 43
No opinion 15

By Age
18–24 Years

Approve 40%
Disapprove 49
No opinion 11

25–29 Years

Approve 47%
Disapprove 42
No opinion 11

30–49 Years

Approve 50%
Disapprove 39
No opinion 11

50 Years and Over

Approve 40%
Disapprove 47
No opinion 13

By Politics
Republicans

Approve 70%
Disapprove 18
No opinion 12

Democrats

Approve 23%
Disapprove 66
No opinion 11

Independents

Approve 47%
Disapprove 41
No opinion 12

Tax reform program?

Approve 37%
Disapprove 37
No opinion 26

By Sex
Male

Approve 42%
Disapprove 35
No opinion 23

Female

Approve 32%
Disapprove 39
No opinion 29

By Ethnic Background
White

Approve 38%
Disapprove 35
No opinion 27

Nonwhite

Approve 23%
Disapprove 59
No opinion 18

Black

Approve 22%
Disapprove 62
No opinion 16

By Education

College Graduate

Approve 49%
Disapprove 39
No opinion 12

College Incomplete

Approve 35%
Disapprove 40
No opinion 25

High-School Graduate

Approve 38%
Disapprove 36
No opinion 26

Less Than High-School Graduate

Approve 28%
Disapprove 36
No opinion 36

By Region

East

Approve 40%
Disapprove 35
No opinion 25

Midwest

Approve 31%
Disapprove 38
No opinion 31

South

Approve 38%
Disapprove 38
No opinion 24

West

Approve 39%
Disapprove 38
No opinion 23

By Age

18–24 Years

Approve 30%
Disapprove 34
No opinion 36

25–29 Years

Approve 38%
Disapprove 37
No opinion 25

30–49 Years

Approve 39%
Disapprove 39
No opinion 22

50 Years and Over

Approve 37%
Disapprove 37
No opinion 26

By Politics

Republicans

Approve 53%
Disapprove 20
No opinion 27

Democrats

Approve 23%
Disapprove 53
No opinion 24

Independents

Approve 36%
Disapprove 38
No opinion 26

Reducing the federal budget deficit?

Approve 37%
Disapprove 46
No opinion 17

By Sex
Male

Approve 41%
Disapprove 48
No opinion 11

Female

Approve 34%
Disapprove 44
No opinion 22

By Ethnic Background
White

Approve 39%
Disapprove 44
No opinion 17

Nonwhite

Approve 24%
Disapprove 60
No opinion 16

Black

Approve 23%
Disapprove 61
No opinion 16

By Education
College Graduate

Approve 42%
Disapprove 46
No opinion 12

College Incomplete

Approve 35%
Disapprove 50
No opinion 15

High-School Graduate

Approve 39%
Disapprove 46
No opinion 15

Less Than High-School Graduate

Approve 34%
Disapprove 42
No opinion 24

By Region
East

Approve 40%
Disapprove 39
No opinion 21

Midwest

Approve 36%
Disapprove 49
No opinion 15

South

Approve 40%
Disapprove 45
No opinion 15

West

Approve 31%
Disapprove 52
No opinion 17

By Age
18–24 Years

Approve 23%
Disapprove 53
No opinion 24

25–29 Years

Approve 37%
Disapprove 48
No opinion 15

30–49 Years

Approve 37%
Disapprove 47
No opinion 16

50 Years and Over

Approve 43%
Disapprove 42
No opinion 15

By Politics
Republicans

Approve 54%
Disapprove 32
No opinion 14

Democrats

Approve 26%
Disapprove 56
No opinion 18

Independents

Approve 34%
Disapprove 51
No opinion 15

Reducing the U.S. trade deficit with other nations?

Approve 38%
Disapprove 40
No opinion 22

By Sex
Male

Approve 42%
Disapprove 42
No opinion 16

Female

Approve 35%
Disapprove 37
No opinion 28

By Ethnic Background
White

Approve 39%
Disapprove 38
No opinion 23

Nonwhite

Approve 28%
Disapprove 56
No opinion 16

Black

Approve 27%
Disapprove 56
No opinion 17

By Education
College Graduate

Approve 45%
Disapprove 36
No opinion 19

College Incomplete

Approve 40%
Disapprove 38
No opinion 22

High-School Graduate

Approve 37%
Disapprove 42
No opinion 21

Less Than High-School Graduate

Approve 33%
Disapprove 41
No opinion 26

By Region

East

Approve 44%
Disapprove 35
No opinion 21

Midwest

Approve 36%
Disapprove 43
No opinion 21

South

Approve 39%
Disapprove 39
No opinion 22

West

Approve 33%
Disapprove 42
No opinion 25

By Age

18–24 Years

Approve 32%
Disapprove 43
No opinion 25

25–29 Years

Approve 45%
Disapprove 35
No opinion 20

30–49 Years

Approve 38%
Disapprove 37
No opinion 25

50 Years and Over

Approve 38%
Disapprove 43
No opinion 19

By Politics

Republicans

Approve 53%
Disapprove 27
No opinion 20

Democrats

Approve 29%
Disapprove 49
No opinion 22

Independents

Approve 33%
Disapprove 44
No opinion 23

Situation in South Africa?

Approve 33%
Disapprove 39
No opinion 28

By Sex

Male

Approve 37%
Disapprove 41
No opinion 22

Female

Approve 30%
Disapprove 37
No opinion 33

By Ethnic Background

White

Approve 36%
Disapprove 35
No opinion 29

Nonwhite

Approve 14%
Disapprove 70
No opinion 16

Black

Approve 13%
Disapprove 77
No opinion 10

By Education
College Graduate

Approve 39%
Disapprove 44
No opinion 17

College Incomplete

Approve 36%
Disapprove 38
No opinion 26

High-School Graduate

Approve 35%
Disapprove 37
No opinion 28

Less Than High-School Graduate

Approve 25%
Disapprove 38
No opinion 37

By Region
East

Approve 38%
Disapprove 38
No opinion 24

Midwest

Approve 30%
Disapprove 38
No opinion 32

South

Approve 30%
Disapprove 41
No opinion 29

West

Approve 38%
Disapprove 37
No opinion 25

By Age
18–24 Years

Approve 28%
Disapprove 42
No opinion 30

25–29 Years

Approve 28%
Disapprove 45
No opinion 27

30–49 Years

Approve 38%
Disapprove 38
No opinion 24

50 Years and Over

Approve 32%
Disapprove 36
No opinion 32

By Politics
Republicans

Approve 47%
Disapprove 27
No opinion 26

Democrats

Approve 23%
Disapprove 50
No opinion 27

Independents

Approve 32%
Disapprove 39
No opinion 29

Situation in the Middle East?

Approve 42%
Disapprove 35
No opinion 23

By Sex
Male

Approve 45%
Disapprove 36
No opinion 19

Female

Approve 39%
Disapprove 35
No opinion 26

By Ethnic Background
White

Approve 44%
Disapprove 34
No opinion 22

Nonwhite

Approve 28%
Disapprove 48
No opinion 24

Black

Approve 26%
Disapprove 51
No opinion 23

By Education
College Graduate

Approve 57%
Disapprove 30
No opinion 13

College Incomplete

Approve 42%
Disapprove 37
No opinion 21

High-School Graduate

Approve 42%
Disapprove 37
No opinion 21

Less Than High-School Graduate

Approve 31%
Disapprove 36
No opinion 33

By Region
East

Approve 42%
Disapprove 36
No opinion 22

Midwest

Approve 41%
Disapprove 35
No opinion 24

South

Approve 42%
Disapprove 35
No opinion 23

West

Approve 44%
Disapprove 36
No opinion 20

By Age
18–24 Years

Approve 32%
Disapprove 44
No opinion 24

25–29 Years

Approve 38%
Disapprove 41
No opinion 21

30–49 Years

Approve 46%
Disapprove 33
No opinion 21

50 Years and Over

Approve 43%
Disapprove 33
No opinion 24

By Politics
Republicans

Approve 58%
Disapprove 24
No opinion 18

Democrats

Approve 29%
Disapprove 46
No opinion 25

Independents

Approve 42%
Disapprove 34
No opinion 24

Note: A solid majority of Americans approves of the way President Ronald Reagan is carrying out the overall duties of his office. However, the president receives less than majority support for his handling of each of seven important issues facing the nation.

In the latest (mid-October) Gallup Poll, 63% approve of Reagan's overall job performance, while 29% disapprove and 8% are undecided. These ratings are not statistically different from those recorded in mid-September, when 60% approved and 30% disapproved.

In terms of specific issues, Reagan fares best for his handling of economic conditions in this country, with 48% approving and 44% disapproving. The president's rating on the economy represents a slight decline from a July survey, when this question was last asked and when his overall performance also stood at 63%. At that time, 53% of the public approved of Reagan's handling of the economy, while 39% disapproved.

The president currently has equal numbers of supporters and detractors (44% each) for his handling of unemployment. In March, when the last public assessment was made, 47% approved and 46% disapproved.

For the situation in the Middle East, Reagan receives a positive grade from 42%, a negative one from 35%, with a large 23% undecided. (The latest survey was conducted shortly after U.S. planes intercepted an Egyptian plane carrying the *Achille Lauro* hijackers and forced it to land in Italy.)

President Reagan receives a mixed reaction for his efforts in reducing the U.S. trade deficit and for his tax reform program. In the case of the former, 38% approve and 40% disapprove. For the latter, positive and negative reactions of 37% each are recorded.

More Americans disapprove (46%) than approve (37%) of Reagan's attempts to reduce the federal budget deficit. His handling of the situation in South Africa also has more detractors (39%) than backers (33%).

Not surprisingly, there is a strong political coloration to the public's assessment of the president's overall job performance, as well as his dealing with specific issues. However, while Republicans strongly endorse Reagan's general leadership (90% approve) and his handling of the economy and unemployment—73% and 70%, respectively, approve—he receives much lower ratings for the other issues studied. For those, none tops 60%. And, in the case of the South African situation, less than a majority of Republicans (47%) approves. The president's overall job rating from Democrats is 39% approval; for his handling of each of the seven issues, his approval ratings are in the 20%–30% range.

NOVEMBER 3
SOUTH AFRICA

Interviewing Date: 10/11–14/85
Survey #258-G

How closely would you say you've followed the recent events in South Africa—very closely, fairly closely, or not very closely?

Very closely 13%
Fairly closely 43
Not very closely 40
Don't know 4

Asked of the aware group (56% of the sample): In the South African situation, are your sympathies more with the black population or more with the South African government?

Black population 63%
South African government 13
Both equally (volunteered) 12
Neither (volunteered) 5
White population (volunteered) 1
Don't know 6

By Sex
Male

Black population 63%
South African government 15
Both equally (volunteered) 11
Neither (volunteered) 5
White population (volunteered) 1
Don't know 5

Female

Black population 63%
South African government 11
Both equally (volunteered) 12
Neither (volunteered) 6
White population (volunteered) 1
Don't know 7

By Ethnic Background
White

Black population 59%
South African government 15
Both equally (volunteered) 12
Neither (volunteered) 6
White population (volunteered) 1
Don't know 7

Nonwhite

Black population 82%
South African government 3
Both equally (volunteered) 11
Neither (volunteered) .... *
White population (volunteered) ......NA
Don't know 4

Black

Black population 85%
South African government 2
Both equally (volunteered) 10
Neither (volunteered) .... *
White population (volunteered) ......NA
Don't know 3

By Education
College Graduate

Black population 66%
South African government 12
Both equally (volunteered) 9
Neither (volunteered) 7
White population (volunteered) 1
Don't know 5

College Incomplete

Black population 65%
South African government 14
Both equally (volunteered) 12
Neither (volunteered) 5
White population (volunteered) 1
Don't know 3

High-School Graduate

Black population 61%
South African government 14
Both equally (volunteered) 10
Neither (volunteered) 6
White population (volunteered) 2
Don't know 7

Less Than High-School Graduate

Black population 57%
South African government 11
Both equally (volunteered) 18
Neither (volunteered) 4
White population (volunteered) ....NA
Don't know 10

By Region
East

Black population 61%
South African government 11
Both equally (volunteered) 14
Neither (volunteered) 7
White population (volunteered) 1
Don't know 6

Midwest

Black population 67%
South African government 11
Both equally (volunteered) 11
Neither (volunteered) 4
White population (volunteered) 2
Don't know 5

South

Black population 60%
South African government 18
Both equally (volunteered) 11
Neither (volunteered) 4
White population (volunteered) 1
Don't know 6

West

Black population 63%
South African government 11
Both equally (volunteered) 13

Neither (volunteered) 7
White population (volunteered) ....NA
Don't know 6

By Age
18–29 Years

Black population 71%
South African government 11
Both equally (volunteered) 10
Neither (volunteered) 4
White population (volunteered) 2
Don't know 2

30–49 Years

Black population 68%
South African government 10
Both equally (volunteered) 9
Neither (volunteered) 7
White population (volunteered) 1
Don't know 5

50 Years and Over

Black population 52%
South African government 17
Both equally (volunteered) 16
Neither (volunteered) 5
White population (volunteered) 1
Don't know 9

By Politics
Republicans

Black population 52%
South African government 18
Both equally (volunteered) 14
Neither (volunteered) 9
White population (volunteered) 1
Don't know 6

Democrats

Black population 73%
South African government 9
Both equally (volunteered) 10
Neither (volunteered) 3
White population (volunteered) .... *
Don't know 5

Independents

Black population 65%
South African government 12
Both equally (volunteered) 9
Neither (volunteered) 5
White population (volunteered) 2
Don't know 7

*Less than 1%

Also asked of the aware group: Do you think the United States should put more pressure on the South African government to end apartheid, less pressure, or about the same amount as now?

More pressure 47%
Less pressure 15
Same as now 30
No opinion 8

By Sex
Male

More pressure 47%
Less pressure 15
Same as now 32
No opinion 6

Female

More pressure 47%
Less pressure 15
Same as now 28
No opinion 10

By Ethnic Background
White

More pressure 42%
Less pressure 17
Same as now 33
No opinion 8

Nonwhite

More pressure 74%
Less pressure 7
Same as now 14
No opinion 5

Black

More pressure 74%
Less pressure 7
Same as now 13
No opinion 6

By Education
College Graduate

More pressure 53%
Less pressure 13
Same as now 28
No opinion 6

College Incomplete

More pressure 52%
Less pressure 13
Same as now 29
No opinion 6

High-School Graduate

More pressure 42%
Less pressure 19
Same as now 30
No opinion 9

Less Than High-School Graduate

More pressure 41%
Less pressure 14
Same as now 34
No opinion 11

By Region
East

More pressure 46%
Less pressure 14
Same as now 33
No opinion 7

Midwest

More pressure 50%
Less pressure 16
Same as now 28
No opinion 6

South

More pressure	42%
Less pressure	15
Same as now	32
No opinion	11

West

More pressure	53%
Less pressure	16
Same as now	24
No opinion	7

By Age

18–29 Years

More pressure	56%
Less pressure	12
Same as now	28
No opinion	4

30–49 Years

More pressure	50%
Less pressure	12
Same as now	30
No opinion	8

50 Years and Over

More pressure	39%
Less pressure	20
Same as now	31
No opinion	10

By Politics

Republicans

More pressure	39%
Less pressure	18
Same as now	37
No opinion	6

Democrats

More pressure	57%
Less pressure	12
Same as now	23
No opinion	8

Independents

More pressure	45%
Less pressure	16
Same as now	30
No opinion	9

Note: Amid growing racial tension and little concrete evidence that the South African government is ready to change its apartheid racial system, the American people say the United States should play a more assertive role in helping to end apartheid. A new (mid-October) Gallup Poll shows that a 47% plurality of "aware" respondents believes the United States should put more pressure on the government of South Africa to end apartheid, while 30% think our present efforts are adequate, 15% would apply less pressure, and 8% are undecided. (The aware group comprises the 56% of the total sample saying they have followed recent events in South Africa very or fairly closely.)

As in an August survey, Americans are strongly supportive of the black majority in South Africa, with 63% saying they sympathize with the black population there. By comparison, 13% side with the South African government and 12% are equally sympathetic to both sides.

NOVEMBER 7
EATING DISORDERS:* YOUNG WOMEN

Interviewing Date: 8/5–8/85
Special Telephone Survey

> Asked of women ages 19 to 39: Would you like to gain weight, lose weight, or would you like your weight to stay the same as it is now?

Gain weight	4%
Lose weight	64
Stay the same	32

> Asked of women ages 19 to 39: Do you think your life would be better if you were thinner, or not?

*This survey was sponsored by the Comprehensive Care Corporation.

Yes, would be 30%
No, would not be 67
No opinion 3

Those Who Would Like
To Lose Weight

Yes, would be 44%
No, would not be 52
No opinion 4

Those Who Would Like
To Stay the Same

Yes, would be 4%
No, would not be 93
No opinion 3

Asked of women ages 19 to 39: About how often, if at all, do you diet—that is, make a serious effort to control the amount and types of food you eat?

Always on a diet 16%
Once a month or more 15
Less than once a month 14
Seldom or never 54
Don't know 1

Asked of women ages 19 to 39: Have you ever gone on food binges in which you ate extremely large quantities of high-calorie foods in a short period of time—say, in less than two hours?

Yes, have 26%
No, have not 74

Asked of those who replied in the affirmative: About how often do you go on food binges?

Once a month or less 16%
More than once a month
  but less than weekly 4
Once a week 3
More than once a week 3
                                    ―――
                                    26%

Asked of women ages 19 to 39: Anorexia nervosa describes someone who is very thin,

but complains about being fat, and often either goes on a very strict diet or refuses to eat at all. Do you, yourself, personally know anyone who has had what you think are the symptoms of anorexia nervosa?

                                           Yes
National 30%

By Education

College graduate 50%
College incomplete 37
High-school graduate 21
Less than high-school graduate 12

By Age

19–29 years 31%
30–39 years 28

By Marital Status

Married 27%
Single 37

By Weight Status

Overweight 34%
About right 21

Asked of women ages 19 to 39: Have you, yourself, ever had what you believe are the symptoms of anorexia nervosa?

                                           Yes
National 3%

By Education

College graduate 4%
College incomplete 7
High-school graduate 1
Less than high-school graduate 2

By Age

19–29 years 3%
30–39 years 3

By Marital Status

Married 2%
Single 4

By Weight Status

Overweight 4%
About right 2

Asked of women ages 19 to 39: Bulimia describes people who go on eating binges, then take laxatives or make themselves throw up. Do you, yourself, personally know anyone who has had what you think are the symptoms of bulimia?

	Yes
National	19%

By Education

College graduate .32%
College incomplete 27
High-school graduate 10
Less than high-school graduate 13

By Age

19–29 years 20%
30–39 years 18

By Marital Status

Married 17%
Single 26

By Weight Status

Overweight 22%
About right 15

Asked of women ages 19 to 39: Have you, yourself, ever had what you believe are the symptoms of bulimia?

	Yes
National	2%

By Education

College graduate 2%
College incomplete 4
High-school graduate 1
Less than high-school graduate 2

By Age

19–29 years 3%
30–39 years 2

By Marital Status

Married 2%
Single 2

By Weight Status

Overweight 3%
About right 2

Note: As many as one-fourth of young American women periodically go on food binges in which they eat extremely large quantities of high-calorie foods in a short space of time. A recent Gallup survey of women ages 19 to 39 found that one woman in ten (10%) indulges in food binges more than once per month, including 6% who do so at least once per week. One in six (16%) goes on a binge once per month or less often. To compensate for these binges, the survey found, almost half the women suffering from this eating disorder resort to extreme measures such as fasting, strenuous exercising, taking purgatives, or self-induced vomiting.

The survey also found that roughly 2 million young women have suffered from the symptoms of anorexia nervosa or bulimia, two serious illnesses mainly affecting women. Victims of anorexia nervosa deliberately starve away one-fifth or more of their normal body weight. An estimated 15% to 20% of anorectics die prematurely due to complications of their illness. Bulimia is a syndrome in which sufferers eat as much as 20,000 calories in one sitting, and then compensate by self-induced vomiting or use of laxatives. Complications of bulimia include damage to the heart and reproductive system, kidney problems, and ulcers of the intestinal tract.

The poll may dispel several theories about anorexia and bulimia, notably the assumption that only white, upper middle-class, college-educated women in their late teens and early twenties are afflicted with these disorders. The poll indicates that young women of all races, educational, and occupational backgrounds are susceptible.

Although about two out of three women (64%) consider themselves overweight, the poll indicates that women generally do not subscribe to the "thinner is better" philosophy. Two-thirds (67%) do not believe that losing weight would improve their lives; even among overweight women, a 52% majority does not subscribe to this belief.

The survey, which also polled women's attitudes toward their body appearance and weight control, found that almost one woman in three (31%) diets at least once per month. One in six (16%) even considers herself a perpetual dieter. However, despite America's preoccupation with weight control, 54% of women say they seldom or never diet.

Other major findings of the poll include: 1) about two single women in five (37%) have gone through periods of binge eating, compared to one in five married women (20%); 2) three women in ten (30%) know someone with the symptoms of anorexia, while one in five (19%) knows someone suffering from bulimia; and 3) college-educated women and those in white-collar occupations are more likely than their counterparts to know someone with an eating disorder.

NOVEMBER 8
EATING DISORDERS:* TEEN-AGERS

Interviewing Date: 5/24–6/30/85
Special Telephone Survey

Asked of teen-agers ages 13 to 18: Would you like to gain weight, lose weight, or would you like your weight to stay the same as it is now?

*This survey was sponsored by the Comprehensive Care Corporation.

Gain weight 18%
Lose weight 39
Stay the same 43

By Sex
Boys

Gain weight 28%
Lose weight 20
Stay the same 52

Girls

Gain weight 8%
Lose weight 59
Stay the same 33

Asked of teen-agers ages 13 to 18: Would you be more pleased about your appearance, or less pleased, if you were thinner than you are now?

More pleased 51%
Less pleased 38
No difference; no opinion 11

By Sex
Boys

More pleased 39%
Less pleased 49
No difference; no opinion 12

Girls

More pleased 65%
Less pleased 25
No difference; no opinion 10

Asked of teen-agers ages 13 to 18: Do you think you would be more healthy, or less healthy, if you were thinner?

More healthy 38%
Less healthy 51
No difference; no opinion 11

By Sex

Boys

More healthy	32%
Less healthy	59
No difference; no opinion	9

Girls

More healthy	44%
Less healthy	41
No difference; no opinion	15

Asked of teen-agers ages 13 to 18: Have you ever gone on food binges in which you ate extremely large quantities of high-calorie foods in a short period of time—say, in less than two hours?

Yes, have	37%
No, have not	63

By Sex

Boys

Yes, have	40%
No, have not	60

Girls

Yes, have	34%
No, have not	66

Asked of teen-agers ages 13 to 18: Anorexia nervosa describes someone who is very thin, but complains about being fat, and often either goes on a very strict diet or refuses to eat at all. Have you, yourself, ever known anyone personally who could be described this way?

	Yes
All teen-agers	43%

By Sex

Boys	39%
Girls	47

By Region

East	40%
Midwest	41
South	41
West	51

By Age

13–15 years	38%
16–18 years	47

By Family Occupation

White collar	43%
Blue collar	42

Asked of teen-agers ages 13 to 18: Have you, yourself, ever had what you believe are the symptoms of anorexia nervosa?

	Yes
All teen-agers	5%

By Sex

Boys	2%
Girls	9

By Region

East	8%
Midwest	5
South	5
West	3

By Age

13–15 years	5%
16–18 years	6

By Family Occupation

White collar	6%
Blue collar	4

Asked of teen-agers ages 13 to 18: Bulimia describes people who go on eating binges, followed by making themselves throw up or by using laxatives. These people usually are always complaining about how fat they are,

*or weigh themselves a lot. Have you, your-
self, ever known anyone personally who could
be described this way?*

	Yes
All teen-agers	23%

By Sex

Boys	21%
Girls	26

By Region

East	28%
Midwest	20
South	24
West	21

By Age

13–15 years	19%
16–18 years	27

By Family Occupation

White collar	23%
Blue collar	22

*Asked of teen-agers ages 13 to 18: Have you,
yourself, ever had what you believe are the
symptoms of bulimia?*

	Yes
All teen-agers	4%

By Sex

Boys	2%
Girls	5

By Region

East	5%
Midwest	2
South	3
West	3

By Age

13–15 years	2%
16–18 years	5

By Family Occupation

White collar	4%
Blue collar	4

Note: Serious eating disorders such as anorexia nervosa and bulimia may afflict as many as 12% of all teen-age girls, according to a recent Gallup survey. The poll, which is thought to be the first nationwide inquiry into adolescents' eating behavior, found that 9% of girls, ages 13 to 18, believe they have had symptoms of anorexia nervosa, an illness in which victims deliberately starve away one-fifth or more of their body weight.

Another 5% of girls think they have had symptoms of bulimia, a syndrome in which those afflicted binge on food containing as many as 20,000 calories in a single sitting, then compensate by self-induced vomiting or by using laxatives. Moreover, 3% report symptoms of both anorexia and bulimia. Although these eating disorders mainly affect girls, the poll found that 4% of teen-age boys claim to have had symptoms of either anorexia or bulimia.

Teen-agers display high awareness of eating disorders among people they know. Almost half the girls (47%) and 39% of the boys say they personally know someone who they believe has had anorexia nervosa. One in four girls (26%) and one in five boys (21%) know someone they believe to be suffering from bulimia.

More than one-third of teen-age boys (40%) and girls (34%) report having gone on food binges, in which they ate extremely large quantities of high-calorie foods in a short period of time. To compensate for having indulged in these binges, more than half of the teen-agers pursue extreme measures such as vigorous exercise, fasting, vomiting, or using purgatives.

Girls are far more concerned about their weight than are boys. Three girls in five (59%) say they would like to lose weight, while 33% are satisfied with their present weight and 8% would like to gain. In sharp contrast, 52% of boys would like their weight to stay the same, 28% would like to gain, and 20%, to lose weight.

Two girls in three (65%) say they would be more pleased about their appearance if they were thinner; only two boys in five (39%) think the same way. By almost a 2-to-1 ratio, boys believe they would be less healthy (59%), rather than more healthy (32%), if they were to lose weight. Girls, on the other hand, are quite evenly divided between those who say that weight loss would make them healthier (44%) and less healthy (41%).

NOVEMBER 10
MOST IMPORTANT PROBLEM

Interviewing Date: 10/11–14/85
Survey #258-G

What do you think is the most important problem facing this country today?

	Oct. 1985	May 1985	Jan. 1985
Unemployment; fear of recession	24%	21%	20%
Threat of war; international tensions	20	23	27
Budget deficit	16	6	16
High cost of living; taxes	7	11	12
Trade deficit	5	*	*
Economy (general)	4	8	6
Moral, religious decline in society	4	6	2
Crime	3	4	4
Drug abuse	3	6	2
Plight of farmers	3	1	2
Poverty; hunger	3	6	6
All others	17	24	16
No opinion	5	3	3
	114%**	119%**	116%**

*First isolated in current survey
**Multiple responses were given.

All those who named a problem were then asked: Which political party do you think can do a better job of handling the problem you have just mentioned—the Republican party or the Democratic party?

	Oct. 1985	May 1985	Jan. 1985
Republican party	32%	37%	39%
Democratic party	32	31	29
No difference (volunteered)	23	23	24
No opinion	13	9	8

Note: Unemployment and international tensions are the most urgent problems facing the nation, according to the latest Gallup Poll. Named next most often is the federal budget deficit.

In the mid-October Gallup survey, 24% cite unemployment as the most important national problem. Almost as many, 20%, name international tensions and the threat of war. (This category includes, for the first time, 5% who specifically cite international terrorism.)

Public concern about the federal budget deficit, currently at 16%, has varied from survey to survey. When this question was asked last May, the deficit was cited by only 6%. Early in the year, however, it ranked a strong third—mentioned by 16%, as at present.

The high cost of living, currently named by 7%, continues to trouble many Americans, with others citing the trade deficit (5%), the economy (4%), and a perceived moral and religious decline in society (4%). Named by 3% each are crime, drug abuse, the farmers' economic plight, and poverty and hunger.

Major differences about which national problems are most urgent are found among demographic groups. College graduates, for example, are twice as likely to name the budget deficit as are persons whose education did not include a college degree, by 27% and 13%, respectively. Similarly, unemployment is a much more pressing priority among blacks (46%), Democrats (35%), and those whose annual family income is less than $25,000 (30%) than it is among whites (22%), Republicans (15%), and those with incomes of $25,000 or more (17%).

In the latest survey, the Republican party has lost the advantage over the Democratic party it held earlier this year as being better able to cope with the problems the public deems most urgent. Currently, equal proportions, 32% each, name the

GOP and the Democratic party as more qualified to deal with the nation's most pressing problems, while 23% think neither party enjoys an edge and 13% are undecided.

In May, the GOP (37%) was more often mentioned as superior in this respect than the Democrats (31%). And in January, the Republican advantage was a full 10 points, with the GOP cited by 39% to the Democrats' 29%.

NOVEMBER 14
PERSONAL FINANCES

Interviewing Date: 10/11–14/85
Survey #258-G

We are interested in how people's financial situation may have changed. Would you say that you are financially better off now than you were a year ago, or are you financially worse off now?

Better	38%
Worse	27
Same (volunteered)	34
No opinion	1

Selected National Trend

	Better	Worse	Same (volunteered)	No opinion
1985				
June	43%	29%	26%	2%
March	48	25	26	1
1984				
Nov./Dec.	43	24	32	1
July	40	25	34	1
March	36	26	37	1
1983				
June	28	39	32	1
March	25	46	28	1

Now looking ahead, do you expect that at this time next year you will be financially better off than now, or worse off than now?

Better	49%
Worse	12
Same (volunteered)	32
No opinion	7

Selected National Trend

	Better	Worse	Same (volunteered)	No opinion
1985				
June	52%	19%	19%	10%
March	57	12	26	5
1984				
Nov./Dec.	50	17	28	5
July	52	12	28	8
March	54	11	28	7
1983				
June	43	19	28	10
March	45	22	24	9

Following is the trend in "super optimists," people who claim to be better off now than they were a year ago and expect to be still better off a year from now:

"Super Optimists" Trend

1985	
October 11–14	28%
June	33
March	37
1984	
Nov./Dec.	32
July	31
March	28
1983	
June	20
March	18

Note: Consumers' financial optimism, which has largely fueled the economic recovery, is now showing signs of cooling off. Still, optimism outweighs pessimism by a large margin.

In the latest (mid-October) Gallup audit of financial expectations, 49% say they expect to be better off a year from now, 32% think their situation will be about the same, and 12% foresee a downturn. The latest figures represent modest declines since June in the proportions who are either optimistic or pessimistic in their financial outlook, but a sharp increase—from 19% to 32%—in those who believe their financial status will not change much in the coming year.

This major shift toward the mid-ground between optimism and pessimism, according to Jay

Schmiedeskamp, senior economist of the Gallup Organization, reflects the slow growth in the nation's economy this year and last. The survey findings also suggest that, although consumers are still optimistic, they are no longer as bullish as they were earlier this year and so may be expected to reduce their discretionary spending.

In response to another survey question, 38% see an improvement in their current financial status vis-à-vis one year ago, 34% perceive no change, and 27% claim to be worse off. Again, comparisons with surveys conducted in June and March reveal a decline in those saying they are better off, and an increase in those who think their financial situation is about the same as it was one year ago. The proportion saying they are worse off has not changed significantly.

The current survey also marks a decline in "super optimists," from 37% in March to 28% at present. These are people who say they are in better financial shape now than they were one year ago and expect to be still more prosperous one year from now. Studies have shown that these super optimists, who tend to be young, well educated, and affluent, are likely to be heavy buyers of big-ticket discretionary items, such as houses, cars, major appliances, and vacations. The current level of extreme optimism is the lowest found in Gallup surveys in over a year; it is, however, far higher than those recorded in 1982 and 1983, when the nation was recovering from a recession.

NOVEMBER 17
"STAR WARS" PROPOSAL

Interviewing Date: 10/11–14/85
Survey #258-G

How closely have you followed the discussions over the administration's so-called "Star Wars" proposal—that is, its proposal to develop a space-based defense against nuclear attack—very closely, fairly closely, or not at all?

Very closely 15%
Fairly closely 46
Not at all 36
No opinion 3

Asked of the aware group (61% of the sample): Would you like to see the United States go ahead with the development of such a program, or not?

Yes, develop 61%
No, don't develop 28
No opinion 11

By Sex
Male

Yes, develop 70%
No, don't develop 23
No opinion 7

Female

Yes, develop 50%
No, don't develop 33
No opinion 17

By Ethnic Background
White

Yes, develop 63%
No, don't develop 26
No opinion 11

Nonwhite

Yes, develop 51%
No, don't develop 37
No opinion 12

Black

Yes, develop 52%
No, don't develop 37
No opinion 11

By Education
College Graduate

Yes, develop 64%
No, don't develop 27
No opinion 9

College Incomplete

Yes, develop 58%
No, don't develop 31
No opinion 11

High-School Graduate

Yes, develop 58%
No, don't develop 31
No opinion 11

Less Than High-School Graduate

Yes, develop 55%
No, don't develop 28
No opinion 17

By Region
East

Yes, develop 61%
No, don't develop 28
No opinion 11

Midwest

Yes, develop 58%
No, don't develop 30
No opinion 12

South

Yes, develop 69%
No, don't develop 20
No opinion 11

West

Yes, develop 56%
No, don't develop 33
No opinion 11

By Age
18–24 Years

Yes, develop 56%
No, don't develop 34
No opinion 10

25–29 Years

Yes, develop 62%
No, don't develop 30
No opinion 8

30–49 Years

Yes, develop 62%
No, don't develop 28
No opinion 10

50 Years and Over

Yes, develop 62%
No, don't develop 24
No opinion 14

By Politics
Republicans

Yes, develop 77%
No, don't develop 13
No opinion 10

Democrats

Yes, develop 51%
No, don't develop 36
No opinion 13

Independents

Yes, develop 56%
No, don't develop 35
No opinion 9

Also asked of the aware group: In your opinion, would the U.S. developing of this system increase or decrease the likelihood of reaching a nuclear arms agreement with the Soviet Union?

Increase likelihood for agreement 48%
Decrease likelihood 36
No difference; no opinion 16

By Sex

Male

Increase likelihood for agreement 54%
Decrease likelihood 35
No difference; no opinion 11

Female

Increase likelihood for agreement 41%
Decrease likelihood 38
No difference; no opinion 21

By Ethnic Background

White

Increase likelihood for agreement 49%
Decrease likelihood 35
No difference; no opinion 16

Nonwhite

Increase likelihood for agreement 44%
Decrease likelihood 40
No difference; no opinion 16

Black

Increase likelihood for agreement 43%
Decrease likelihood 39
No difference; no opinion 18

By Education

College Graduate

Increase likelihood for agreement 50%
Decrease likelihood 33
No difference; no opinion 17

College Incomplete

Increase likelihood for agreement 51%
Decrease likelihood 33
No difference; no opinion 16

High-School Graduate

Increase likelihood for agreement 47%
Decrease likelihood 41
No difference; no opinion 12

Less Than High-School Graduate

Increase likelihood for agreement 46%
Decrease likelihood 34
No difference; no opinion 20

By Region

East

Increase likelihood for agreement 50%
Decrease likelihood 36
No difference; no opinion 14

Midwest

Increase likelihood for agreement 51%
Decrease likelihood 35
No difference; no opinion 14

South

Increase likelihood for agreement 50%
Decrease likelihood 31
No difference; no opinion 19

West

Increase likelihood for agreement 42%
Decrease likelihood 43
No difference; no opinion 15

By Age

18–24 Years

Increase likelihood for agreement 33%
Decrease likelihood 60
No difference; no opinion 7

25–29 Years

Increase likelihood for agreement 43%
Decrease likelihood 45
No difference; no opinion 12

30–49 Years

Increase likelihood for agreement 51%
Decrease likelihood 34
No difference; no opinion 15

50 Years and Over

Increase likelihood for agreement 51%
Decrease likelihood 28
No difference; no opinion 21

By Politics
Republicans

Increase likelihood for agreement 57%
Decrease likelihood 27
No difference; no opinion 16

Democrats

Increase likelihood for agreement 44%
Decrease likelihood 43
No difference; no opinion 13

Independents

Increase likelihood for agreement 44%
Decrease likelihood 36
No difference; no opinion 20

Also asked of the aware group: In your opinion, would developing this system make the world safer from nuclear destruction, or less safe?

Make world safer 58%
Make world less safe 29
No difference; no opinion 13

By Sex
Male

Make world safer 64%
Make world less safe 25
No difference; no opinion 11

Female

Make world safer 50%
Make world less safe 34
No difference; no opinion 16

By Ethnic Background
College Graduate

Make world safer 59%
Make world less safe 28
No difference; no opinion 13

College Incomplete

Make world safer 63%
Make world less safe 28
No difference; no opinion 9

High-School Graduate

Make world safer 54%
Make world less safe 34
No difference; no opinion 12

Less Than High-School Graduate

Make world safer 57%
Make world less safe 21
No difference; no opinion 22

By Region
East

Make world safer 57%
Make world less safe 32
No difference; no opinion 11

Midwest

Make world safer 57%
Make world less safe 28
No difference; no opinion 15

South

Make world safer 63%
Make world less safe 23
No difference; no opinion 14

West

Make world safer 53%
Make world less safe 33
No difference; no opinion 14

By Age

18–24 Years

Make world safer 44%
Make world less safe 43
No difference; no opinion 13

25–29 Years

Make world safer 56%
Make world less safe 37
No difference; no opinion 7

30–49 Years

Make world safer 61%
Make world less safe 28
No difference; no opinion 11

50 Years and Over

Make world safer 60%
Make world less safe 22
No difference; no opinion 18

By Politics

Republicans

Make world safer 72%
Make world less safe 13
No difference; no opinion 15

Democrats

Make world safer 46%
Make world less safe 42
No difference; no opinion 12

Independents

Make world safer 56%
Make world less safe 32
No difference; no opinion 12

Asked of the entire sample: Soviet leader Mikhail Gorbachev has proposed that the United States and the Soviet Union agree to cut their strategic missile forces by 50% and to negotiate a total ban on the development and deployment of space-based weapons. Do you favor or oppose this proposal?

Favor 47%
Oppose 32
No opinion 21

By Sex

Male

Favor 48%
Oppose 37
No opinion 15

Female

Favor 46%
Oppose 27
No opinion 27

By Ethnic Background

White

Favor 47%
Oppose 31
No opinion 22

Nonwhite

Favor 44%
Oppose 34
No opinion 22

Black

Favor 43%
Oppose 35
No opinion 22

By Education

College Graduate

Favor 50%
Oppose 36
No opinion 14

College Incomplete

Favor 49%
Oppose 32
No opinion 19

High-School Graduate

Favor 46%
Oppose 32
No opinion 22

Less Than High-School Graduate

Favor 43%
Oppose 28
No opinion 29

By Region
East

Favor 48%
Oppose 27
No opinion 25

Midwest

Favor 50%
Oppose 30
No opinion 20

South

Favor 41%
Oppose 35
No opinion 24

West

Favor 49%
Oppose 35
No opinion 16

By Age
18–24 Years

Favor 51%
Oppose 22
No opinion 27

25–29 Years

Favor 37%
Oppose 34
No opinion 29

30–49 Years

Favor 50%
Oppose 32
No opinion 18

50 Years and Over

Favor 46%
Oppose 34
No opinion 20

By Politics
Republicans

Favor 52%
Oppose 25
No opinion 23

Democrats

Favor 47%
Oppose 31
No opinion 22

Independents

Favor 44%
Oppose 36
No opinion 20

Also asked of the entire sample: Do you feel that Gorbachev's recent proposals mean that the Soviet Union now is really serious about a major nuclear arms reduction agreement, or are his proposals mainly intended to influence world opinion in his nation's favor?

Really serious 14%
Influence world opinion 60
Both (volunteered) 6
No opinion 20

By Sex
Male

Really serious 16%
Influence world opinion 64
Both (volunteered) 6
No opinion 14

Female

Really serious 12%
Influence world opinion 56
Both (volunteered) 7
No opinion 25

Less Than High-School Graduate

Really serious 14%
Influence world opinion 51
Both (volunteered) 6
No opinion 29

By Ethnic Background
White

Really serious 14%
Influence world opinion 61
Both (volunteered) 6
No opinion 19

By Age
18–24 Years

Really serious 17%
Influence world opinion 52
Both (volunteered) 10
No opinion 21

Nonwhite

Really serious 15%
Influence world opinion 55
Both (volunteered) 7
No opinion 23

25–29 Years

Really serious 11%
Influence world opinion 60
Both (volunteered) 8
No opinion 21

Black

Really serious 13%
Influence world opinion 38
Both (volunteered) 5
No opinion 24

30–49 Years

Really serious 14%
Influence world opinion 59
Both (volunteered) 7
No opinion 20

By Education
College Graduate

Really serious 14%
Influence world opinion 64
Both (volunteered) 8
No opinion 14

50 Years and Over

Really serious 13%
Influence world opinion 64
Both (volunteered) 5
No opinion 18

College Incomplete

Really serious 17%
Influence world opinion 61
Both (volunteered) 6
No opinion 16

By Politics
Republicans

Really serious 12%
Influence world opinion 68
Both (volunteered) 6
No opinion 14

High-School Graduate

Really serious 11%
Influence world opinion 63
Both (volunteered) 7
No opinion 19

Democrats

Really serious 16%
Influence world opinion 54
Both (volunteered) 7
No opinion 23

Really serious 12%
Influence world opinion 61
Both (volunteered) 8
No opinion 19

Note: On the eve of the summit meeting in Geneva on November 19–20 between President Ronald Reagan and Soviet leader Mikhail Gorbachev, a growing majority of Americans familiar with the administration's "Star Wars" proposal favors the development of such a system. Of the six in ten who have followed the discussions about "Star Wars" very or fairly closely, 61% want to see the United States go ahead with development, up from 52% in January.

Those who favor the development of this system believe it would increase the likelihood of reaching a nuclear arms agreement with the Soviet Union (48% say increase, 36% decrease). These respondents also believe it would improve the chances for peace (58%), rather than make the world less safe (29%). Public opinion on the prospect of "Star Wars" increasing the chances for an arms pact has changed little since January, but an increase is noted in those who think it would make the world safer—from 50% in January to 58% today.

The issue of "Star Wars" has been a major area of contention between the two superpowers, with Reagan stating his commitment to this program on many occasions and Gorbachev insisting that the program be abandoned before any meaningful arms agreement can be reached. In early October, Gorbachev proposed that the United States and the Soviet Union agree to cut their strategic missile forces by half and negotiate a total ban on the development and deployment of space-based weapons.

Americans like his proposal (47% favor it, 32% are opposed) and might be willing to back off from their support of "Star Wars" if the Soviet Union would, indeed, reduce its missiles by half. But many U.S. citizens remain distrustful of the intentions of the Soviet leader.

In the current survey, for example, only 14% think Gorbachev's recent proposals mean that his nation is really serious about a major nuclear arms

reduction agreement, while 60% see them as a propaganda ploy. Lack of trust has been the basic reason why Americans have been wary of entering into any bilateral or unilateral disarmament treaties with the Soviet Union. If assured of verification, the vast majority of U.S. citizens would support such treaties.

NOVEMBER 18
NUCLEAR STRENGTH

Interviewing Date: 10/11–14/85
Survey #258-G

At the present time, which nation do you feel is stronger in terms of nuclear weapons, the United States or the Soviet Union—or do you think they are about equal in nuclear strength?

United States 21%
Soviet Union 27
About equal 40
No opinion 12

By Sex
Male

United States 23%
Soviet Union 28
About equal 40
No opinion 9

Female

United States 18%
Soviet Union 27
About equal 40
No opinion 15

By Ethnic Background
White

United States 20%
Soviet Union 28
About equal 40
No opinion 12

Nonwhite

United States	23%
Soviet Union	24
About equal	41
No opinion	12

Black

United States	23%
Soviet Union	25
About equal	39
No opinion	13

By Education
College Graduate

United States	20%
Soviet Union	28
About equal	44
No opinion	8

College Incomplete

United States	21%
Soviet Union	32
About equal	36
No opinion	11

High-School Graduate

United States	19%
Soviet Union	28
About equal	43
No opinion	10

Less Than High-School Graduate

United States	23%
Soviet Union	21
About equal	36
No opinion	20

By Region
East

United States	25%
Soviet Union	25
About equal	36
No opinion	14

Midwest

United States	18%
Soviet Union	28
About equal	43
No opinion	11

South

United States	24%
Soviet Union	26
About equal	37
No opinion	13

West

United States	15%
Soviet Union	31
About equal	44
No opinion	10

By Age
18–29 Years

United States	21%
Soviet Union	26
About equal	42
No opinion	11

30–49 Years

United States	20%
Soviet Union	29
About equal	41
No opinion	10

50 Years and Over

United States	21%
Soviet Union	27
About equal	37
No opinion	15

By Politics
Republicans

United States	21%
Soviet Union	35
About equal	34
No opinion	10

Democrats

United States 23%
Soviet Union 23
About equal 41
No opinion 13

Independents

United States 16%
Soviet Union 26
About equal 46
No opinion 12

Selected National Trend

	United States	Soviet Union	About equal	No opinion
February 1985	24%	23%	44%	9%
March 1983	15	42	35	8

In your opinion, which of the following increases the chances of nuclear war more— a continuation of the nuclear arms buildup here and in the Soviet Union, or the United States falling behind the Soviet Union in nuclear weaponry?

Continuation of arms buildup 33%
U.S. falling behind 45
No opinion 22

By Sex
Male

Continuation of arms buildup 32%
U.S. falling behind 50
No opinion 18

Female

Continuation of arms buildup 33%
U.S. falling behind 41
No opinion 26

By Ethnic Background
White

Continuation of arms buildup 33%
U.S. falling behind 45
No opinion 22

Nonwhite

Continuation of arms buildup 31%
U.S. falling behind 46
No opinion 23

Black

Continuation of arms buildup 31%
U.S. falling behind 45
No opinion 24

By Education
College Graduate

Continuation of arms buildup 36%
U.S. falling behind 46
No opinion 18

College Incomplete

Continuation of arms buildup 35%
U.S. falling behind 47
No opinion 18

High-School Graduate

Continuation of arms buildup 35%
U.S. falling behind 45
No opinion 20

Less Than High-School Graduate

Continuation of arms buildup 26%
U.S. falling behind 42
No opinion 32

By Region
East

Continuation of arms buildup 32%
U.S. falling behind 41
No opinion 27

Midwest

Continuation of arms buildup 35%
U.S. falling behind 43
No opinion 22

South

Continuation of arms buildup 29%
U.S. falling behind 49
No opinion 22

West

Continuation of arms buildup 36%
U.S. falling behind 48
No opinion 16

By Age
18–29 Years

Continuation of arms buildup 38%
U.S. falling behind 42
No opinion 20

30–49 Years

Continuation of arms buildup 35%
U.S. falling behind 46
No opinion 19

50 Years and Over

Continuation of arms buildup 28%
U.S. falling behind 46
No opinion 26

By Politics
Republicans

Continuation of arms buildup 31%
U.S. falling behind 52
No opinion 17

Democrats

Continuation of arms buildup 35%
U.S. falling behind 39
No opinion 26

Independents

Continuation of arms buildup 33%
U.S. falling behind 47
No opinion 20

Selected National Trend

	Continu- ation of arms buildup	U.S. falling behind	No opinion
February 1985	41%	43%	16%
March 1983	38	47	15

Note: The Geneva summit meetings between President Ronald Reagan and Soviet leader Mikhail Gorbachev will begin at a time when American public opinion leans to the view that a Soviet advantage in nuclear weapons would increase the possibility of a nuclear conflict, more than would a continuation of the arms buildup by both superpowers. The latest Gallup Poll found that 45% say our falling behind the Soviet Union in nuclear weaponry would pose a greater threat to peace than would an extension of the arms race, cited by 33%. This is the largest difference between these divergent views recorded in surveys conducted during the last three years. As recently as last February, statistically equal proportions named our falling behind (43%) and the arms race (41%) as the greater threat.

A 40% plurality currently believes the United States and the USSR are about equal in nuclear strength, while 27% think the Soviets are stronger and 21% that the United States holds an edge. These figures represent a slight shift since February toward the view that the Soviet Union holds the upper hand in nuclear might. In March 1983, however, Americans were far more inclined to believe the Soviets (42%), rather than this country (15%), enjoyed a nuclear edge, with substantially fewer (35%) seeing nuclear parity between the two nations.

NOVEMBER 24
CRIME

Interviewing Date: 10/11–14/85
Survey #258-G

During the last twelve months, have any of these happened to you? [Respondents were handed a card listing crimes.]

	Yes
Money or property stolen	9%
Property vandalized	7
Home broken into or attempt made	5
Car stolen	1
Personal assault	3
One or more incidents	18

By Sex

Male

Money or property stolen	10%
Property vandalized	8
Home broken into or attempt made	7
Car stolen	1
Personal assault	3
One or more incidents	20

Female

Money or property stolen	7%
Property vandalized	6
Home broken into or attempt made	4
Car stolen	2
Personal assault	3
One or more incidents	15

By Ethnic Background

White

Money or property stolen	8%
Property vandalized	7
Home broken into or attempt made	5
Car stolen	1
Personal assault	2
One or more incidents	17

Nonwhite

Money or property stolen	12%
Property vandalized	5
Home broken into or attempt made	8
Car stolen	1
Personal assault	4
One or more incidents	21

Black

Money or property stolen	12%
Property vandalized	5
Home broken into or attempt made	7
Car stolen	2
Personal assault	5
One or more incidents	21

By Education

College Graduate

Money or property stolen	9%
Property vandalized	7
Home broken into or attempt made	5
Car stolen	1
Personal assault	2
One or more incidents	20

College Incomplete

Money or property stolen	11%
Property vandalized	10
Home broken into or attempt made	10
Car stolen	2
Personal assault	3
One or more incidents	23

High-School Graduate

Money or property stolen	8%
Property vandalized	7
Home broken into or attempt made	3
Car stolen	1
Personal assault	3
One or more incidents	16

Less Than High-School Graduate

Money or property stolen	7%
Property vandalized	4
Home broken into or attempt made	5
Car stolen	1
Personal assault	2
One or more incidents	14

By Region

East

Money or property stolen	6%
Property vandalized	9
Home broken into or attempt made	5
Car stolen	1
Personal assault	3
One or more incidents	18

Midwest

Money or property stolen 7%
Property vandalized 7
Home broken into or attempt made 2
Car stolen 2
Personal assault 1
One or more incidents 14

South

Money or property stolen 8%
Property vandalized 5
Home broken into or attempt made 8
Car stolen 2
Personal assault 3
One or more incidents 18

West

Money or property stolen 17%
Property vandalized 8
Home broken into or attempt made 7
Car stolen 1
Personal assault 4
One or more incidents 24

By Age
18–29 Years

Money or property stolen 11%
Property vandalized 10
Home broken into or attempt made 7
Car stolen 1
Personal assault 4
One or more incidents 22

30–49 Years

Money or property stolen 9%
Property vandalized 8
Home broken into or attempt made 6
Car stolen 1
Personal assault 3
One or more incidents 20

50 Years and Over

Money or property stolen 7%
Property vandalized 3
Home broken into or attempt made 4

Car stolen 2
Personal assault 1
One or more incidents 13

By Income
$50,000 and Over

Money or property stolen 9%
Property vandalized 11
Home broken into or attempt made 4
Car stolen 1
Personal assault 2
One or more incidents 21

$35,000–$49,999

Money or property stolen 9%
Property vandalized 8
Home broken into or attempt made 4
Car stolen 1
Personal assault 1
One or more incidents 18

$25,000–$34,999

Money or property stolen 9%
Property vandalized 6
Home broken into or attempt made 5
Car stolen 1
Personal assault 2
One or more incidents 15

$15,000–$24,999

Money or property stolen 10%
Property vandalized 9
Home broken into or attempt made 5
Car stolen 2
Personal assault 4
One or more incidents 22

$10,000–$14,999

Money or property stolen 9%
Property vandalized 4
Home broken into or attempt made 5
Car stolen . . . . *
Personal assault 3
One or more incidents 13

Under $10,000

Money or property stolen 6%
Property vandalized 5
Home broken into or attempt made 6
Car stolen 2
Personal assault 3
One or more incidents 15

*Less than 1%

Selected National Trend

	1984	1982	1979	1975
Money or property stolen	12%	14%	11%	11%
Property vandalized	12	11	10	10
Home broken into or attempt made	9	7	7	8
Car stolen	3	2	2	2
Personal assault	4	3	3	2
One or more incidents	24	25	22	25

Asked of those who experienced a crime: Did you happen to report this to the police, or not?

	Crime incidence	Reported to police
Money or property stolen	9%	5%
Property vandalized	7	5
Home broken into or attempt made	5	4
Car stolen	1	1
Personal assault	3	2

Note: The latest Gallup crime audit shows that about one-sixth of U.S. households (18%) were victimized by crime during the twelve months preceding the survey. This not only marks a sharp decline from the 24% victimized in 1984 but also is the lowest figure recorded since these studies began in 1972.

The 1985 audit, which covered the twelve-month period ending in October, found declines in most major classifications of crimes against property (money or property stolen or vandalized). The reported drop in the incidence of crimes against persons (assaults and robberies) is too small to be statistically significant.

Coincidentally, the U.S. Bureau of Justice Statistics recently reported that the number of crimes in 1984 fell to the lowest level in the twelve years these records have been kept. The bureau's latest figures, however, showed little change from 1983 in the incidence of violent crimes: rapes, robberies, and assaults.

NOVEMBER 28
DEATH PENALTY

Interviewing Date: 11/11–18/85
Special Telephone Survey

Do you favor or oppose the death penalty for persons convicted of murder?

Favor 75%
Oppose 17
No opinion 8

By Sex
Male

Favor 78%
Oppose 15
No opinion 7

Female

Favor 73%
Oppose 20
No opinion 7

By Ethnic Background
White

Favor 78%
Oppose 15
No opinion 7

Nonwhite

Favor 50%
Oppose 37
No opinion 13

Black

Favor 46%
Oppose 43
No opinion 11

By Education
College Graduate

Favor 71%
Oppose 22
No opinion 7

College Incomplete

Favor 76%
Oppose 19
No opinion 5

High-School Graduate

Favor 79%
Oppose 15
No opinion 6

Less Than High-School Graduate

Favor 72%
Oppose 15
No opinion 13

By Region
East

Favor 75%
Oppose 21
No opinion 4

Midwest

Favor 74%
Oppose 19
No opinion 7

South

Favor 74%
Oppose 17
No opinion 9

West

Favor 78%
Oppose 12
No opinion 10

By Age
18–29 Years

Favor 69%
Oppose 23
No opinion 8

30–49 Years

Favor 75%
Oppose 18
No opinion 7

50 Years and Over

Favor 80%
Oppose 12
No opinion 8

Selected National Trend

	Favor	Oppose	No opinion
1985	72%	20%	8%
1981	66	25	9
1978	62	27	11
1976	65	28	7
1972	57	32	11
1971	49	40	11
1969	51	40	9
1966	42	47	11
1965	45	43	12
1960	51	36	13
1953	68	25	7
1937	65	35	*
1936	61	39	*

*Not included

Do you favor or oppose the death penalty for persons convicted of rape?

Favor 45%
Oppose 45
No opinion 10

By Sex
Male
Favor 47%
Oppose 43
No opinion 10

Female
Favor 43%
Oppose 46
No opinion 11

By Ethnic Background
White
Favor 46%
Oppose 44
No opinion 10

Nonwhite
Favor 37%
Oppose 51
No opinion 12

Black
Favor 35%
Oppose 56
No opinion 9

By Education
College Graduate
Favor 37%
Oppose 55
No opinion 8

College Incomplete
Favor 43%
Oppose 47
No opinion 10

High-School Graduate
Favor 49%
Oppose 41
No opinion 10

Less Than High-School Graduate
Favor 48%
Oppose 38
No opinion 14

By Region
East
Favor 42%
Oppose 50
No opinion 8

Midwest
Favor 46%
Oppose 46
No opinion 8

South
Favor 47%
Oppose 41
No opinion 12

West
Favor 45%
Oppose 41
No opinion 14

By Age
18–29 Years
Favor 48%
Oppose 43
No opinion 9

30–49 Years
Favor 42%
Oppose 50
No opinion 8

50 Years and Over
Favor 47%
Oppose 39
No opinion 14

Selected National Trend

	Favor	Oppose	No opinion
1981	37%	53%	10%
1978	32	56	12

Do you favor or oppose the death penalty for persons convicted of attempting to assassinate the president?

Favor 57%
Oppose 37
No opinion 6

By Sex
Male

Favor 63%
Oppose 31
No opinion 6

Female

Favor 52%
Oppose 41
No opinion 7

By Ethnic Background
White

Favor 58%
Oppose 36
No opinion 6

Nonwhite

Favor 50%
Oppose 43
No opinion 7

Black

Favor 44%
Oppose 49
No opinion 7

By Education
College Graduate

Favor 45%
Oppose 46
No opinion 9

College Incomplete

Favor 52%
Oppose 43
No opinion 5

High-School Graduate

Favor 63%
Oppose 31
No opinion 6

Less Than High-School Graduate

Favor 63%
Oppose 30
No opinion 7

By Region
East

Favor 56%
Oppose 38
No opinion 6

Midwest

Favor 57%
Oppose 38
No opinion 5

South

Favor 55%
Oppose 38
No opinion 7

West

Favor 60%
Oppose 32
No opinion 8

By Age
18–29 Years
Favor 50%
Oppose 41
No opinion 9

30–49 Years
Favor 55%
Oppose 41
No opinion 4

50 Years and Over
Favor 64%
Oppose 29
No opinion 7

Do you favor or oppose the death penalty for persons convicted of spying for a foreign nation during peacetime?

Favor 48%
Oppose 47
No opinion 5

By Sex
Male
Favor 56%
Oppose 41
No opinion 3

Female
Favor 40%
Oppose 53
No opinion 7

By Ethnic Background
White
Favor 48%
Oppose 47
No opinion 5

Nonwhite
Favor 40%
Oppose 52
No opinion 8

Black
Favor 37%
Oppose 57
No opinion 6

By Education
College Graduate
Favor 36%
Oppose 57
No opinion 7

College Incomplete
Favor 42%
Oppose 54
No opinion 4

High-School Graduate
Favor 52%
Oppose 43
No opinion 5

Less Than High-School Graduate
Favor 58%
Oppose 38
No opinion 4

By Region
East
Favor 45%
Oppose 51
No opinion 4

Midwest
Favor 44%
Oppose 51
No opinion 5

South
Favor 51%
Oppose 44
No opinion 5

West

Favor 49%
Oppose 43
No opinion 8

Female

Favor 42%
Oppose 51
No opinion 7

By Age
18–29 Years

Favor 40%
Oppose 54
No opinion 6

By Ethnic Background
White

Favor 47%
Oppose 46
No opinion 7

30–49 Years

Favor 42%
Oppose 54
No opinion 4

Nonwhite

Favor 33%
Oppose 60
No opinion 7

50 Years and Over

Favor 59%
Oppose 35
No opinion 6

Black

Favor 29%
Oppose 66
No opinion 5

Selected National Trend*

	Favor	Oppose	No opinion
1981	39%	49%	12%
1978	36	50	14

*Question asked was: "Do you favor or oppose the death penalty for persons convicted of treason?"

By Education
College Graduate

Favor 37%
Oppose 55
No opinion 8

Do you favor or oppose the death penalty for persons convicted of airplane hijacking?

Favor 45%
Oppose 48
No opinion 7

College Incomplete

Favor 40%
Oppose 53
No opinion 7

High-School Graduate

Favor 46%
Oppose 48
No opinion 6

By Sex
Male

Favor 48%
Oppose 45
No opinion 7

Less Than High-School Graduate

Favor 57%
Oppose 34
No opinion 9

By Region

East

Favor 47%
Oppose 48
No opinion 5

Midwest

Favor 46%
Oppose 49
No opinion 5

South

Favor 45%
Oppose 49
No opinion 6

West

Favor 43%
Oppose 44
No opinion 13

By Age

18–29 Years

Favor 34%
Oppose 60
No opinion 6

30–49 Years

Favor 42%
Oppose 52
No opinion 6

50 Years and Over

Favor 57%
Oppose 35
No opinion 8

Selected National Trend

	Favor	Oppose	No opinion
1981	22%	68%	10%
1978	37	52	11

Note: In the last seven years, public support for the death penalty for a variety of serious crimes has increased sharply.* Three Americans in four, for example, now favor the death penalty for murder—the largest proportion to do so in the Gallup Poll's fifty-year history—up from 62% in 1978. Twenty years ago a 47% plurality opposed the death penalty for murder.

The current survey also reveals growing public support for the death penalty for persons convicted of rape or hijacking an airplane. In addition, a high level of support is found for two crimes studied for the first time: attempting to assassinate the president and espionage during peacetime.

With each recent week bringing new revelations of Americans spying for the Soviet Union, Israel, and most recently, China, 48% in the new poll favor, while 47% oppose, capital punishment for espionage during peacetime. As a capital offense, espionage is seen as less serious than either murder or attempting to assassinate the president; 75% and 57%, respectively, advocate the death penalty for these crimes.

Spying for a foreign power during peacetime ranks with rape and hijacking an airplane as crimes meriting the death penalty; slightly less than one-half the public favors capital punishment for persons convicted of each type of crime. Public support for the death penalty for persons convicted of airplane hijacking has doubled since 1981, when 22% believed that this crime should be punishable by death. Today, 45% think this way.

*Twenty-three percent favor the death penalty in all cases, while 14% oppose it.

DECEMBER 1
FEDERAL BUDGET DEFICIT

Interviewing Date: 11/11–18/85
Special Telephone Survey

In your opinion, is the current federal budget deficit a very serious problem for the country, a fairly serious problem, not a serious problem, or is this something you haven't thought much about?

Very serious 61%
Fairly serious 23
Not serious 3
Not thought much about; no opinion 13

By Sex

Male

Very serious 65%
Fairly serious 20
Not serious 5
Not thought much about; no opinion 10

Female

Very serious 58%
Fairly serious 25
Not serious 2
Not thought much about; no opinion 15

By Ethnic Background

White

Very serious 62%
Fairly serious 25
Not serious 3
Not thought much about; no opinion 10

Nonwhite

Very serious 56%
Fairly serious 15
Not serious 4
Not thought much about; no opinion 25

Black

Very serious 58%
Fairly serious 14
Not serious 3
Not thought much about; no opinion 25

By Education

College Graduate

Very serious 62%
Fairly serious 32
Not serious 3
Not thought much about; no opinion 3

College Incomplete

Very serious 65%
Fairly serious 22
Not serious 3
Not thought much about; no opinion 10

High-School Graduate

Very serious 57%
Fairly serious 24
Not serious 3
Not thought much about; no opinion 16

Less Than High-School Graduate

Very serious 62%
Fairly serious 14
Not serious 5
Not thought much about; no opinion 19

By Region

East

Very serious 60%
Fairly serious 23
Not serious 4
Not thought much about; no opinion 13

Midwest

Very serious 66%
Fairly serious 21
Not serious 2
Not thought much about; no opinion 11

South

Very serious 61%
Fairly serious 21
Not serious 4
Not thought much about; no opinion 14

West

Very serious 58%
Fairly serious 28
Not serious 5
Not thought much about; no opinion 9

By Age

18–29 Years

Very serious 43%
Fairly serious 34
Not serious 3
Not thought much about; no opinion 20

30–49 Years

Very serious 62%
Fairly serious 22
Not serious 4
Not thought much about; no opinion 12

50 Years and Over

Very serious 73%
Fairly serious 16
Not serious 3
Not thought much about; no opinion 8

By Politics

Republicans

Very serious 60%
Fairly serious 29
Not serious 4
Not thought much about; no opinion 7

Democrats

Very serious 64%
Fairly serious 19
Not serious 3
Not thought much about; no opinion 14

Independents

Very serious 60%
Fairly serious 22
Not serious 3
Not thought much about; no opinion 15

National Trend

	Very serious	Fairly serious	Not serious	No opinion
Aug. 1985 ...	57%	21%	2%	20%
Apr. 1985	58	23	5	14
Dec. 1984	54	29	5	12

Would you approve or disapprove of raising personal income taxes to reduce the federal budget deficit?

Approve 29%
Disapprove 67
No opinion 4

By Sex

Male

Approve 32%
Disapprove 65
No opinion 3

Female

Approve 25%
Disapprove 69
No opinion 6

By Ethnic Background

White

Approve 30%
Disapprove 66
No opinion 4

Nonwhite

Approve 18%
Disapprove 75
No opinion 7

Black

Approve 18%
Disapprove 75
No opinion 7

By Education

College Graduate

Approve 41%
Disapprove 57
No opinion 2

College Incomplete

Approve 30%
Disapprove 66
No opinion 4

High-School Graduate

Approve 22%
Disapprove 73
No opinion 5

Less Than High-School Graduate

Approve 26%
Disapprove 68
No opinion 6

By Region

East

Approve 30%
Disapprove 64
No opinion 6

Midwest

Approve 30%
Disapprove 65
No opinion 5

South

Approve 30%
Disapprove 67
No opinion 3

West

Approve 22%
Disapprove 74
No opinion 4

By Age

18–29 Years

Approve 30%
Disapprove 66
No opinion 4

30–49 Years

Approve 27%
Disapprove 68
No opinion 5

50 Years and Over

Approve 29%
Disapprove 67
No opinion 4

By Politics

Republicans

Approve 29%
Disapprove 68
No opinion 3

Democrats

Approve 29%
Disapprove 68
No opinion 3

Independents

Approve 28%
Disapprove 66
No opinion 6

Note: Congressmen pondering legislation that would mandate a balanced federal budget by the early 1990s may find it helpful to consider the growing popular consensus that the current deficit represents a serious threat to the nation. In the latest Gallup Poll, 61% characterize the deficit as a very serious national problem and an additional 23% call it fairly serious. Merely 3% say it is not serious, while 13% have not given the matter much thought or do not express an opinion.

The proportion who now describe the deficit as very serious is the highest recorded since this measurement was begun one year ago. At that time, 54% believed that the deficit was very serious. Despite the political implication that the Reagan administration deserves much of the blame for the current deficit, Democrats are only slightly more likely (64%) than Republicans or independents (60% each) to say the deficit is a very serious problem.

The extent of the public's concern is reflected by the fact that almost three in ten (29%) would approve of raising personal income taxes to reduce the federal deficit. Among college graduates, the proportion rises to four in ten (41%). Respondents of all political stripes favor a tax increase to the same degree.

The House and Senate have approved legislation to require a balanced federal budget, beginning in the early 1990s. Both versions require automatic cuts in spending if Congress and the White House are unable to arrive at budgets within predetermined limits each year. House and Senate negotiators are now working on reconciliation of the two considerably different versions.

DECEMBER 5
STATE "WORKFARE" LAWS

Interviewing Date: 11/11–18/85
Special Telephone Survey

> Some states have laws requiring people on welfare who have completed job search and training programs and still can't find jobs, to work at public service or nonprofit jobs without additional pay. Would you like to see such a law in your state, or not?

Favor 69%
Oppose 25
No opinion* 6

*Includes a small percentage, 1% nationally, who volunteered the information that their state already has such a law.

By Sex
Male

Favor 71%
Oppose 25
No opinion 4

Female

Favor 68%
Oppose 24
No opinion 8

By Ethnic Background
White

Favor 71%
Oppose 23
No opinion 6

Nonwhite

Favor 54%
Oppose 39
No opinion 7

Black

Favor 53%
Oppose 41
No opinion 6

By Education
College Graduate

Favor 76%
Oppose 19
No opinion 5

College Incomplete

Favor 73%
Oppose 20
No opinion 7

High-School Graduate

Favor 70%
Oppose 25
No opinion 5

Less Than High-School Graduate

Favor 59%
Oppose 34
No opinion 7

By Region

East

Favor 72%
Oppose 23
No opinion 5

Midwest

Favor 74%
Oppose 22
No opinion 4

South

Favor 67%
Oppose 26
No opinion 7

West

Favor 63%
Oppose 28
No opinion 9

By Age

18–29 Years

Favor 68%
Oppose 27
No opinion 5

30–49 Years

Favor 74%
Oppose 22
No opinion 4

50 Years and Over

Favor 67%
Oppose 25
No opinion 8

By Politics

Republicans

Favor 70%
Oppose 24
No opinion 6

Democrats

Favor 65%
Oppose 29
No opinion 6

Independents

Favor 73%
Oppose 22
No opinion 5

Note: A proposal for state "workfare" laws that would require welfare recipients to perform public service or nonprofit jobs has the backing of two out of three Americans, including statistically equivalent proportions of Democrats, Republicans, and independents. The proposed program, which stipulates that people on welfare must have completed job search and training programs before becoming eligible for workfare jobs, is similar in nature to those now in effect in seven states, soon to be joined by California.

The goal of these programs is to break the familiar pattern of welfare dependency caused, at least in part, by a loss of benefits for welfare recipients who become employed. Critics of workfare programs, however, fear that welfare workers may displace public employees in their jobs.

Currently, 69% nationwide say they would like to see their states enact work-for-welfare laws, while 25% are opposed. When a similar question was asked in 1969, it received comparable public support. The present proposal is favored by 70% of Republicans, 65% of Democrats, and 73% of independents; these differences are not large enough to be statistically significant.

Somewhat greater opposition to the proposal is expressed by persons from population groups with above average representation on the unemployment rolls, notably nonwhites and those whose formal education ended before graduation from high school. Nevertheless, majorities in both groups favor the workfare proposal.

DECEMBER 8
SATISFACTION INDEX

Interviewing Date: 11/11–18/85
Special Telephone Survey

In general, are you satisfied or dissatisfied with the way things are going in the United States at this time?

Satisfied 51%
Dissatisfied 46
No opinion 3

By Sex
Male

Satisfied 53%
Dissatisfied 43
No opinion 4

Female

Satisfied 48%
Dissatisfied 49
No opinion 3

By Ethnic Background
White

Satisfied 53%
Dissatisfied 44
No opinion 3

Nonwhite

Satisfied 30%
Dissatisfied 65
No opinion 5

Black

Satisfied 28%
Dissatisfied 67
No opinion 5

By Education
College Graduate

Satisfied 62%
Dissatisfied 36
No opinion 2

College Incomplete

Satisfied 50%
Dissatisfied 48
No opinion 2

High-School Graduate

Satisfied 56%
Dissatisfied 40
No opinion 4

Less Than High-School Graduate

Satisfied 31%
Dissatisfied 65
No opinion 4

By Region
East

Satisfied 53%
Dissatisfied 44
No opinion 3

Midwest

Satisfied 49%
Dissatisfied 48
No opinion 3

South

Satisfied 51%
Dissatisfied 45
No opinion 4

West

Satisfied 50%
Dissatisfied 47
No opinion 3

By Age

18–29 Years

Satisfied 61%
Dissatisfied 37
No opinion 2

30–49 Years

Satisfied 54%
Dissatisfied 44
No opinion 2

50 Years and Over

Satisfied 40%
Dissatisfied 55
No opinion 5

By Politics

Republicans

Satisfied 66%
Dissatisfied 32
No opinion 2

Democrats

Satisfied 37%
Dissatisfied 58
No opinion 5

Independents

Satisfied 51%
Dissatisfied 47
No opinion 2

Selected National Trend

	Satisfied	Dis-satisfied	No opinion
1984			
December	52%	40%	8%
September	48	45	7
February	50	46	4
1983			
August	35	59	6
1982			
November	24	72	4
April	25	71	4
1981			
December	27	67	6
June	33	61	6
January	17	78	5
1979			
November	19	77	4
August	12	84	4
February	26	69	5

In general, are you satisfied or dissatisfied with the way things are going in your own personal life?

Satisfied 82%
Dissatisfied 17
No opinion 1

By Sex

Male

Satisfied 82%
Dissatisfied 16
No opinion 2

Female

Satisfied 82%
Dissatisfied 17
No opinion 1

By Ethnic Background

White

Satisfied 85%
Dissatisfied 14
No opinion 1

Nonwhite

Satisfied 66%
Dissatisfied 31
No opinion 3

Black

Satisfied 64%
Dissatisfied 22
No opinion 4

By Education

College Graduate

Satisfied 91%
Dissatisfied 8
No opinion 1

College Incomplete

Satisfied 82%
Dissatisfied 16
No opinion 2

High-School Graduate

Satisfied 81%
Dissatisfied 18
No opinion 1

Less Than High-School Graduate

Satisfied 76%
Dissatisfied 22
No opinion 2

By Region

East

Satisfied 83%
Dissatisfied 17
No opinion .... *

Midwest

Satisfied 82%
Dissatisfied 17
No opinion 1

South

Satisfied 82%
Dissatisfied 16
No opinion 2

West

Satisfied 83%
Dissatisfied 16
No opinion 1

By Age

18–29 Years

Satisfied 83%
Dissatisfied 16
No opinion 1

30–49 Years

Satisfied 80%
Dissatisfied 19
No opinion 1

50 Years and Over

Satisfied 85%
Dissatisfied 14
No opinion 1

By Politics

Republicans

Satisfied 83%
Dissatisfied 16
No opinion 1

Democrats

Satisfied 83%
Dissatisfied 15
No opinion 2

Independents

Satisfied 84%
Dissatisfied 15
No opinion 1

*Less than 1%

Selected National Trend

	Satisfied	Dis-satisfied	No opinion
1984			
December	79%	17%	4%
February	79	19	2
1983			
August	77	20	3
1982			
November	75	23	2
April	76	22	2

December	81	17	2
June	81	16	3
January	81	17	2
1979			
November	79	19	2
July	73	23	4
February	77	21	2

Note: The mood of the nation today is far brighter than it was just two years ago, with 51% now saying they are satisfied with the way things are going, compared to 35% in August 1983. Satisfaction with trends in the nation has increased from 12% in August 1979, the year this measurement was started, to 50% in February 1984 and has remained at about this level in subsequent measurements.

Satisfaction with the way things are going in one's personal life, already high, also has grown. Today, 82% say they are satisfied in this respect, representing the highest level since the first measurement. Interestingly, young adults 18 to 29 are more likely than persons 30 and older to express satisfaction with what is happening in the nation but are equally satisfied with trends in their personal lives.

Much of the growth in optimism in recent years appears to be economically based. For example, in March 1983, 25% of Americans said they were financially better off than one year earlier. The comparable figure today is 38%.

DECEMBER 12
HOMOSEXUALITY

Interviewing Date: 11/11–18/85
Special Telephone Survey

Do you think homosexual relations between consenting adults should or should not be legal?

Should 44%
Should not 47
No opinion 9

By Sex
Male

Should 41%
Should not 53
No opinion 6

Female

Should 46%
Should not 42
No opinion 12

By Ethnic Background
White

Should 43%
Should not 47
No opinion 10

Nonwhite

Should 49%
Should not 44
No opinion 7

Black

Should 48%
Should not 45
No opinion 7

By Education
College Graduate

Should 60%
Should not 31
No opinion 9

College Incomplete

Should 51%
Should not 43
No opinion 6

High-School Graduate

Should 42%
Should not 46
No opinion 12

Less Than High-School Graduate

Should 21%
Should not 70
No opinion 9

By Region

East

Should 43%
Should not 44
No opinion 13

Midwest

Should 44%
Should not 49
No opinion 7

South

Should 40%
Should not 50
No opinion 10

West

Should 50%
Should not 42
No opinion 8

By Age

18–29 Years

Should 52%
Should not 41
No opinion 7

30–49 Years

Should 52%
Should not 41
No opinion 7

50–64 Years

Should 32%
Should not 53
No opinion 15

65 Years and Over

Should 25%
Should not 65
No opinion 10

By Family Income

$35,000 and Over

Should 62%
Should not 31
No opinion 7

$15,000–$34,999

Should 43%
Should not 48
No opinion 9

Under $15,000

Should 33%
Should not 55
No opinion 12

By Religion

Protestants

Should 38%
Should not 53
No opinion 9

Catholics

Should 51%
Should not 40
No opinion 9

Selected National Trend

	Should	Should not	No opinion
1982	45%	39%	16%
1977	43	43	14

Would you say the AIDS epidemic has changed your opinion about homosexuals for the better, for the worse, or has it not made any difference in the way you feel?

Better 2%
Worse 37
No difference 59
No opinion 2

By Sex

Male

Better 3%
Worse 38
No difference 58
No opinion 1

Female

Better 2%
Worse 36
No difference 59
No opinion 3

By Ethnic Background

White

Better 2%
Worse 36
No difference 60
No opinion 2

Nonwhite

Better 4%
Worse 44
No difference 51
No opinion 1

Black

Better 3%
Worse 38
No difference 58
No opinion 1

By Education

College Graduate

Better 3%
Worse 25
No difference 71
No opinion 1

College Incomplete

Better 1%
Worse 38
No difference 60
No opinion 1

High-School Graduate

Better 3%
Worse 37
No difference 59
No opinion 1

Less Than High-School Graduate

Better 2%
Worse 47
No difference 47
No opinion 4

By Region

East

Better 2%
Worse 39
No difference 57
No opinion 2

Midwest

Better 3%
Worse 33
No difference 63
No opinion 1

South

Better 2%
Worse 41
No difference 55
No opinion 2

West

Better 2%
Worse 33
No difference 63
No opinion 2

By Age

18–29 Years

Better	4%
Worse	34
No difference	62
No opinion	*

30–49 Years

Better	1%
Worse	32
No difference	66
No opinion	1

50–64 Years

Better	4%
Worse	39
No difference	55
No opinion	2

65 Years and Over

Better	*%
Worse	52
No difference	42
No opinion	6

By Family Income

$35,000 and Over

Better	2%
Worse	33
No difference	64
No opinion	1

$15,000–$34,999

Better	2%
Worse	34
No difference	63
No opinion	1

Under $15,000

Better	3%
Worse	45
No difference	50
No opinion	2

By Religion

Protestants

Better	2%
Worse	38
No difference	58
No opinion	2

Catholics

Better	1%
Worse	38
No difference	58
No opinion	3

*Less than 1%

Note: Six in ten American adults report that the AIDS epidemic has not changed their basic attitudes toward homosexuals. And, although about one-third say they are now less favorably disposed toward gays than they were before the disease became widely publicized, other survey evidence suggests that newly formed antihomosexual attitudes may not be deeply held.

First, the latest Gallup Poll found no decrease since 1982 in the proportion who believe that homosexual relations between consenting adults should be legal, and only a minor increase in those who disagree. Second, the survey found no increase since 1982 in job discrimination against homosexuals. Third, a recent *Newsweek* Poll conducted by the Gallup Organization found an increase since 1983 in the view that homosexuals as a group are becoming more, rather than less, accepted in American society.

In the latest Gallup Poll, 59% say the AIDS epidemic has made no difference in the way they think about homosexuals, while 37% report their opinions have changed for the worse. Merely 2% say they now are more sympathetic toward gays, and 2% have no opinion.

Public opinion on this issue is conditioned by age, education, and income, with persons 65 and older, those whose formal education ended before graduation from high school, and those in the lower-income brackets more likely to say their attitudes toward homosexuals have worsened because of the AIDS epidemic.

In the Gallup Poll's first (1977) sounding of public opinion, equal proportions said homosexual relations between consenting adults should and should not be legal. In 1982, a 45% plurality favored legalization, while 39% were opposed. The current survey found no significant decline in those favoring legalization, a slight upturn in opposition, and a concomitant decline in the no opinion vote.

DECEMBER 13
JOBS FOR HOMOSEXUALS

Interviewing Date: 11/11–18/85
Special Telephone Survey

Do you think homosexuals should or should not be hired for each of the following occupations:

Salespersons?

Should	71%
Should not	22
No opinion	7

The armed forces?

Should	55%
Should not	38
No opinion	7

Doctors?

Should	52%
Should not	41
No opinion	7

The clergy?

Should	41%
Should not	53
No opinion	6

Elementary schoolteachers?

Should	36%
Should not	60
No opinion	4

Selected National Trend

(Percent Saying Homosexuals Should Be Hired for Each Occupation)

	1982	1977
Salespersons	70%	68%
Armed forces	52	51
Doctors	50	44
Clergy	38	36
Elementary schoolteachers	32	27

The following summarizes those who say homosexuals should be hired for all five occupations versus those who believe that they should not be hired for any of the occupations tested.

	Should be hired for all	Should not be hired for any
National	26%	17%

By Sex

Male	24%	24%
Female	28	12

By Ethnic Background

White	25%	19%
Nonwhite	36	9
Black	32	10

By Education

College graduate	40%	10%
College incomplete	30	12
High-school graduate	19	20
Less than high-school graduate	21	27

By Region

East	29%	10%
Midwest	28	20
South	20	22
West	29	17

By Age

18–29 years	28%	16%
30–49 years	34	13
50–64 years	18	19
65 years and over	17	28

By Income

$35,000 and over	40%	11%
$15,000–$34,999	23	18
Under $15,000	22	22

By Religion

Protestants	20%	21%
Catholics	31	15

Note: Although Americans consistently have upheld the principle of equal job opportunities for homosexuals, a substantial number would withhold this right from homosexuals seeking employment in certain occupations, including the clergy and elementary schoolteachers. The latest Gallup Poll, however, found no evidence of increased job discrimination against gays since 1982, before the AIDS epidemic.

In the latest survey, 71% say homosexuals should be hired as salespersons, 55% as members of the armed forces, and 52% as doctors. Less than a majority believes homosexuals should be hired as clergy (41%) or elementary schoolteachers (36%). In the case of each of the five occupations tested, the latest figures are as high or higher than those recorded in surveys conducted in 1982 and 1977.

DECEMBER 19
POLITICAL AFFILIATION

Interviewing Date: July–September 1985
Various Surveys

In politics, as of today, do you consider yourself a Republican, a Democrat, or an independent?*

Republican 32%
Democrat 37
Independent 31

*Those saying they have no party preference or who named other parties (3% in the latest surveys) are excluded.

By Sex
Male

Republican 32%
Democrat 35
Independent 33

Female

Republican 33%
Democrat 39
Independent 28

By Ethnic Background
White

Republican 35%
Democrat 33
Independent 32

Black

Republican 7%
Democrat 76
Independent 17

Hispanics

Republican 22%
Democrat 48
Independent 30

By Education
College Graduate

Republican 40%
Democrat 31
Independent 29

College Incomplete

Republican 37%
Democrat 29
Independent 34

High-School Graduate

Republican 32%
Democrat 38
Independent 30

Less Than High-School Graduate

Republican 22%
Democrat 49
Independent 29

By Region

East

Republican 33%
Democrat 36
Independent 31

Midwest

Republican 31%
Democrat 33
Independent 36

South

Republican 32%
Democrat 41
Independent 27

West

Republican 33%
Democrat 37
Independent 30

By Age

18–29 Years

Republican 34%
Democrat 29
Independent 37

30–49 Years

Republican 30%
Democrat 36
Independent 34

50 Years and Over

Republican 33%
Democrat 44
Independent 23

By Income

$35,000 and Over

Republican 39%
Democrat 30
Independent 31

$15,000–$34,999

Republican 31%
Democrat 36
Independent 33

Under $15,000

Republican 28%
Democrat 44
Independent 28

By Occupation

Professional and Business

Republican 39%
Democrat 31
Independent 30

Other White Collar

Republican 33%
Democrat 39
Independent 28

Blue Collar—Total

Republican 27%
Democrat 38
Independent 35

Skilled Blue Collar

Republican 27%
Democrat 34
Independent 39

Unskilled Blue Collar

Republican 27%
Democrat 41
Independent 32

By Labor Union Household

Labor Union Members

Republican 22%
Democrat 42
Independent 36

Nonlabor Union Members

Republican 34%
Democrat 36
Independent 30

Selected National Trend

	Republican	Democrat	Independent
1985 (2d quarter)	32%	37%	31%
1985 (1st quarter)	35	37	28
1984	31	40	29
1982	26	45	29
1980	24	46	30
1978	23	48	29
1976	23	47	30
1972	28	43	29
1968	27	46	27
1964	25	53	22
1960	30	47	23
1954	34	46	20
1950	33	45	22
1946	40	39	21
1940	38	42	20
1937	34	50	16

Note: The Republican party has suffered some erosion in popular support since the political realignment associated with President Ronald Reagan's reelection last November. During the six-month period ending last March, nearly equal proportions of voting-age Americans described themselves as either Republicans or Democrats.

In 3,500 face-to-face interviews, conducted during the July–September quarter, 32% of American adults claimed allegiance to the Republican party, while 37% said they were Democrats and 31% independents. Almost identical figures were recorded during the previous three months. In contrast, in the January–March quarter, 35% claimed affiliation with the GOP, 37% with the Democrats, and 28% independents. This is the closest the Republican party has been to numerical parity with the Democrats since 1946, when 40% described themselves as Republicans and 39% as Democrats.

Gallup surveys during the last half century have shown that political party allegiance tends to ebb and flow with the fortunes of the party controlling the White House. Thus, Republican affiliation rose to 28% at the time of President Reagan's election in 1980. After the onset of the recession, however, it declined steadily to the 23% level until mid-1983, when there was clear evidence of economic recovery. The proportion of the electorate claiming Republican allegiance had been on a slow but steady upturn until recent months. The minor, but statistically significant, recent slippage in Republican membership has not been accompanied by an increase in Democratic affiliation, with the GOP loss traceable to an increase in independents.

During the January quarter, the Republicans claimed a numerical advantage over the Democrats among whites, 18 to 29 year olds, persons who attended college, those in upper-income groups, midwesterners, and persons from households in which the chief wage earner is employed in business or the professions. In addition, the two parties were at a virtual standoff, not only nationally and among voters of both sexes but also among high-school graduates, westerners, and skilled blue-collar workers.

In the latest surveys, the GOP has retained an edge only among 18 to 29 year olds, the college educated, business and professional people, and the affluent. And parity with the Democrats has been lost among women, high-school graduates, and, most notably, skilled workers.

As was the case nationwide, little benefit has accrued directly to the Democrats. Instead, most of the GOP defectors noted above have swung over to the independent ranks. For example, party identification among skilled workers during the first three months of 1985 was 35% Republicans,

34% Democrats, and 31% independents; the third quarter figures for this group were 27%, 34%, and 39%, respectively.

DECEMBER 22
CHURCH ATTENDANCE

Interviewing Date: Four Selected Weeks During 1985
Various Surveys

Did you, yourself, happen to attend church or synagogue in the last seven days?

	Yes
National	42%

By Sex

Male	36%
Female	47

By Ethnic Background

White	42%
Black	42
Hispanic	45

By Education

College graduate	45%
College incomplete	44
High-school graduate	39
Less than high-school graduate	39

By Region

East	41%
Midwest	44
South	46
West	34

By Age

18–24 years	31%
25–29 years	33
30–49 years	42
50–64 years	47
65 years and over	49

By Religion

Protestants	42%
Catholics	53
Jews	23

Selected National Trend

	Yes
1984	40%
1983	40
1981	41
1979	40
1977	41
1969	42
1967	43
1962	46
1958	49
1955	49
1954	46
1950	39
1940	37
1939	41

Do you happen to be a member of a church or synagogue?

	Yes
National	71%

Selected National Trend

	Yes
1984	68%
1983	69
1982	67
1981	68
1980	69
1978	68
1976	71
1965	73
1952	73
1947	76

1942	75
1939	72
1937	73

Note: Four adults in every ten (42%) attended church or synagogue in a typical week in 1985. Churchgoing has remained remarkably constant since 1969, after having declined from the high point of 49% recorded in 1955 and 1958.

The level of churchgoing in 1985 was higher among women (47% attended in a typical week) than among men (36%), and among older persons than younger. Nationally, 53% of Catholics and 42% of Protestants attended.

Persons who attended college reported somewhat higher levels of churchgoing than did those whose formal education did not include college. Southerners and midwesterners were more likely to attend church weekly, while westerners had the lowest level of attendance. No significant differences in attendance were reported by persons from different racial or ethnic backgrounds.

The proportion of U.S. adults who say they are church members also has changed in recent years, with seven in ten (71%) now claiming membership in a church or synagogue. The highest level of membership (76%) was found in 1947, close to the 73% recorded in the first Gallup audit in 1937.

It is important to bear in mind that the membership figures reported here are self-classifications, representing the proportion of people who say they are members of a church or synagogue, and may include some who are not actually on the rolls of local churches. It should also be noted that adherents of certain faiths—for example, the Roman Catholic and Eastern Orthodox churches—are considered members at birth.

DECEMBER 26
MOST ADMIRED WOMAN

Interviewing Date: 11/11–18/85
Special Telephone Survey

What woman whom you have heard or read about, living today in any part of the world, do you admire the most? Who is your second choice?

The following are listed in order of frequency of mention, with first and second choices combined:

Nancy Reagan
Margaret Thatcher
Mother Teresa of Calcutta
Geraldine Ferraro
Princess Diana
Jeane Kirkpatrick
Betty Ford
Queen Elizabeth II
Jacqueline Kennedy Onassis
Sandra Day O'Connor

Note: First Lady Nancy Reagan, British Prime Minister Margaret Thatcher, and Mother Teresa of Calcutta top the list of women most admired by the American people, as determined by these annual Gallup contests conducted since the late 1940s. Receiving frequent mentions in the 1985 survey, but not included in the top ten, are, in alphabetical order: Shirley Chisholm, Jane Fonda, Katharine Hepburn, Coretta King, and Barbara Walters.

Survey respondents in this study, which the Gallup Poll has conducted for more than three decades, are asked to give their choices without the aid of a prearranged list of names. This procedure, while opening the field to all possible choices, tends to favor those who are currently or have recently been in the news.

DECEMBER 29
MOST ADMIRED MAN

Interviewing Date: 11/11–18/85
Special Telephone Survey

What man whom you have heard or read about, living today in any part of the world, do you admire the most? Who is your second choice?

The following are listed in order of frequency of mention, with first and second choices combined:

Ronald Reagan
Pope John Paul II
Lee Iacocca
Jesse Jackson
Billy Graham
Edward Kennedy
Desmond Tutu
Jimmy Carter
Prince Charles
George Bush

Note: President Ronald Reagan, Pope John Paul II, and Lee Iacocca, chairman of the Chrysler Corporation, top the list of men most admired by the American people. President Reagan and Pope John Paul II were also number one and two in the 1984, 1983, 1982, and 1981 audits.

Receiving honorable mention this year, but not in the top ten are, in alphabetical order: Mario Cuomo, Gerald Ford, Henry Kissinger, Richard Nixon, Pat Robertson, and Jimmy Swaggart.

Index

A

Abortion
  in instructional program at public elementary schools, 19, 232
  in instructional program in public high schools, 19, 233
Accounting
  as career choice for young men and women, 226
Advertising practitioners
  honesty rating, 193
  profession rated by teachers and public, 17
Aerobics and dancercize
  participated in, 1, 215
    by women, 216
AIDS (Acquired Immune Deficiency Syndrome)
  epidemic has changed your opinion about homosexuals, 284–86
  heard or read about, 193
  statements about, true or false, 194
  in what way is it spread, 194
  who is most likely to get, 193
Alcohol abuse
  dealing with, as goal of education, 20
Alcoholic beverages
  drinking, as cause of trouble in your family, 81, 185
    national trend, 81
    survey in twenty-two nations, 185
  drinking, as problem in public schools, 15
  you plan to cut down or quit drinking, 82
  your use of, 80, 185
    national trend, 81
    survey in twenty-two nations, 185–86
  you sometimes drink more than you should, 81–82, 186
    national trend, 82
    survey in twenty-one nations, 186

Alcoholism
  how serious a problem, 186
    survey in twelve nations, 186
  as problem in public schools, 14
Anorexia nervosa. *See* Eating disorders
Argentina, questions asked in
  approval rating of United Nations, 84
  chances of world war breaking out, 2
  drinking as cause of trouble in your family, 185
  1985 as peaceful or troubled year, 3
  predictions for 1985, 6
  world as better place to live in ten years than now, 79
  your use of alcoholic beverages, 185
  you sometimes drink more than you should, 186
Armed forces
  homosexuals in, 287
Assault
  incidence of, 45, 265–68
    national trend, 268
  reported to police, 268
Atomic bomb
  forty years ago (special report), 188
Australia, questions asked in
  approval rating of United Nations, 84
  chances of world war breaking out, 2
  drinking as cause of trouble in your family, 185
  1985 as peaceful or troubled year, 3
  predictions for 1985, 7
  world as better place to live in ten years than now, 79
  your use of alcoholic beverages, 185
  you sometimes drink more than you should, 186
Austria, questions asked in
  chances of world war breaking out, 3
  1985 as peaceful or troubled year, 3
  predictions for 1985, 7
Auto mechanics
  as career choice for young men, 226
Auto racing
  favorite sport to watch, 223

B

Babbitt, Bruce
  as nominee for Democratic presidential candidate, 161
Baker, Howard
  approval rating by degree, 195
  as convention choice vs. Bush and Dole, 160
  as nominee for Republican presidential candidate, 159, 160
Baker, James
  as nominee for Republican presidential candidate, 159, 160

Bankers
  honesty rating, 191
  profession rated by teachers and public, 17
Banks and banking
  confidence in, 164
    national trend, 164
Baseball
  favorite sport to watch, 223–24
    national trend, 224
  participated in, 1, 215
Basketball
  favorite sport to watch, 223–24
    national trend, 224
  participated in, 1, 215
    by men, 216
    national trend, 1
Belgium, questions asked in
  approval rating of United Nations, 84
  chances of world war breaking out, 3
  drinking as cause of trouble in your family, 185
  how serious a problem is alcoholism, 186
  1985 as peaceful or troubled year, 3
  predictions for 1985, 7
  world as better place to live in ten years than now, 79
  your use of alcoholic beverages, 185
  you sometimes drink more than you should, 186
Bicycling
  participated in, 1, 215
    by men and women, 216
    national trend, 1
Biden, Joseph
  as nominee for Democratic presidential candidate, 161
Billiards
  participated in, 1, 215
    by men, 216
Birth control
  in instructional program at public elementary schools, 19, 232
  in instructional program at public high schools, 19, 233
Birth control pills
  health risks from childbearing compared to health risks from taking, 55
  substantial risks with using, 54–55
Blacks
  interests served by Republican and Democratic parties, 27
  more likely to receive death penalty, 37
  satisfaction with income, housing, and job, compared to whites, 41
Bowling
  participated in, 1, 215
    frequency of participation, 1
    by men and women, 216

national trend, 1, 216
Boxing
  favorite sport to watch, 223
Bradley, Bill
  as nominee for Democratic presidential candidate, 161
Bradley, Tom
  as nominee for Democratic presidential candidate, 161
Brazil, questions asked in
  approval rating of United Nations, 84
  chances of world war breaking out, 2
  drinking as cause of trouble in your family, 185
  1985 as peaceful or troubled year, 3
  predictions for 1985, 6
  world as better place to live in ten years than now, 79
  your use of alcoholic beverages, 186
  you sometimes drink more than you should, 186
Brock, William
  as nominee for Republican presidential candidate, 159, 160
Budget (federal)
  proposed amendment requiring government to balance, 211–12
  Reagan administration policy on chances for balancing, 61
    compared to 1982, 63
Budget deficit (federal)
  larger a year from now than it is now, 208–09
  as most important problem 52, 139, 253
    national trend, 52
  reduce by making cuts in defense spending, 29–30, 98–100
    national trend, 100
  reduce by making cuts in "entitlement" programs, 30, 100–01
    national trend, 101
  reduce by making cuts in social programs, 29, 96–98
    national trend, 98
  reduce by raising income taxes, 28–29, 95–96, 209–10, 276–77
    national trend, 96
  reducing, handled by Reagan, 238–39
  as serious problem for country, 93–95, 207–08, 274–76
    national trend, 276
Building contractors
  honesty rating, 192
Bulimia. See Eating disorders
Bumpers, Dale
  as nominee for Democratic presidential candidate, 161
Burglary (home broken into)
  incidence of, 265–68
    national trend, 268
  reported to police, 268

D

national trend, 73, 170
nominees for presidential candidate, 161
serves interests of blacks, 27
serves interests of business and professional people, 26
    national trend, 26
serves interests of farmers, 26
    national trend, 26
serves interests of labor union members, 26
serves interests of people like yourself, 24–26
serves interests of retired, 27
serves interests of skilled workers, 26
    national trend, 26
serves interests of small business people, 27
serves interests of unemployed, 27
serves interests of unskilled workers, 26
    national trend, 26
serves interests of white collar workers, 26
    national trend, 26
serves interests of women, 27
    see also Presidential trial heats
Denmark, questions asked in
    chances of world war breaking out, 3
    how serious a problem is alcoholism, 186
    1985 as peaceful or troubled year, 3
    predictions for 1985, 7
Dentists
    honesty rating, 191
Diana, Princess of Wales
    as most admired woman, 292
Doctors and physicians
    homosexuals as, 287
    honesty rating, 191
    profession rated by teachers and public, 17
Dole, Elizabeth
    as nominee for Republican presidential candidate, 159, 160
Dole, Robert
    approval rating by degree, 195
    as convention choice vs. Baker and Bush, 160
    as nominee for Republican presidential candidate, 159, 160
Domenici, Pete
    as nominee for Republican presidential candidate, 159, 160
Drug abuse
    dealing with, as goal of education, 20
    as most important problem, 139, 253
Druggists and pharmacists
    honesty rating, 191
Drug use
    as problem in public schools, 14, 15
    users most likely to get AIDS, 193, 194

E

Eating disorders in teen-agers
    ever gone on food binges, 251
    ever known anyone with anorexia nervosa, 251
    ever known anyone with bulimia, 251–52
    have you had symptoms of anorexia nervosa, 251
    have you had symptoms of bulimia, 252
    like to gain or lose weight, 250
    more healthy if you were thinner, 250–51
    more pleased about your appearance if you were thinner, 250
Eating disorders in young women
    ever gone on food binges, 248
    have you had symptoms of anorexia nervosa, 248–49
    have you had symptoms of bulimia, 249
    how often do you diet, 248
    how often do you go on food binges, 48
    know anyone with symptoms of anorexia nervosa, 248
    know anyone with symptoms of bulimia, 249
    like to gain or lose weight, 247
    your life better if you were thinner, 247–48
Economic conditions
    handled by Reagan, 34, 76, 178–79, 234–35
    national trend, 34, 76, 179
Economy
    house values will continue to go up, 9
    national trend, 10
    how long recovery will last, 7–8, 212–14
    national trend, 8, 215
    income to go up more than prices, 10
    national trend, 10
    as most important problem, 52, 139, 253
    national trend, 52
    time to buy big things for the house, 8–9
    national trend, 9
    see also Interest rates; Personal finances
Education
    goals of, rated by teachers, 19–20
Eisenhower, Dwight
    approval rating vs. Reagan and other presidents, 28, 34, 78, 202, 223
    as greatest president, 168
    choice of Democrats, 168
    choice in 1975, 168
    choice of Republicans, 168
Electoral reforms
    four regional presidential primaries, 122–23
    national trend, 123
Electric chair
    as most humane form of punishment, 38

Electronics
  as career choice for young men and women, 226
Elizabeth II, Queen
  as most admired woman, 292
Energy situation
  Reagan administration policy on, 60
    compared to 1982, 63
Engineering
  as career choice for young men and women, 226
Engineers
  honesty rating, 191
"Entitlement" programs
  make cuts in, to reduce federal budget deficit, 30, 100–01
  national trend, 101
Environmental situation
  Reagan administration policy on, 60–61
    compared to 1982, 63

F

Family life
  satisfaction with, 40
Family size
  ideal number of children, 63
    national trend, 63
    national trend for Protestants and Catholics, 64
Farmers
  interests served by Republican and Democratic parties, 26
    national trend, 26
  plight of, as most important problem, 253
Feinstein, Dianne
  as nominee for Democratic presidential candidate, 161
Ferraro, Geraldine
  as most admired woman, 292
  as nominee for Democratic presidential candidate, 161
Finland, questions asked in
  chances of world war breaking out, 3
  drinking as cause of trouble in your family, 185
  1985 as peaceful or troubled year, 3
  predictions for 1985, 7
  your use of alcoholic beverages, 185
  you sometimes drink more than you should, 186
Firing squad
  as most humane form of punishment, 38
Fishing
  participated in, 1, 215
    frequency of participation, 1
    by men and women, 216
    national trend, 1, 216
Football
  favorite sport to watch, 223–24

national trend, 224
Ford, Betty
  as most admired woman, 292
Ford, Gerald
  approval rating vs. Reagan and other presidents, 28
  how he will go down in history, compared to Reagan and Carter, 48
Foreign policy
  handled by Reagan, 33, 76, 179–80
    national trend, 33, 76, 180
France, questions asked in
  chances of world war breaking out, 2
  how serious a problem is alcoholism, 186
  1985 as peaceful or troubled year, 3
  predictions for 1985, 7
Free time
  satisfaction with, 40–41
Frisbee tossing
  participated in, 215
Funeral directors
  honesty rating, 192
  profession rated by teachers and public, 17
Future
  world a better place to live in ten years than now, 78–79
    survey in sixteen nations, 79–80

G

Gas chamber
  as most humane form of punishment, 38
Gingrich, Newt
  as nominee for Republican presidential candidate, 160
Golf
  favorite sport to watch, 223
  participated in, 1, 215
    frequency of participation, 1
    national trend, 1, 216
Gorbachev, Mikhail
  his proposals mean Soviet Union is serious about nuclear arms reduction, 260–62
  proposal by, that U.S. and Soviet Union ban space-based weapons, 259–60
Government
  big, as threat to country, 140–41
    national trend, 141
  satisfaction with way nation is governed, 31–32
Government size
  Reagan administration policy on chances for reducing, 61–62
    compared to 1982, 63
Government spending
  amount for national defense and military purposes, 53

national trend, 53–54
amount for social programs, 54
excessive, as most important problem, 52, 139
national trend, 52
Graham, Billy
as most admired man, 293
Great Britain (United Kingdom), questions asked in
approval rating of United Nations, 84
chances of world war breaking out, 3
distribution of money is fair in, 85; *see also* Poverty
drinking as cause of trouble in your family, 185
how serious a problem is alcoholism, 186
1985 as peaceful or troubled year, 3
predictions for 1985, 7
world as better place to live in ten years than now, 79
your use of alcoholic beverages, 185
you sometimes drink more than you should, 186
Greece, questions asked in
approval rating of United Nations, 84
chances of world war breaking out, 3
drinking as cause of trouble in your family, 185
1985 as peaceful or troubled year, 3
predictions for 1985, 7
world as better place to live in ten years than now, 79
your use of alcoholic beverages, 185
you sometimes drink more than you should, 186
Gymnastics
favorite sport to watch, 223

H

Handguns
law banning sale and possession of, 118–19
registration of all, 116–18
Hanging
as most humane form of punishment, 38
Hart, Gary
approval rating by degree, 195
as convention choice vs. Kennedy, 161
as nominee for Democratic presidential candidate, 161
in trial heats vs. Bush, 190
Health
satisfaction with, 40
Helms, Jesse
as nominee for Republican presidential candidate, 159, 160
Hiking
participated in, 215
by women, 216
Hockey
favorite sport to watch, 223

Homosexuality
in instructional program at public elementary schools, 19, 232
in instructional program at public high schools, 19, 233
relations legal between consenting adults, 283–84
national trend, 284
Homosexuals
AIDS epidemic has changed your opinion about, 284–86
in armed forces, 287
national trend, 287
as clergy, 287
national trend, 287
as doctors, 287
national trend, 287
as elementary schoolteachers, 187
national trend, 187
as most likely to get AIDS, 193, 194
as salespersons, 287
national trend, 287
Honesty and ethical standards
ratings by professions, 191–93
Hoover, Herbert
as greatest president, 168
Horseback riding
participated in, 1, 215
frequency of participation, 1
national trend, 1
Housewife
as career choice for young women, 226
Housing
satisfaction with, 39
by whites and blacks, 41
Hunger
as most important problem, 52, 139, 253
national trend, 52
Hunting
participated in, 1, 215
frequency of participation, 1
by men, 216
national trend, 1

I

Iacocca, Lee
approval rating by degree, 195
as most admired man, 293
as nominee for Democratic presidential candidate, 161
in trial heats vs. Bush, 189
Iceland, questions asked in
drinking as cause of trouble in your family, 185
your use of alcoholic beverages, 185
you sometimes drink more than you should, 186

Ice skating
    favorite sport to watch, 223
    participated in, 216
Income
    satisfaction with your household, 39–40
        by whites and blacks, 41
Independents
    affiliation with, 23–24, 86–87, 288–90
        national trend, 24, 87–88, 290
        quarterly, 88
Inflation
    Reagan administration policy on, 59–60
        compared to 1982, 63
Inflation rate
    by this time next year, 129
        misery index, 129–30
        misery index trend, 130
Insurance salesmen
    honesty rating, 193
Interest rates
    during next twelve months, 8
        national trend, 8
International tensions
    as most important problem, 52, 139, 253
        national trend, 52
Ireland, Northern, questions asked in
    how serious a problem is alcoholism, 186
Ireland, Republic of, questions asked in
    chances of world war breaking out, 2
    drinking as cause of trouble in your family, 185
    how serious a problem is alcoholism, 186
    1985 as peaceful or troubled year, 3
    predictions for 1985, 7
    your use of alcoholic beverages, 185
    you sometimes drink more than you should, 186
Israel, questions asked in
    drinking as cause of trouble in your family, 185
    your use of alcoholic beverages, 186
    you sometimes drink more than you should, 186
Italy, questions asked in
    chances of world war breaking out, 3
    how serious a problem is alcoholism, 186
    1985 as peaceful or troubled year, 3
    predictions for 1985 in, 7

J

Jackson, Jesse
    approval rating by degree, 195
    as most admired man, 293
    as nominee for Democratic presidential candidate, 161
    in trial heats vs. Bush, 189

Japan, questions asked in
    approval rating of United Nations, 84
    chances of world war breaking out, 3
    drinking as cause of trouble in your family, 185
    how serious a problem is alcoholism, 186
    1985 as peaceful or troubled year, 3
    predictions for 1985, 7
    world as better place to live in ten years than now, 80
    your use of alcoholic beverages, 185
    you sometimes drink more than you should, 186
Jefferson, Thomas
    as greatest president, 168
        choice of Democrats, 168
        choice in 1975, 168
        choice of Republicans, 168
Job
    better, as advantage of college education, 228
    satisfaction with, 41
        by whites and blacks, 41
    to get good, as goal of education, 20
    see also Careers
Jogging
    happen to jog, 173
        national trend, 173
    how far do you usually jog, 173
        national trend, 173
    how often do you jog, 173
    participated in, 1, 215
        frequency of participation, 1
        by men and women, 216
John Paul II, Pope
    as most admired man, 293
Johnson, Lyndon
    approval rating vs. Reagan and other presidents, 28,
        34, 78, 202, 223
    as greatest president, 168
        choice in 1975, 168
Journalists
    honesty rating, 192
Judges
    profession rated by teachers and public, 17

K

Kean, Thomas
    as nominee for Republican presidential candidate, 160
Kemp, Jack
    as nominee for Republican presidential candidate, 159,
        160
Kennedy, Edward
    approval rating by degree, 195

N

Netherlands, questions asked in
  approval rating of United Nations, 84
  chances of world war breaking out, 3
  drinking as cause of trouble in your family, 185
  how serious a problem is alcoholism, 186
  1985 as peaceful or troubled year, 3
  predictions for 1985, 7
  world as better place to live in ten years than now, 79
  your use of alcoholic beverages, 185
  you sometimes drink more than you should, 186
Newspaper reporters
  honesty rating, 192
Newspapers
  confidence in, 165–66
    national trend, 166
Nicaragua
  approval of Reagan's embargo on trade with, 127–28
  favor U.S. economic assistance to, 71
  favor U.S. military advisers to, 71
  favor U.S. military supplies to, 71
  favor U.S. moral, diplomatic support of, 71
  favor U.S. troops to, 71
  Sandinista type of government will spread, 72
    views of those who favor and oppose, 72
  situation in, handled by Reagan, 76, 182–83
    national trend, 77, 183
  United States should help rebel forces, or stay out, 70–71
  U.S. involvement could turn into another Vietnam, 71–72
    views of those who favor and oppose, 72
  which side the United States is backing, 70
Nixon, Richard
  approval rating vs. Reagan and other presidents, 28, 34, 78, 202, 223
  as greatest president, 168
    choice of Democrats, 168
    choice in 1975, 168
    choice of Republicans, 168
Norway, questions asked in
  chances of world war breaking out, 3
  drinking as cause of trouble in your family, 185
  1985 as peaceful or troubled year, 3
  predictions for 1985, 7
  your use of alcoholic beverages, 185
  you sometimes drink more than you should, 186
Nuclear arms agreement. *See* "Star Wars" proposal
Nuclear disarmament
  Reagan administration policy on, 62–63
  negotiations handled by Reagan, 33, 77, 183–84

national trend, 77, 184
Nuclear weapons
  arms buildup here and in Soviet Union increases chances of war, 57, 264–65
    national trend, 57, 265
  United States or Soviet Union stronger in, 56, 262–64
    national trend, 56, 264
Nunn, Sam
  as nominee for Democratic presidential candidate, 161
Nursing
  as career choice for young women, 226

O

O'Connor, Sandra Day
  as most admired woman, 292
Onassis, Jacqueline Kennedy
  as most admired woman, 292

P

Packwood, Robert
  as nominee for Republican presidential candidate, 160
Parochial schools
  government "voucher system" for sending child to, 220–21
    national trend, 221
  proposed amendment permitting government financial aid to, 219
    national trend, 220
Peace
  chances of world war breaking out, in opinion of twenty-seven nations, 2–3
  1985 as peaceful or troubled year, in opinion of twenty-seven nations, 3
  Reagan administration policy on chances for world, 62 compared to 1982, 63
  "Star Wars" proposal would make world safer, 51
  United States doing all it can to keep, 3–4
  USSR doing all it can to keep, 4–6
Peace (keeping out of war)
  Republican or Democratic party more likely to keep United States out of war, 73, 169–70
    national trend, 73, 170
Personal finances
  better off next year than now, 68–69, 187, 254
    national trend, 69–70, 187, 254
    national trend by optimists and pessimists, 70, 187–88, 254
  better off now than a year ago, 66–67, 187, 254
    national trend, 67–68, 187, 254
    national trend by optimists and pessimists, 70, 187–88, 254

R

Racquetball
   participated in, 1, 215
Reagan, Nancy
   as most admired woman, 292
Reagan, Ronald
   approval of his embargo on trade with Nicaragua, 127–28
   approval of his visiting Bitburg cemetery, 125–26
   approval rating, 33, 46, 74–75, 92, 123–25, 176–77, 202, 221–23, 233
      for last six months, 92
      national trend, 33, 46, 75–76, 125, 177–78, 233–34
      percentage among men and women, 92
   approval rating by degree, 195
   approval rating vs. predecessors, 28, 34, 202, 223
   and economic conditions, 34, 76, 178–79, 234–35
      national trend, 34, 76, 179
   and foreign policy, 33, 76, 179–80
      national trend, 33, 76, 180
   as greatest president, 168
      choice of Democrats, 168
      choice of Republicans, 168
   and his plan for overhauling federal tax system, 141–42, 203–05, see also Taxes and Taxation, proposed changes
   how will he go down in history, 46–48
      compared to Carter and Ford, 48
   more effective in second term than in first, 202–03
   as most admired man, 293
   and nuclear disarmament negotiations with Soviet Union, 33, 77, 183–84
      national trend, 77, 184
   and reducing federal budget deficit, 238–39
   and reducing U.S. trade deficit, 239–40
   and relations with Soviet Union, 33, 77, 180–82
      national trend, 77, 182
   and situation in Middle East, 242–43
   and situation in Nicaragua, 76, 182–83
      national trend, 77, 183
   and situation in South Africa, 240–42
   and tax reform program, 236–38
   and unemployment, 235–36
Reagan administration
   approval rating of way it is dealing with South African situation, 201–02
Reagan administration policies
   on ability of nation to defend itself, 61
      compared to 1982, 63
   on chances for balancing national budget, 61
      compared to 1982, 63
   on chances for nuclear disarmament, 62–63

on chances for reducing federal taxes of average citizen, 62
   compared to 1982, 63
on chances for reducing size of government, 61–62
   compared to 1982, 63
on chances for world peace, 62
   compared to 1982, 63
on energy situation, 60
   compared to 1982, 63
on environmental situation, 60–61
   compared to 1982, 63
on increasing respect for United States abroad, 61
   compared to 1982, 63
on inflation, 59–60
   compared to 1982, 63
on unemployment, 60
   compared to 1982, 63
Realtors
   honesty rating, 192
   profession rated by teachers and public, 17
Recession
   fear of, as most important problem, 253
Religion
   aware of presence or power different from everyday self, 108
   can answer all problems, 120
      national trend, 120
   church or synagogue attendance, 291
      national trend, 291
   church or synagogue membership, 291
      national trend, 291–92
   confidence in church or organized, 162
      national trend, 162
   effect of presence or power on your life, 108–09
   influence on American life, 120
      national trend, 120
   presence or power described, 108
   views on premarital sex, by importance of religion in life, 111
   see also Moral decline in society
Reproduction, biology of
   in instructional program at public elementary schools, 18, 19, 232
   in instructional program at public high schools, 18, 19, 233
Republican party
   affiliation with, 23–24, 86–87, 288–90
      national trend, 24, 87–88, 290
      quarterly, 88
      Republican gains, 88–89
   better for handling most important problem, 52, 139, 253
      national trend, 52

Skiing
  participated in, 1, 215
    frequency of participation, 1
    national trend, 1
Skilled work (crafts)
  as career choice for young men and women, 226
Skilled workers
  interests served by Republican and Democratic parties,
    26
    national trend, 26
Small business people
  interests served by Republican and Democratic parties,
    27
Social programs
  amount government should spend for, 54
  make cuts in, to reduce federal budget deficit, 29, 96–
    98
    national trend, 98
Social Security
  make cuts in, to reduce federal budget deficit, 30, 100–
    01
    national trend, 101
Social service
  yourself involved with, 44
Social work
  as career choice for young women, 226
Softball
  participated in, 1, 215
    by men and women, 216
    national trend, 1, 216
South Africa
  approval rating of way Reagan administration is deal-
    ing with situation in, 201–02
  followed recent events in, 195–97, 244
  situation in, handled by Reagan, 240–42
  United States should put more pressure on, to end
    apartheid, 246–47
  what proportion of South Africans is black, 198–99
  what the United States should do next in, 202
  whether black South Africans have right to vote, 197–
    98
  your sympathies more with black population or with
    government, 199–201, 244–46
South Africa, questions asked in
  approval rating of United Nations, 84
  world as better place to live in ten years than now,
    80
South Korea, questions asked in
  chances of world war breaking out, 3
  drinking as cause of trouble in your family, 185
  1985 as peaceful or troubled year, 3
  predictions for 1985, 6
  your use of alcoholic beverages, 185

you sometimes drink more than you should, 186
Soviet Union (USSR)
  arms buildup in, increases chances of nuclear war, 57,
    264–65
    national trend, 57, 265
  doing all it can to keep peace, 4–6
  Gorbachev's proposal that U.S. and Soviet Union ban
    space-based weapons, 259–60
  relations with, handled by Reagan, 33, 77, 180–82
    national trend, 33, 77, 182
  serious about nuclear arms reduction, 260–62
  stronger than United States in nuclear weapons, 56,
    262–64
    national trend, 56, 264
  United States falling behind, increases chances of
    nuclear war, 57
    national trend, 57
  U.S. development of "Star Wars" would increase like-
    lihood of nuclear arms agreement with, 51, 256–
    58
  see also Nuclear disarmament, negotiations handled by
    Reagan
Spain, questions asked in
  chances of world war breaking out, 2
  how serious a problem is alcoholism, 186
  1985 as peaceful or troubled year, 3
  predictions for 1985, 7
Spiritual experiences. See Religion
Sports
  to promote physical development through, as goal of
    education, 20
  which have you participated in, 1, 215–16
    by frequency, 1
    by men and women, 216
    national trend, 1, 216
  your favorite to watch, 223–24
    national trend, 224
Standard of living
  satisfaction with, 39
"Star Wars" proposal
  developing this system would make world safer, 51,
    258
  Gorbachev's proposal that U.S. and Soviet Union ban
    space-based weapons, 259–60
  Gorbachev's proposals mean Soviet Union is serious
    about nuclear arms reduction, 260–62
  how closely have you followed, 49–50, 255
  U.S. development would increase likelihood of nuclear
    arms agreement with Soviet Union, 51, 256–58
  would like to see the United States develop such a pro-
    gram, 50–51, 255–56
Stockbrokers
  honesty rating, 192

Teachers' additudes toward (*continued*)
    sex education included in grades 4 through 8, 18
    sex education included in high schools, 18
    students who fail required to take remedial classes, 16
    subjects listed, required of high-school student who
        plans to go to college, 17
    subjects listed, required of high-school students who do
        not plan to go to college, 18
    subjects listed, with number of years required for stu-
        dent who plans to go to college, 17–18
    subjects listed, with number of years required for stu-
        dents who do not plan to go to college, 18
    teachers permitted to strike, 16
    teachers required to pass state board examination, 16
    unionization helped quality of education, 16
Teaching
    as career choice by teachers for daughter or son, 16
    as career choice for young men and women, 226
    rated by teachers and public, 17
Teen-agers
    lowering minimum wage for teen-agers during summer,
        114–16
    see also Eating disorders in teen-agers
Television
    confidence in, 166–67
        national trend, 167
Television reporters and commentators
    honesty rating, 192
Tennis
    favorite sport to watch, 223
    participated in, 1, 215
        frequency of participation, 1
        national trend, 1, 216
Thatcher, Margaret
    as most admired woman, 292
Theft of car
    incidence of, 265–68
        national trend, 268
    reported to police, 268
Theft of money or property
    incidence of, 265–68
        national trend, 268
    as problem in public schools, 15
    reported to police, 268
Thompson, James
    as nominee for Republican presidential candidate, 160
Thornburgh, Richard
    as nominee for Republican presidential candidate, 159,
        160
Touch football
    favorite sport to watch, 223
    participated in, 1, 216

Trade deficit
    as most important problem, 253
    reducing, handled by Reagan, 239–40
Truman, Harry
    approval rating vs. Reagan and other presidents, 28,
        34, 78, 202, 223
    as greatest president, 168
        choice of Democrats, 168
        choice in 1975, 168
        choice of Republicans, 168
Turkey, questions asked in
    approval rating of United Nations, 84
    world as better place to live in ten years than now, 79
Tutu, Desmond
    as most admired man, 293

U

Unemployed people
    interests served by Republican and Democratic parties,
        27
    plan to invite, to move where job opportunities are bet-
        ter, 174–75
Unemployment
    handled by Reagan, 235–36
    as most important problem, 52, 139, 253
        national trend, 52
    Reagan administration policy on, 60
        compared to 1982, 63
Unemployment rate
    by this time next year, 129
    misery index, 129–30
    misery index trend, 130
United Nations
    approval rating, 82–84, 229–30
        national trend, 84, 230
        surveyed in sixteen nations, 84
    name any agencies, 231
        national trend, 84, 230
        surveyed in sixteen nations, 84
    United States should give up membership in, 230–31
        national trend, 231
United States
    confidence in ability of, to deal with world problems,
        130–32
    gone up or gone down, 132–33
    doing all it can to keep peace, 3–4
    Reagan administration policy on increasing respect for,
        abroad, 61
        compared to 1982, 63
    satisfaction with its ability to care for poor, 32

satisfaction with way things are going, 31, 280–81
national trend, 31, 281
and Soviet Union *see* Soviet Union
on worst or best step of ladder representing U.S. situation, 121
national trend, 121
Unskilled workers
interests served by Republican and Democratic parties, 26
national trend, 26
Uruguay, questions asked in
approval rating of United Nations, 84
chances of world war breaking out, 2
drinking as cause of trouble in your family, 185
1985 as peaceful or troubled year, 3
predictions for 1985, 7
world as better place to live in ten years than now, 79
your use of alcoholic beverages, 185
you sometimes drink more than you should, 186

V

Vandalism of property
incidence of, 265–68
national trend, 268
as problem in public schools, 14, 15
reported to police, 268
Venereal disease
in instructional program at public elementary schools, 18, 19, 232
in instructional program at public high schools, 18, 19, 233
Vigilantism
have you been assaulted or mugged, 45
heard about incident in New York City subway, 45
taking the law into one's own hands is sometimes justified, 45
Volleyball
participated in, 1, 215
national trend, 1, 216
by women, 216

W

War
arms buildup here and in Soviet Union increases chances of nuclear, 57
national trend, 57
chances of world war breaking out, in opinion of twenty-seven nations, 2–3
1985 as peaceful or troubled year, in opinion of twenty-seven nations, 3

threat of, as most important problem, 52, 139, 253
national trend, 52
United States falling behind Soviet Union increases chances of nuclear, 57
national trend, 57
Washington, George
as greatest president, 168
choice of Democrats, 168
choice in 1975, 168
choice of Republicans, 168
Waterskiing
participated in, 1, 215
national trend, 1
Wealth
distribution of money is fair, 41–42, 85
surveyed in Great Britain, 85
Wealthy families
affected by Reagan tax plan, 142
Weight training
participated in, 1, 215
by men, 216
Welfare. *See* "Workfare" laws
West Germany, questions asked in
approval rating of United Nations, 84
chances of world war breaking out, 3
drinking as cause of trouble in your family, 185
how serious a problem is alcoholism, 186
1985 as peaceful or troubled year, 3
predictions for 1985, 7
world as better place to live in ten years than now, 80
your use of alcoholic beverages, 185
you sometimes drink more than you should, 186
White, Mark
as nominee for Democratic presidential candidate, 161
White collar workers
interests served by Republican and Democratic parties, 26
national trend, 26
Wilson, Woodrow
as greatest president, 168
choice in 1975, 168
Woman, most admired
choice for, 292
Women
career choices listed for young, 226
ideal life-style, 105–07
national trend, 107
interests served by Republican and Democratic parties, 27
participation in sports by, 216
see also Eating disorders in young women